Pointing the Way

Pointing the Way

collected essays by Martin Buber

Edited and Translated
by MAURICE S. FRIEDMAN

Essay Index

Essay Index Reprint Series

 BOOKS FOR LIBRARIES PRESS
FREEPORT, NEW YORK

INTERNATIONAL STANDARD BOOK NUMBER:
0-8369-2149-6

LIBRARY OF CONGRESS CATALOG CARD NUMBER:
77-134063

PRINTED IN THE UNITED STATES OF AMERICA

Contents

v

Contents

Acknowledgements

THE author wishes to acknowledge the kind permission of Henry Regnery Company to reprint the essay 'Goethe's Concept of Humanity' from *Goethe and the Modern Age*, edited by Arnold Bergstraesser, 1949; and to Schocken Books Inc. for permission to reprint the essay 'Plato and Isaiah' from *Israel and the World*; *Essays in a Time of Crisis*, by Martin Buber, translated by Olga Marx, 1948. The latter is included as a part of the longer essay, 'The Demand of the Spirit and Historical Reality.' 'Society and the State' is reprinted from the *World Review*, May 1951 (New Series 27).

Foreword

IN this selection of my essays from the years 1909 to 1954, I have, with *one* exception, included only those that, in the main, I can also stand behind today.

The one exception is 'The Teaching of the Tao,' the treatise which introduced my 1909 translation of selected *Talks and Parables of Chuang-tzu*. I have included this essay because, in connection with the development of my thought, it seems to me too important to be withheld from the reader in this collection. But I ask him while reading it to bear in mind that this small work belongs to a stage that I had to pass through before I could enter into an independent relationship with being. One may call it the 'mystical' phase if one understands as mystic the belief in a unification of the self with the all-self, attainable by man in levels or intervals of his earthly life. Underlying this belief, when it appears in its true form, is usually a genuine 'ecstatic' experience. But it is the experience of an exclusive and all-absorbing unity of his own self. This self is then so uniquely manifest, and it appears then so uniquely existent, that the individual loses the knowledge, 'This is my self, distinguished and separate from every other self.' He loses the sure knowledge of the *principium individuationis*, and understands this precious experience of his unity as the experience of *the* unity.

When this man returns into life in the world and with the world, he is naturally inclined from then on to regard everyday life as an obscuring of the true life. Instead of bringing into unity his whole existence as he lives it day by day, from the hours of blissful exaltation unto those of hardship and of sickness, instead of living this existence as unity, he constantly flees from it into the experience of unity, into the detached feeling of unity of being, elevated above life. But he thereby turns away from his existence as a man, the existence into which he has been set, through conception and birth, for life and death in this unique personal form. Now he no longer stands in the dual basic attitude that is destined to him as a man: carrying being in his person, wishing to complete it, and ever again going forth to meet worldly and above-worldly being over against him, wishing to be a helper to it. Rather in the 'lower' periods he regards everything as preparation for the 'higher.' But in these 'higher hours' he no longer knows anything over against him: the great dialogue between I and Thou is silent; nothing else exists than his self, which he experiences as *the* self. That is certainly an exalted form of being untrue, but it is still being untrue. Being true to the being in which and before which I am placed is the one thing that is needful.

I recognized this and what follows from it five years after setting down this small work. It took another five years for this recognition to ripen to expression. The readers for whom I hope are those who see my way as one, parallel to their own way towards true existence.

Martin Buber

Jerusalem, Israel
  June 1957

I

Towards Authentic Existence

Books and Men

(1947)

I<small>F</small> I had been asked in my early youth whether I preferred to have dealings only with men or only with books, my answer would certainly have been in favour of books. In later years this has become less and less the case. Not that I have had so much better experiences with men than with books; on the contrary, purely delightful books even now come my way more often than purely delightful men. But the many bad experiences with men have nourished the meadow of my life as the noblest book could not do, and the good experiences have made the earth into a garden for me. On the other hand, no book does more than remove me into a paradise of great spirits, where my innermost heart never forgets I cannot dwell long, nor even wish that I could do so. For (I must say this straight out in order to be understood) my innermost heart loves the world more than it loves the spirit. I have not, indeed, cleaved to life in the world as I might have; in my relations with it I fail it again and again; again and again I remain guilty towards it for falling short of what it expects of me, and this is partly, to be sure, because I am so indebted to the spirit. I am indebted to the spirit as I am to myself, but I do not, strictly speaking, love it, even as I do not, strictly speaking, love myself. I do not in reality love him who has seized me with his heavenly clutch and holds me fast; rather I love her, the 'world', who comes again and again to meet me and extends to me a pair of fingers.

Both have gifts to share. The former showers on me his manna of books; the latter extends to me the brown bread on whose crust I break my teeth, a bread of which I can never have enough: men. Aye, these tousle-heads and good-for-nothings, how I love

3

them! I revere books—those that I really read—too much to be able to love them. But in the most venerable of living men I always find more to love than to revere: I find in him something of this world, that is simply there as the spirit never can be there. The spirit hovers above me powerfully and pours out his exalted gift of speech, books; how glorious, how weird! But she, the human world, needs only to cast a wordless smile, and I cannot live without her. She is mute; all the prattle of men yields no word such as sounds forth constantly out of books. And I listen to it all in order to receive the silence that penetrates to me through it, the silence of the creature. But just the human creature! That creature means a mixture. Books are pure, men are mixed; books are spirit and word, pure spirit and purified word; men are made up of prattle and silence, and their silence is not that of animals but of men. Out of the human silence behind the prattle the spirit whispers to you, the spirit *as soul*. She, she is the beloved.

Here is an infallible test. Imagine yourself in a situation where you are alone, wholly alone on earth, and you are offered one of the two, books or men. I often hear men prizing their solitude, but that is only because there are still men somewhere on earth, even though in the far distance. I knew nothing of books when I came forth from the womb of my mother, and I shall die without books, with another human hand in my own. I do, indeed, close my door at times and surrender myself to a book, but only because I can open the door again and see a human being looking at me.

4

Productivity and Existence

(1914)

'A REMARKABLE and charming man, your friend,' said the professor; 'but what does he really *do*? I mean . . . in the intellectual sphere?'

'In the intellectual sphere . . .' I answered. 'H'mm . . . in the intellectual sphere . . . he is simply there.'

'How do you mean?'

'Well, his occupation is not, in fact, of a very intellectual nature, and one cannot really assert that he makes anything out of his leisure time.'

'But his thoughts?'

'He contents himself for the most part with images. When they want to combine and condense into a thought, he gladly helps them and is pleased if something real comes out of them. At times, in conversation, as just now, he also shares some of these clear and fulfilled images.'

'Then he does not write?'

'Oh, he once confessed to me, almost against his will, that occasionally, now and then, when his thoughts congeal, he enters a few lines in a secret book, in order, as he put it, to distinguish from then on what is actually won from what is merely *possible*.'

'Then will he perhaps eventually publish something comprehensive?'

'I do not believe that he has that in mind. He has no need to enter into relation with men other than the friends life has brought him in contact with. He trusts life like a child. He said once that intensity is the only dimension that unceasingly rewards travelling.'

'But why do not you, his friends, persuade him to collect his

5

thoughts and share them with the general public? I have heard enough of them to say with certainty that they are worth while.'

'We feel that his real unity lies in his personality and that only there can it exist. And we feel that we would injure his vitality, which means more to us than any book, if we induced him to store it between covers instead of pouring it into our souls, repaying living with living. He does not give away any part of himself; he only lends it, to receive it back transformed, so that all being then blooms in his presence as young faces, young gestures. That alone makes the blessing of his sharing; that calls up and enlivens ever new levels in him and renews him, indeed, time after time. In the sureness of our glance, in the buoyancy of our plan, in the sacrificial power of our undertaking, he reads the fiery writing of his transformed words. When one of our circle died, I marked that our friend went on reading him in an immortal sphere.'

'But the world—you forget the world! You speak as if a book were an end in itself, whereas it is only a transmitter that bears our voices to unknown ears and hearts. I write what I am inspired to; I fling it out beyond all that is personal, into the whirl of the market, and the whirl carries it into reading-rooms and lamp-lit parlours where men whom I have never seen and never will see hear my words—and perhaps really understand. Is a book not a significant mixture of the personal and the impersonal? The book works and woos out there, and yet it is also myself. Thus separated from myself, I flow into all the world—into distant houses and perhaps into distant generations also—elevating, pleasing, angering who knows, but always in some way educating the human spirit. This thousandfold journey, this victory over all limits of individual existence, this bond with the unknown—for ever misused by vanity and yet never wholly desecrated—this is the predestined way of the thinker.'

'I am familiar with this way, for at times I, too, publish a book. I know the joy of it and its terror—yes, its terror; for it is something dreadful to know that the ghost of my thought hovers in the dreams of confused and impure men, confused and impure as they. But I also know its joy—I remember how it moved me when an old beekeeper wrote me that he had read my book every day for a week on a bench in his garden in the bright hours of the afternoon, from the coming of the apple-blossoms till their withering. And, in order to be entirely fair, I shall also recall the great and creative gifts which I myself owe to books. Now I feel wholly what they are. And yet—more powerful and more holy than all writing is the presence of a man who is simply and immediately present. He need not cry through the loud-speaker of a book to that special circle of contemporary and future readers the writer calls the world. He has spoken without a medium, from mouth to ear, silently and overpoweringly, from his countenance to an eye and to an entranced soul; he has spoken in the magic fullness of togetherness to those men he calls his friends—and who are now full of the spirit because it has laid its hands upon them. Such a man will rarely produce a book. And if he does anything of this sort, the original source of the book is the life of a man who is present only in a direct way.'

'Then all those who are not among the friends of such a man must remain excluded from his teaching?'

'Not at all, for those who are transformed through his teaching are forthwith, one and all, apostles—even though they do not repeat anything of it, nor even proclaim the name of the teacher; as transformed men, they are apostles through their existence, and whatever they do is done in apostleship, through the essence of his teaching which they express therein. In the life of his friends, in the life of all who meet him, and thus to distant generations, immediacy is transmitted.'

'You wish, then, if I understand you rightly, to regard productivity as a lower rung of existence?'

'Rather, I regard productivity, in general, as existence only when it is rooted in the immediacy of lived life. If the man whom you call productive, the one who expresses himself in a creative work, is inferior in power, in holiness, to him who only expresses himself in his life, he is still, in so far as he is grounded in immediacy, superior to him in the noble faculty of creating form. But if you consider an individual who has shrunk to mere form the streaming, living potency, there stands before us a masquerading hobgoblin who cannot form himself but can only disguise himself in forms. No, what I said of the immediate man was not said against the productive one: I was attacking the dominant delusion of our time, that creativity is the criterion of human worth. But illegitimate creativity, creation without immediacy, is no criterion, for it is no reality. It is an illusion— and I believe in the absolute eye before which it cannot stand for a moment. Only that can be a criterion from which genuine creativity arises: that is, the immediate.'

'Certainly, man can be judged only by what he is. But does not his creating, along with his acting, belong to his being?'

'Yes, when it functions as a valid organ of the living body; no, when it indicates a mere excrescence. Artifice has so much got the upper hand that the fictitious dares to usurp the place of the real. The overvaluation of productivity that is afflicting our age has so thrived and its par-technical glance has set up a senseless exclusiveness of its own that even genuinely creative men allow their organic skills to degenerate into an autonomous growth to satisfy the demand of the day. What the born deceivers never had, they give up: the ground where the roots of a genuinely lived life alone can grow. They mean, they strive for, and at last they contain nothing but creativity. Instead of bringing forth a natural creation, in a gradual selective progression from experiences to thoughts, from thoughts to words, from words to writing, and from writing to public communication, they wear themselves out turning all experience to account as public communication; they renounce true necessity and give themselves over to the arbitrary. They poison experience, for already while it is taking place they are dominated by the will to produce. Thus they prostitute their lives and are cheated of the reward for their ignominy; for how can they expect to create anything save the artificial and the transitory? They forfeit both life and art, and all that they gain is the applause of their production-mad contemporaries.'

'But it appears to me that the will to create is a legitimate part of the experience of every productive man. Thus the painter is the man who paints with all his senses. His seeing is already a painting, for what he sees is not merely what his physical sight receives: it is something, two-dimensionally intensified, that vision produces. And this producing does not come later, but is present in his seeing. Even his hearing, his smelling, are already painting, for they enrich for him the graphic character of the thing; they give him not only sensations but also stimulations. In the same way the poet creates poetry with all his senses; in each of his experiences the form in which it will be phrased is immediately announced. His perceiving is already a transformation of the thing perceived into the stuff of poetry, and in its becoming each impression presents itself to him as an expression of rhythmic validity.'

'That is indeed so. But this dynamic element that you find in the experience of the creative is no will to create but an ability to create. This potentiality of form also accompanies every experience that befalls the non-artistic man and is given an issue as often as he lifts an image out of the stream of perception and inserts it into his memory as something single, definite, and meaningful in itself. For the creative man this potentiality of form is a specific one, directed into the language of his particular art. If an intention is expressed in this direction, it is that of his genius, not that of a self-conscious resolution. The dynamic element of his experience does not affect its wholeness and purity. It is otherwise when in perceiving he already cherishes the deliberate intention of utilizing what he perceives. Then he disturbs the experience, stunts its growth, and taints the process of its becoming. Only the unarbitrary can grow properly and bear mature and healthy fruit. That man is legitimately creative who experiences so strongly and formatively that his experiences unite into an image that demands to be set forth, and who then works at his task with full consciousness of his art. But he who interferes with the spontaneity of perceiving, who does not allow the inner selection and formation to prevail, but instead inserts an aim from the beginning, has forfeited the meaning of this perception, the meaning that lies above all aims. And he who meets men with a double glance, an open one that invites his fellows to sincerity and the concealed one of the observer stemming from a conscious aim; he who in friendship and in love is cleft into two men, one who surrenders himself to his feelings and another who is already standing by to exploit them—this man cannot be delivered by any creative talent from the blight that he has brought upon himself and his work, for he has poisoned the springs of his life.'

'You wish, then, to reintroduce into æsthetics the ethical principle that we have finally succeeded in banishing from it?'

'What was banished from æsthetics was an ideology that had degenerated into rhetoric and had thereby become false. It certainly signified a conquest of sure ground when the perspective was established that evaluated a work of art—approving or rejecting it—not by its relation to the aspirations of the artist but by its intrinsic qualities. Now for the first time we can, without promoting misunderstanding, strive towards the deeper insight: that this approval affords entrance into the outer circle only, but in the inner circle those works alone count that have given form to the meaning of being. Similarly, a gain in clarity and solidity was achieved when it was recognized that the significance of an artist does not depend upon his morals: now for the first time we can attain the deeper clarity that in inner development mastery and power accrue only to that artist who is worthy of his art.'

The Demon in the Dream

(1914)

'WHAT do you see?' asked the demon in the dream.

'A very long wall,' I said.

'That is,' he explained, 'the boundary wall between the land of things and the land of thoughts. On this wall we demons live. It seems narrow to you, does it not, and not very roomy? But for us it is broad and comfortable enough. And we feel at home on it as well. Yes, I even allow myself to fancy that our feelings are better than yours, for you think yourself at home in both lands and are really at home in neither.

'You man! You act as if this wall were only a boundary which is otherwise not there, so to speak; as if one could neither squat on the wall, as I am squatting on it now, nor dance on it, as you saw me doing a moment ago. You believe such a foolish thing only because you know nothing of us. And if one knows nothing of us, how shall he know anything of the world or of the subtlest of its kingdoms, this wall?

'You know nothing of us. You only "suspect" something. Oh, your suspicions! They arouse disgust in all beings—things and thoughts and demons. There, out of the darkness, a slimy grasping arm shoots towards you and then past you. Ugh, man, how unappetizing! I should rather be a crude tree-trunk and experience only what is necessary than be a being full of suspicions.

'You have a suspicion of us, then. But we know you to your very ground and deeper, too. We know you better than anything else, and in another way. But you are also more important to us than anything else. Yes, reluctantly I admit it, we are directly dependent on you. For we live off you. We can receive the strength of the world only through you. We can enjoy all things only through you. Your experience is our food, and we have no other.

'The more forcefully you live, the more avidly do we enjoy ourselves. The content of your living does not much matter to us; your joy and anger, sin and holiness, heroism and despair, are all the same to us. But whether you live fully or faintly, that does concern us. Your moderation is a meagre crumb, your temperance a tough morsel that sticks in the throat. But where some fellow is horrified at the world and rushes against it and rages over all its appeasements and is shattered on the wall of the great indifference; or where some fellow falls madly in love and again and again draws forth new power from out of his extravagance and converts it into amorousness until he revolves around some envisioned axis like a hundred-spoked fire-wheel, flaring up and crackling in a blissful smoke—there we feast, there we thrive.

'What you call contents is for us only gaily-coloured variety, a cupboard of agreeable spices, no more. It does not occur to us to prefer one kind to another. Whether your passion pursues sensuality or politics, business or deeds of mercy, that does not affect our enjoyment; it only plays round it. But on the violence of your passion, on that we do depend.

'You have a No for every Yes, and for every value a disvalue. You effect transitions from one to the other, and you call the Yes good and the No bad, or vice versa, and are very concerned about whether your passion is on the side of the Yes or on the side of the No. But we are not especially interested in all this. The juggling amuses us, yet I assure you that we cannot otherwise express our esteem for your virtue and your moderate high-mindedness than by leaving it alone.

'But you must not think that we amuse ourselves on this wall and coolly await what ascends to us from excited human power. We would have a hard life then! For you are accustomed to "let things happen" and to allow the possibilities in you to remain merely possibilities. It is fatiguing and disagreeable, you think, to give all of yourself; it is not even seemly. If it were not for us you would sleep through all your opportunities. We descend to you, we become things or thoughts in order not to startle you, we mingle with you, and—we tempt you. We taste the food, and when we find it flat we undertake the temptation: thereupon the bite becomes tasty. We rustle your passion out of its hiding-place. We inflame to feeling your capacity to feel. We actualize you. Naturally we do all this for our own sake; but, incidentally, what would become of you if we did not stir you up!

'There are some among you who imagine that one is tempted only to sin. That attitude fits them well, my dear: for they possess no other art than that which inclines them towards what they call sin. But in reality we are not at all specialized: we desire that out of your *potentia* should come *actus*, nothing more. We do not mix in your sophistries.

'We have, indeed—I may not conceal it from you—our sad chapter. We consume ourselves in the act of tempting. To tempt men is no child's play. We spring head over heels into each new undertaking, and it swallows all we are and all we can be. We could, in fact, say that we risk ourselves. Yes, we do enjoy it; but the enjoyment is exclusive and pitiless. When we are finished with this enjoyment, we collapse into ourselves. This collapsing of ours is not like your sleep; it is a dispersion, a scattering, a being wiped away. It lasts until a desire for fresh enjoyment steals over us and collects us. From this you can well imagine how much continuity there is in our lives. Hardly a vague trace remains in memory from one adventure to another! We seem continually to be starting life over again. Indeed it appears each time as if the escapade were really worth while—but that is, after all, a moot point.

'Though we are constantly starting all over again, we cannot remember a real beginning in our lives. Seriously, it seems to me as if we had nothing that might be called a real beginning. At times there descends on me a dull feeling as if I already always existed. But we do have an end, that is certain. Sometimes a final enjoyment will arrive which will swallow me and not deliver me up again. And until then . . . ! Well, it is a melancholy bliss, I cannot deny it.

'And once there was even one among us who . . . I shall tell you about it although I can hardly believe you capable of fully

13

understanding; for it is a story with long roots—but you have a nice way of looking at one, as if you . . . no matter!

'There was one demon who was discontented. He longed for continuity. Moments—he loathed moments if he could not advance upright from one to another, but one lay there and was more insignificant than a drunken man! He refused to take part any longer in this foolish rhythm of power and weakness. But you must not fancy that he conducted himself like your famous human rebels and harangued some god. When he realized he was fed up, he stood up and took a step outside of time. Once outside he sat down again.

'There he sat and was no longer affected by the whole game. There was no enjoyment, but there was no more emptiness—for where time no longer beats there is no emptiness, only the shape of the stillness. Thus he who had been discontented waxed in power and in duration. He took on security as a tree takes on rings. His power became ever stronger until he became aware that it could never again flag. Confident that he was wholly his own, it seemed to him as if the world was wholly his possession. You should have seen him when he stepped back into time!

'He began to tempt men again. But because his power had grown so great, each of his temptations drove his victim to his uttermost. Each ability of this man was intensified to the maximum, every longing was strained to its extreme. The uttermost of man, as you may well know, is a wonderful thing. The uttermost of man creates. That is a dangerous activity. It creates modes of being, essence, immortality. It lures men into madness and destruction, but it transforms the uttermost moment into eternity. And it cannot be exhausted through our enjoyment of it; its deep sweetness remains untasted, an eternally inaccessible remainder.

'He who had come back had been able to enjoy himself despite this remainder before he stepped out of time. Now he could do so no longer. Now, under the influence of the stillness, something greater than enjoyment sprang up in him: he sensed the inexhaustible over against him; he suffered, he burned. He was no longer merely discontented as before; he was wretched and alien.

And he grew ever more miserable the higher his temptations reached on the ladder of creativeness. His strength, his capacity for enjoyment, was not impaired; it even grew from time to time without slackening. He went upright from one adventure to the next, yet each time the remainder pained him ever more acutely. Ever more silly the enjoyment appeared that could only satiate itself through intensity; ever more furiously he longed for the vision. To grasp the remainder, to fathom the qualities, to take possession of creativity, to see! But a demon can see as little as he can create.

'And while my brother's great game kindled awesome raptures, triumphs, downgoings on earth, driving the human soul upward to perform its greatest deed; while a gigantic burnt offering ascended to the tempter out of tumult and beauty, tyranny and grace, my brother recognized: "What I enjoy is not the essence, the essence is beyond my reach; the essence is given to this little man with whom I play. While I play with him I evoke in him the essence, I make the essence in him alive." And in the tempter there awoke this desire: "I want to become a man: man, plaything—I want immortality—I want a creating soul!" For immortality, he perceived, is nothing but the creating soul.'

The demon in my dream had altered. His grin had turned into an awkward smile, like the first smile on an infant's face, and his initially strident voice now sounded like the voice of the wine-growers I once heard sing the ancient melody of the dead to the words of a harvest song. Then sleep loosened, and the intertwined worlds slipped away from each other's embrace.

The Altar

(1914)

THAT is the altar of the spirit in the West erected at one time by the master Matthias Grünewald in an Alsatian monastic church, this altar now to be seen in another Alsatian monastic church. But it is more powerful than any church, like the sermons of Meister Eckhart who preached two centuries before in the same Alsatian cloisters. These two, Eckhart and Matthias, are brothers, and their teachings are fraternally related, though Grünewald taught in the language of colour, with a magic such as no German before or after him achieved.

That is the altar of the spirit in the West. Only the pilgrim who is summoned by its speech finds genuine access to it.

Like so many great old masterpieces, the Isenheim Altar has been dismantled in our own time. Before this happened, one saw it closed upon approaching it. On the closed wings was the crucifixion.

In this painting, a Christ with the bloodless flesh of a martyr and the outstretched fingers of the nailed hands is set before the night of the world. On one side of him a red John the Baptist points to him like a raucous market crier and recites his speech; on the other side a disciple staggers, wind-blown, like a will-o'-the-wisp; and in front of him are two women, the two women of the earth, the twin souls of the world, Mary standing and Magdalene kneeling.

Mary's eyes are closed; Magdalene's are open. Mary's pale hands are stiffly pressed into each other without individuality; Magdalene's hands, the blood glimmering through, are so savagely entwined that each finger sticks forth like a fierce young animal. On Mary colour has vanished from the flesh in the arms, over the breast, and at the border of the clothes—before the terrible deathly white of the mantle covering her completely like a shroud. On Magdalene there is no spot of flesh, and clothes from which colour does not shout and sing; her bright-red gown is girdled by a deep-red cord, a golden yellow serves for the streaming blondness of her hair, and even the dark veil is iridescent. She is vowed to manifold colourfulness as Mary is to the simple absence of colour; but her variegated appearance is not bound by sense, and Mary's whiteness is sundered from life. These are the two souls; neither of them is the spirit of the world. Before the night of the world they shine forth at the feet of the crucified one in different and yet related attitudes, as the question of man.

When the triptych is opened, the back walls of the wings appear as sides of the centre. Here the heart of the altar is revealed.

At the left is the annunciation of the answer.

In the centre the nativity. There on crystalline mountains glows the morning of creation; below them sits the virgin with the child and, high above the scene, an infinite bloom, the divine glory of bands of angels bursts forth. Their glory is above colour, united in the radiant light; but as they undulate downward into the intermediate realm of becoming, each angel gleams forth in colour; thus in the portal on the left they hover and kneel, playing music, each a colour. 'For this is the final stage, that a thing stands alone in its self and rejoices in its exaltation.' That is the miracle of the becoming of colour, the emanation of the many out of the one: that is the first mystery. This mystery is only revealed, not allotted, to us. The glory that is above colour is the spirit of heaven; it is not the spirit of earth to which it does not disclose itself. The angels burst forth from it, but they do not behold it. We cannot penetrate behind the multiplicity to find the living unity. If we remove the colours, we do not behold the light but only darkness, be this darkness ever so intoxicating and full of enchantment. He who puts on the white mantle is cut off from life, and he experiences the truth only so long as he shuts his eyes. Our world, the world of colours, is *the* world.

Are we, then, like Magdalene, abandoned to the manifold? If we do not strive to turn away from the actual and to deny the fullness of our experience, must we be dispersed in things and exiled to the conditioned? Must we for ever stray, then, from being to being and from happening to happening, incapable of grasping their unity?

On the right side of the altar is the resurrection. Here the night and day of the world are merged into one: in the centre of the starry space is a huge sun, swollen with colour as if with running sap, extended from the light yellow centre over a red circle of rays to the blue rim which reaches into the darkness. Amid this, above a turned-up grave and guards who have sunk to earth, is the risen one. Ascending steeply in a mantle composed of the red of the morning, violet thunderclouds, lightning flashes, and the light distant blue of heaven, he is himself aflame with colour from his sunlit countenance to the humble red of his feet. How can Magdalene's variegated colour compare with his world spectrum; what is Mary's white unity before his all-embracing unity? He includes all hues of being in his unity of spirit, each tone pure and intensified, all fused in his world-uniting person. The shades are not iridescent; they sparkle in themselves, ranged round a higher self that has received them all, all colours and angels and beings, and bears them upward. That is the miracle of the coming to be of glory, the becoming of one out of the many: this is the other mystery. This mystery is ours, it is allotted to us. This all-coloured glory that opens and ascends in all direction, the glory of things, is the spirit of the earth.

This is not the Jew Jeshua, trodding the soil of Galilee and teaching in his day; it is also Jeshua. This is not the incarnate *Logos*, descending from timeless pre-existence into time; it is also the *Logos*. This is the man, the man of all times and of all places, the man of the here and now, who perfects himself into the *I* of the world. This is the man who, embracing the world, does not become manifold in its manifoldness; but rather, out of the strength of his world-embracing, has himself become unified, a united doer.

He loves the world, he rejects none of its colours. But he can receive none of them before it is pure and intensified. He loves the world, but he fights for its unconditionality against all that is conditioned. He loves the world towards the Unconditioned, he bears the world upward to its Self. He, the united one, shapes the world to unity.

Our world, the world of colours, is *the* world; but it is so in its mystery, in its glory—this glory is not that of the primal unity, but that of a unified glory achieved out of becoming and out of deed.

We cannot penetrate behind the manifold to find living unity. But we can create living unity out of the manifold.

Brother Body

(1914)

THE dancer* is sick. I sense it, reflect on it awhile, think about something else, and suddenly the wonder of the contemporary strikes me, as though I had not read it, but perceived it through the distance: he who resided in my memory only as a picture I now experience in the depths of his bodily life. From there I feel his illness, for a decisive moment I feel an angry impulse rush from the spinal marrow to the resisting muscles. And in this same moment the mystery of the dancer overpowers me. I live the ineffable unfolding of the movement.

In this dancer the gesture of man liberates itself.

Here are the playing and the expressing gestures that, joined in primitive dance, then long separated, have again become united. But the new movement of the dancer is of a different nature from that of the primitive; it is liberated.

The primitive man plays: the body celebrates its strength. The power of surplus and of possibility surges through him, all things move around him as if they were his outposts, the air whirs as though a thousand arrows flew; the earth quakes as though a thousand wild horses ran, and there, in the depths of his bodily life, a volcanic becoming inflicts itself on him. He flings out his arms, spreads his fingers, a singing shriek shakes him from his neck to the soles of his feet.

The primitive man expresses: the body reports the onrushing happening; braced, tense, he receives the impact of the threatening, the unknown, the wooing occurrences. He has seen a large, many-coloured beast in the forest, an unfamiliar one; it stood silently breathing and cast the firebrand of its glance upon him.

* Nijinsky.

20

What does the beast want of him? And he has it in some way in himself, has brought away something of it. The beast horrifies him, the image burns from his seeing into his whole flesh, burns in the depths of his bodily life, and the transformation is completed, the command takes hold of him, he must make the image. He does not imitate the animal, he only bends the breast to the standstill that precedes a spring, he merely turns the head to a lurking pose, and he has announced the animal to his comrades, to the gods, to himself.

Thus the playing and the expressing gestures become a part of human existence, the body's enjoyment of itself and its spirituality. Each builds its world in soul and form; they meet each other, co-operate with each other, but they do not unite. Newly combined in the cradle life of each child, sundered in the life of the man, they ally themselves in art for common work; but they do not wed—unless it be in those rare beings of wonder, one of whom is this dancer. His dancing body is at once wholly its own and wholly interpenetrated by the spirit. His attitude comprehends playing gestures and expressing gestures, but both thoroughly transformed.

Play is the exultation of the possible.

In all other movements of man the gesture is determined by the sensation to which it responds or by the end towards which it strives. In play the body is autonomous, independent of world and spirit. What it does there is dictated to it by nothing else than the situation of its moment. It is its surplus that moves it, its latent fullness of gestures that drives it to pour them out; to do justice to it the body must execute at once all the movement of which it is capable; for play does not demand of it, as do sensation and end, the choice of a suitable response or act, but the working out of all movement. Thus around every gesture that it makes there whirls a glimmering vortex, the possible. Man becomes master of the measureless impulse. He masters it through rhythm and through line; he forms it through the discipline of the ear and the eye that now separates out the possible and commands the 'beautiful'; he creates convention and tradition, he restrains the fullness through precepts. But the origin does not let itself be disowned; the element of play, the exultation of the possible, breaks through ever again, and still swirls around the step of the most disciplined, most controlled of dancers, especially where he throws off the limits of tradition—the glimmering vortex of the possible, visible in a barely noticeable undulation in the outlines of the movement.

But it is not so with this dancer. His gesture of the possible is stripped naked without a remainder. Each one penetrates the beholder with the felt conviction of its necessity. For none may a variant be imagined, an ever-so-delicate nuance of deflection to the side. Around none of them does there play the uncertain shimmer of otherness.

Necessity! No combination of sensation and reaction, of end and fulfilment, can create this. For everywhere there is still an external, a cleavage, a duality of body and world, of body and spirit. But here the united necessity of a human body reveals itself —of this human body which is only determined by itself, out of itself, yet in which there is no arbitrariness of play, only meaning, only essence.

But this play is also expression.

None of his gestures, to be sure, means anything other than itself. None refers to anything that is external to it, to an object, a relation, a feeling, to anything of all that which the gestures of men usually mean. None points beyond itself. As the gesture of the dancer is liberated from the possibility swinging round, so it is liberated from the meaning that swings with it. It is pure and bounded in its form; it is single and free. It recalls nothing but the gesture preceding it, it announces nothing but the gesture following it. It does not entice memory, imagination, sensibility—it entices the glance; it does not delight anything separate in us but our total system of movement, concentrated in the glance that sees its released perfection. It has absorbed the essence, the character, of the expressing movement; but this character cannot be detached and isolated from it.

And yet this dance is an expression. It would not be one if it were only the sum of its moments. But it is something else. It has a line which is not in space but in time. This line realizes itself in none of the moments; it realizes itself in their succession and in their unison.

No matter how delightful the individual gestures of this dancer may be, it is not their singleness that makes them essentially significant. None falls down, each flows into the next, and the most image-like attitudes are not end-points but junctures of movement; only the last, intensified or fading away, is insurpassable conclusion. The dancer does not trace the outline of his image in space but in time. He who, following him, is able to trace this line after him with glance and life, recognizes its creative strictness and virtue. It is not formed out of images; it is one single image in time, a totality, uninterpretable, untranslatable, unique and unrelated, yet expressive. But the truth that it expresses cannot be stated, only experienced. It is thus that the symbol expresses.

To divulge the mystery is called, in the speech of the ancient Greeks as in that of some primitive peoples, to 'dance it out.'

What is it that taught men to master the impulse of play through rhythm and line and to originate the dance? To interweave the gestures of expression in the dance and otherwise coordinate them as was necessary for their utterance?

The decisive power in the development of the dance was neither play nor expression, but what bound them both and gave them law: magic. That is the response to the chaotic and furiously inrushing happening through the bound, lawful movement, through movement as form. The bound binds.

In this dancer the deep origin returns; movement as form, magically-formed time. It enables him who can blend all impulse of play and of expression to liberate the play from the possibility that swings around it, to liberate the expression from the accompanying meaning. Time after time it makes a symbol out of a man of our generation.

Francis did not call to you, Brother Body, among his brothers and sisters. How should he, indeed; he who was wholly united in you, who ate from one bowl with lepers and felt the agony of the crucifixion break out in his own flesh? He did not stand shuddering before your countenance; you served him as his very self.

He did not need to conscript your voice for his song, for it was born in it. But I, a too-late one, a too-early one, a more separated one, I look at you and call to you, Brother Body, and praise you more than sun and wind.

With a Monist

(1914)

RECENTLY I made the acquaintance of a monist. I noticed at the first glance that he was an excellent man. Excellence, by the way, seems to be essentially facilitated by monism. We others can only offer difficulties.

'You are a mystic,' said the monist, looking at me more resignedly than reproachfully. It is thus that I would represent to myself an Apollo who disdained to flay a Marsyas. He even omitted the question mark. But his voice was affable. Indeed, he achieved the feat of being at once sublime and excellent.

'No, a rationalist,' I said.

He fell out of his splendid composure. 'How? . . . I mean . . .' he stammered.

'Yes,' I affirmed, 'that is the only one of my world views that I have allowed to expand into an "ism." I am in favour of reason absorbing everything, mastering everything, working up everything. Nothing can withstand it, nothing can hide from it. I find that splendid. Only no half-way work, no nine-tenths work! Overlook nothing, spare nothing, leave nothing standing! Reason has done something only when it has done it completely. It goes to work on the world, and it sets it right, a masterpiece of the times, this rationalized world! A world without gaps and without contradiction! The world as syllogism!'

'No, but . . .' he objected.

'Entirely so,' I conceded. 'You would formulate it differently, such as: the world as the completed series of inductions. It does not matter to me; in any case, I agree. If only the work is done thoroughly! There exist, of course, those who efface the boundaries. I do not like them. But I am predisposed in favour of you, save that to me you are not, despite all your claims, complete enough. You persist in occasionally letting in shamefaced teleologies. That should not be. If the human will is entirely determined, then it is a matter of complete indifference that one cannot survey this determinism, that he conceives of the future as dependent on him, and imagines himself to be not the channel but the source. From the viewpoint of your ideal, the observer of the completed series of inductions, man is unfree, and must therefore be so for you as well.'

'However . . .' he interjected.

'Certainly,' I replied, 'the ethical. . . . But this cannot affect my inclination towards unrestricted rationalism. I think of it as a close-meshed net that catches all phenomena and from which none of them can escape. Concede to the soul no special place! "Reduce" it till it can be reduced no further! Press it against the wall! Tolerate nothing that evades your tabulations! Do not rest until the world unrolls before your probing glance as a well-ordered registry! Then you shall have proved that the *mind* is master and that he need only send forth the first of his daughters that happens along, and she will bind the world and her father along with it. Thus it must happen ever anew, from generation to generation. Until he again raises a finger and all fetters fall off and the world stretches itself and the chains of your categories fly about wildly in the raging storm.'

'So therefore . . .' he interposed in annoyance.

'Yes,' I confirmed, and denied nothing. 'You have seen through me. And we do not need to wait at all. What takes place in the human sphere from one time to another takes place at all times. When the circle is described, the pure circle of world-comprehensibility, and when everything is contained in it and all thinking is unmasked as a form of energy and all will as a form of causality, then self, the hidden lark, soars upward out of the circle and warbles. You have dissected and partitioned the I, yet there it soars untouched above your artifices, the untouchable one. You may unmask my soul as a loose aggregate of sensations; then it bestirs itself and feels the splendour of the night or the affection of a child, and is firm as a crystal. And when it sleeps, all your

26

formulas and calculations fly like moths about its fiery dream. You may exhibit the elements of which I am composed, the transformations which take place in me, the laws which compel me; yet when I, a whole unique form, arise to deed and take my choice, then I myself am element, transformation, law, and the lightning of creation flashes out of my originating hands. Of what materials I am composed, from what animal I am descended, of what functions I am the slave, it is salutary for me to hear— still that means nothing to me when I dare to think the infinite, to behold the infinite, and, interwoven with the infinite, experience myself as infinite. That there was a time when man was not on earth, this information I readily receive—but I no longer know its voice when eternity beats against me in the flame of the lived moment. That the earth will someday grow cold and man will disappear, I willingly accept; but I have forgotten and annihilated this knowledge when my deed surges outward in shoreless becoming.

'This is the glorious paradox of our existence that all comprehensibility of the world is only a footstool of its incomprehensibility. But this incomprehensibility has a new, a wonderful secret to bestow; it is like Adam's knowledge when he "knew" his wife Eve. What the most learned and ingenious combination of concepts denies, the humble and faithful beholding, grasping, knowing of any situation bestows. The world is not comprehensible, but it is embraceable: through the embracing of one of its beings. Each thing and being has a twofold nature: the passive, absorbable, usable, dissectible, comparable, combinable, rationalizable, and the other, the active, non-absorbable, unusable, undissectible, incomparable, noncombinable, nonrationalizable. This is the confronting, the shaping, the bestowing in things. He who truly experiences a thing so that it springs up to meet him and embraces him of itself has in that thing known the world.'

'So for all that you are a mystic,' said the monist as I paused. He smiled. Was it because he could put in a word? Because he carried his point? Or because a monist must smile when a fellow like me, after diffuse dissembling, in the end turns out to be a hopeless reactionary? Let us not probe for motives, let us be glad of every human smile so long as it is not downright malicious.

'No,' I answered, and looked at him in a friendly way, 'for I still grant to reason a claim that the mystic must deny to it. Beyond this, I lack the mystic's negation. I can negate convictions but never the slightest actual thing. The mystic manages, truly or apparently, to annihilate the entire world, or what he so names—all that his senses present to him in perception and in memory—in order, with new disembodied senses or a wholly supersensory power, to press forward to his God. But I am enormously concerned with just this world, this painful and precious fullness of all that I see, hear, taste. I cannot wish away any part of its reality. I can only wish that I might heighten this reality. For what is this world? It is the contact between the inexpressible revolving of things and the experiencing powers of my senses, which are more than and different from the vibration of the ether, the nervous system, sensations and combinations of sensations—embodied spirit. And the reality of the experienced world is so much the more powerful the more powerfully I experience it and realize it. Reality is no fixed condition, but a quantity which can be heightened. Its magnitude is functionally dependent upon the intensity of our experiencing. There is an ordinary reality which suffices as a common denominator for the comparison and ordering of things. But the great reality is another. And how can I give this reality to my world except by seeing the seen with all the strength of my life, hearing the heard with all the strength of my life, tasting the tasted with all the strength of my life? Except by bending over the experienced thing with fervour and power and by melting the shell of passivity with the fire of my being until the confronting, the shaping, the bestowing side of things springs up to meet me and embraces me so that I know the world in it? The actual world is the manifest, the known world. And the world cannot be known through response to the things by the active sense-spirit of the loving man.'

'But then . . .' asserted the monist.

'No, no,' I protested. 'You are mistaken. This is not in any sense to be taken as agreeing with your theses. The loving man is one who grasps non-relatively each thing he grasps. He does not think of inserting the experienced thing into relations to other things; at the moment of experience nothing else exists, nothing save this beloved thing, filling out the world and indistinguishably coinciding with it. Where you with agile fingers draw out the qualities common to all things and distribute them in ready-made categories, the loving man's dream-powerful and primally-awake heart beholds the non-common. This, the unique, is the bestowing shape, the self of the thing, that cannot be detained within the pure circle of world comprehensibility. What you extract and combine is always only the passivity of things. But their activity, their effective reality, reveals itself only to the loving man who knows them. And thus he knows the world. In the features of the beloved, whose self he realizes, he discerns the enigmatic countenance of the universe.

'True art is a loving art. To him who pursues such art there appears, when he experiences an existent thing, the secret shape of that thing which appeared to none before him. This he does not see only with his eyes, rather he feels its outlines with his limbs; a heart beats against his heart. Thus he learns the glory of things so that he expresses them and praises them and reveals their shape to others.

'True science is a loving science. The man who pursues such science is confronted by the secret life of things which has confronted none before him; this life places itself in his hands, and he experiences it, and is filled with its happening to the rim of his existence. Then he interprets what he has experienced in simple and fruitful concepts, and celebrates the unique and incomparable that happened to him with reverent honesty.

'True philosophy is a loving philosophy. To him who pursues such philosophy a secret meaning opens, when he experiences a thing of the world—the law of that thing that opened itself to none before him. This meaning comes not as an object but as something that shatters him and discloses to him his own meaning —the meaning of all the years of his life and all its destiny, the meaning of his sorrowful and exalted thinking. So he receives the law of the thing which he perceived with obedient and creative soul, and establishes it as a law of the world; in so doing he has not been presumptious but worthy and faithful.

'Every true deed is a loving deed. All true deeds arise from contact with a beloved thing and flow into the universe. Any true deed brings, out of lived unity, unity into the world. Unity is not a property of the world but its task. To form unity out of the world is our never-ending work.

'And for the sake of this monism, dear monist . . .

He stood up and extended his hand.

We looked at each other.

Let us believe in man!

The Teaching of the Tao

(1910)

I

A MID our theories of races and cultures, our time has lost sight of the old knowledge that the Orient forms a natural unity, expressed in its values and workings; that despite their differences the peoples of the East possess a common reality that sunders them in unconditional clarity from the destiny and genius of the West. The genetic explanation for this distinction, with which we are not here concerned, has its foundation, naturally, in the different conditions not only of space but also of time, for the spiritually determining epoch of the Orient belongs, in fact, to a moment of mankind other than that of the West.

Here I can only indicate the unity of the Orient through a single manifestation, which is, however, the most essential of all—that of the teaching.

In its primal state the spirit of the West is what all human spirit is in its primal state—magic. That is its essence, that it can encounter the thousandfold menace of the instorming freedom of nature with its constraint, the binding in which dwells magic power. Regulated word, ordered movement, magic speech, and magic gesture compel the demonic element under rule and order. All primitive technique and all primitive organization are magic; tools and arms, language and play, customs and bonds, arise out of magical intention, and serve in their initial period a magical meaning from which their own life only gradually detaches itself and becomes independent.

This process of detaching and becoming independent is accomplished much more slowly in the Orient than in the West. In the West the magical endures in a living form only in the folk religiousness which has preserved the undifferentiated wholeness of life; in all other spheres the detachment is rapid and complete. In the Orient it is slow and incomplete: a magical character adheres for a long while to the products of the separation. The art of the Orient, for example, perseveres in many ways in its magical intention even after the attainment of artistic freedom and power; whereas in that of the West, reaching this height confers its own right and its own aim.

Among the three basic forces out of which the indicating spirit of the East (I do not consider here the forming spirit) builds itself, of which the Occident only possesses two creatively— called science and law—it is the third, called the teaching, that is able to detach itself most completely from the magical primal ground.

In order to understand the Orient it is necessary, in my view, to bring these three basic forces into the clearest possible contrast with one another.

'Science' includes all information about the 'is,' whether earthly or heavenly, these two being never and nowhere separated, but uniting into the sphere of being which is the subject of science.

'Law' includes all the commands of an 'ought', human and divine, these two being never and nowhere separated from one another, but uniting into the sphere of ought which is the subject of law.

Science and law always belong together so that the 'is' verifies itself in the 'ought,' the 'ought' grounds itself on the 'is.' The growing cleavage between is and ought, between science and law, that characterizes the spiritual history of the Occident is alien to the Orient.

To science and law there belongs, as the third basic force of the Eastern spirit, the teaching.

The teaching includes no subjects, it has only *one* subject— itself: the one thing needful. It stands beyond 'is' and 'ought,' information and command; it knows how to say only one thing, the needful that must be realized in genuine life. The needful is in no way accessible to an 'is,' and it is not obtainable through information; it is not already in existence either on earth or in heaven, rather it is possessed and lived. The genuine life is in no wise an ought, nor is it subject to a command. Authentic life is not taken over either from men or from God, rather it can be fulfilled only out of itself, and is nothing whatever other than fulfilment. Science rests upon the duality of demand and deed; the teaching rests wholly upon the unity of the one thing needful.

One can always transform fundamentally the meanings the words 'is' and 'ought' have in science and law, and describe the needful as an 'is' that is accessible to no information and the genuine life as an 'ought' that is subject to no command, and the teaching consequently is a synthesis of 'is' and 'ought'. But if one does this, one should not thereby make this way of speaking—which is nonsense to science and law—idle, of no account, and presentable through replacing information and command by an 'inner' information, and an 'inner' command with which the teaching has to do. These phrases of a hackneyed rhetoric, used to explain belief, signify only confusion and delusion. The dialectic opposition of *inner* and *outer* can serve only symbolically for the elucidation of this experience; it cannot set the teaching in contrast to the other basic forces of the spirit. The teaching is not peculiar in that it concerns itself with the inner or receives its measure and sanction from it. To wish to narrow science and law for the sake of an 'inner knowledge' that is not at all separable from the outer, for an 'inner command' that is not separable from the outer would be senseless. What is peculiar to the teaching, rather, is that it is not concerned with the manifold and the individual but with the One, and that it therefore demands neither belief nor action, both of which are rooted in multiplicity and individuality. The teaching, in general, demands nothing; instead it simply proclaims itself.

This essential difference of the teaching from science and law is amply documented by history. The teaching forms itself independently of science and law until it finds its pure fulfilment in a central human life. Only in its decline that begins soon after this fulfilment does the teaching mingle with elements of science and law. Out of such intermixture there arises a religion: a product of the contamination in which information, command, and the necessary are welded into a contradictory and effective whole. Now belief and action are demanded: the One has disappeared.

Neither teaching nor religion are partial forces, like science and law; both represent the wholeness of life. But in the teaching all opposites of the wholeness are elevated into the One as the seven colours of the spectrum fuse into white light. In religion these are joined in community like the seven colours in the rainbow. The magic that borders science and law but cannot touch the teaching assumes control of religion. Its binding power unites the contending elements into an iridescent, magic vortex that rules the ages.

Between the teaching and religion, leading from the one to the other, stand parable and myth. These attach themselves to the central human life in which the teaching has found its purest fulfilment: the parable as the word of this man himself, the myth as the impact of this life on the consciousness of the age. The parable, accordingly, still appears to stand wholly on the side of the teaching, myth already wholly on the side of religion. None the less, each carries mediation in itself. This must be understood through the essence of the teaching when it is considered in its relation to man.

The teaching has only *one* subject: the needful. It is realized in genuine life. From the standpoint of man, this realization means nothing other than unity. But that is not, as it might seem, an abstract conception, but the most concrete living. For the unity that is meant is not, in fact, any comprehensive unity of a world or of a body of knowledge, not the established unity of the spirit or of being or of anything that is thought or felt or willed, but the unity of this human life and this human soul that fulfils itself in itself, the unity of your life and your soul, you who are seized by the teaching. Genuine life is united life.

Just as there are two kinds of goodness and two kinds of wisdom, the elemental and the achieved, so also there are two kinds of unity in man, as the consecration of which the teaching can verify and realize itself: the unity of the simple man and the unity of the man who has become unified. But as soon as the central man appears, whose achieved unity has the purity and the ingenuous power of the elemental, he must seek out the simple, his poor brothers in spirit, so that their deep unity, which preserves in its bosom all their sins and follies, may sanctify itself beyond sin and folly. And he speaks to them in the language that they can hear: in parable. And when he dies, the memory of his life becomes a parable itself. But a life that has become parable is called myth.

The parable is the insertion of the absolute into the world of events. The myth is the insertion of the world of things into the absolute.

So long as the teaching speaks only to those who have become unified, it cannot dispense with parable. For naked unity is dumb. Only out of things, events, and relations can it attain to speech; there is no human speech beyond these. As soon as the teaching comes to the things, it comes as parable. So long, however, as the teaching speaks only to those who have become unified, the parable is only a glass through which one beholds the light framed in a border of colours. But as soon as the teaching begins to address the simple through its central men, the parable becomes a prism. Thus the fulfilment leads across to the dissolution, and in the parable of the master there already rests in seed all the intoxication of ritual and the madness of dogma.

Again, the *life*, too, of the central man is not seen as reflected in a mirror, but as refracted in a prism: it is mythicized. *Mythus* does not mean that one brings the stars down to earth and allows them to tread it in human shape; rather in it the bliss-bestowing human shape is elevated to heaven, and moon and sun, Orion and the Pleiades, serve only to adorn it. Myth is not an affair of yonder and of old, but a function of today and of all times, of this city where I write and of all places of men. This is an eternal function of the soul: the insertion of what is experienced into the world process that is perceived as now more driving, now more thoughtful, but even in the dullest still in some way perceived— its insertion into the magic of existence. The stronger the tension and intensity of the experience, the greater the experienced shape, the experienced event, so much the more compelling the myth-forming power. Where the highest shape, the hero and saviour, the sublimest event, the life that he has lived, and the mightiest tension, the profound emotion of the simple, meet, the myth arises which compels all the future. Thus the way of dissolution proceeds; for the myth of the saviour already contains in germ the faith in the insignificant miracle and the misuse of the truth of salvation and redemption.

The dissolution takes place in religion, and is consummated in that perpetuated act of violence that calls itself religion yet holds religiousness in chains. Ever again there awakens in the souls of the religious the ardour for freedom—for the teaching; ever again reformation—restoration—renewal of the teaching—is ventured; ever again this venture must miscarry, ever again the fervent movement must issue not in the teaching but in a mixture of science and law, the so-called purified religion. For the teaching cannot be restored, cannot be renewed. Eternally the same, still it must eternally begin anew. This is the course taken by the history of the highest manifestation of the Eastern spirit.

2

That the teaching perpetually begins anew is in no way to be understood as meaning that it has one content that takes different forms, as those believe who investigate and compare the various teachings to find what is common to them. The opposition of content and form appears here as a dialectical one that does not clarify history but rather confuses it, just as it does not clarify but confuses the apperception of art. The Logos of the Johannine Gospel, the symbol of primal existence taken significantly from the world of speech, is erected as a sign of truth against the encroachment of this dialectic. 'The Word' is 'in the beginning' because it is the unity that is dialectically dissected. Just for this reason the word is the mediator: because it presents to the products of this dissection, e.g. to divinity and humanity, or otherwise regarded, to 'God the Father' and to 'the Holy Ghost,' the bond that unites them, the original unity that, divided and become flesh, once again reconciles the elements. 'The Word' is thereby the companion of every genuine human word, which also is not a content that has taken on a form, but a unity that has been dissected into content and form—a dissection that does not clarify but confuses the history of the human word and the history of each single human word, and whose claim, therefore, cannot reach beyond the province of conceptual classification. The same holds with the teaching.

The teaching proclaims that it is the unity as the necessary. But this is no wise a content that assumes different forms. When we dissect each teaching into content and form, we obtain as the 'content' not the unity, but the talk about the kingdom of heaven and the adoption by God, or the talk about the release from suffering and the holy path, or the talk about Tao and non-action. This cannot be otherwise; for the unity was even more than the content of Jesus or Buddha or Lao-tzu, more than they strove to express; it was their meaning and ground. It was more than the content of their word, it was the life of this word and this word itself in its unity. Therefore the fundamental relation with which we are here concerned is not that of content and form but, as is yet to be shown, that of the teaching and the parable.

Some have tried yet again to make unity into a content, into a 'common' content, but making the unity of genuine life into the unity of God or of the spirit or of being, common to the teachings—somewhat after the analogy of modern monism which decrees a 'unity of being' constituted in one way or another. But it is definitely not essential to the teaching to concern itself about the essence of God. With the Buddha this is, indeed, fully clear; but in the Upanishads, too, the significance of the teaching of the Atman does not lie in the fact that a statement is made thereby about the unity of being, but that what one calls being is nothing other than the unity of the self and that the unified one thereby encounters the world as being, as unity, as his self. Even so, primitive Christianity is not concerned with the unity of God but with the likeness of the unified man to God; here, too, the existent divine is only there, so to speak, for the sake of the necessary.

37

And the same holds with the teaching of the Tao, where all that is said of the 'path' of the world points to the path of the perfected man, and receives from it its verification and fulfilment.

It must be difficult, of course, for a modern Westerner to realize this fully, especially for those schooled in philosophy to whom the necessary is, perhaps, being seen *sub specie æterni*, and unity, perhaps, a synthetic act of knowledge. The teaching concerns itself with being even as little as it concerns itself with the ought. It is concerned only with the reality of genuine life, which is primary and cannot be subsumed. It is inaccessible, therefore, through the distinction between subject and object by which, perhaps, one no longer finds the unity in the object but instead removes it into the subject. This distinction is either not present for the man of the teaching, or he regards it only as an abstract formula for that manifold dialectical opposition on whose surpassing the teaching is built.

3

The way of the teaching is, accordingly, not that of the development of knowledge but that of pure fulfilment in human life. That is to be perceived with greater or lesser clarity in the three manifestations of the teaching that have come down to us with sufficient documentation.

These three manifestations are the Chinese teaching of the Tao, the Indian teaching of liberation, the Jewish and early Christian teaching of the Kingdom of God. The documentation of even these manifestations is insufficient to enable us to survey the whole of their way. Thus we know of the developing Jewish and early Christian teaching something of the living community that bore it—from the Rechabites (Jeremiah 35) to the Essenes, to whom ancient tradition, despite all exaggerations, probably refers correctly—but very little of the words of this, so-to-speak, underground Judaism that we can only thirstily surmise or infer from late sources. In the writings of the Tao-teaching, on the other hand, sayings of the 'Old Ones' are handed down to us that conceal the long pre-existence of the teaching, and this is also corroborated through statements of its opponents; but of the life forms in which it was transmitted we have entirely inadequate information. Not even the Indian literature, despite its incomparable vastness, offers a complete view of the links.

Yet the material suffices to show how the teaching takes form independently of science and law and how it fulfils itself in the central man, who conquers science and law without a battle, simply through his teaching and his life. Thus Buddha overcame the Vedic science through the elevation of the 'view' that does not concern the perfected man into the 'path,' and the Brahmanical law through the elevation of the castes into the order. And Lao-tzu overcame the official wisdom through the teaching of 'non-being,' the official virtue through 'non-action.'

And we can also see from these manifestations that the central man brings no new element to the teaching, but rather fulfils it. 'I am not come to destroy but to fulfil.' Lao-tzu also says of himself that he has only to fulfil the unrecognized of earlier times, the faint notion of the One that is contained in the word of the people. He once quotes the saying, 'Those who do deeds of violence do not reach their natural death,' and adds to it, 'What the others teach, I also teach: I shall make out of it a father-ground of the teaching.' This corresponds to the saying of the Sermon on the Mount, 'But I say unto you'; for violence, to Lao-tzu, is already in itself dead, lifeless because it is Tao-less. To fulfil means here as there to raise something that has been handed down out of the conditioned into the unconditioned.

The central man brings to the teaching no new element, rather he fulfils it; he raises it out of the unrecognized into the recognized and out of the conditioned into the unconditioned.

This unconditionality of the fulfilling man, which sets the world of the conditioned against him, and this his power of fulfilment manifest themselves in his life. For him, in incomparably higher measure than for the great ruler, the great artist, and the great philosopher, all that is scattered, fleeting, and fragmentary grows together into unity; this unity is his life. The ruler has his organization of peoples, the artist has his work, the philosopher has his system of ideas; the fulfilling man has only his life. His words are elements of this life, each an executor and originator, each inspired by destiny and caught up by destiny, the multitude of voices transformed through this human body into a conclusive harmony, the weak movement of many dead joined in him into might, he who is the crossroads of the teaching, of fulfilment and dissolution, salvation and degeneration. There are, therefore, logia that no doubt can touch, and that, striding through the generations without being written down, preserve themselves unmixed, by the strength of their stamp of destiny and the elementary uniqueness of their fulfilling speech. For the fulfilling man, who is assembled out of everything and yet comes out of nothing, is the most unique of men. Though all seeking desires him and all self-communion foresees him, he is recognized by few when he appears, and these few are probably not at all those who foresaw and desired him: so great is his uniqueness— so unoriginal, so unpretentious, so wholly the final genuineness of mankind.

This is most apparent with Jesus whose witness was perfected through death, the sole absolute that man has to offer. Next to him stands Buddha. Lao-tzu's life holds out least, because his life was just that of his teaching, a hidden life. In the scanty report of the historian all that is necessary is said concerning it; of his life: 'His teaching was the concealment of self: what he strove for was to be nameless'; and of his death: 'No one knows where he died: Lao-tzu was a hidden wise man.'

4

Like his life, his teaching also is the most hidden, for it is the most lacking in parable.

Naked unity is dumb. As soon as the unity becomes teaching out of the ground and goal of a separated man, submerged in wordless wonder, as soon as the word stirs in this man—in the hour of stillness, before the break of day, where there is yet no Thou other than the I, and the lonely talk in the dark traverses the abyss across and back—the unity is already touched by parable. Man utters his words as the *Logos* utters men: his words no longer proceed from pure unity—the manifold, the parable, is already therein. But as the multiplicity of men, so long as they are children, is still tied to the unity, and parable only rests on them as the smile on their lips, so in the hour of stillness the speech of the separated man is only touched at first by the parable as by a smile. And as, when men awaken and themselves beget children, their multiplicity detaches itself from the unity, and the parable flows in them as the blood in their veins, so the parable flows like blood through the speech of the fulfilling man when he goes out to meet his fellows.

But as between the time of childhood and manhood stands youth, the tragedy that is reconciled unperceived, so between solitude and sermon there stands the time of transition which, to be sure, is not reconciled unperceived, but comes to a decision. Buddha calls it the time of temptation. He says to the tempter: 'I shall not go into Nirvana, O evil one, before this, my irreproachable way of life, shall have thrived and come to flower, disseminated far, found by many, richly unfolded, so that it is beautifully manifested by men.' In this period the parable is no longer the smile, not yet the blood; it still rests upon the spirit already in the spirit—like a dream. Like youth, the transition stands in a dream. Therefore the word of the solitude is the cry and the word of the sermon is the narrative; but the word of the transition is the image.

There is a life, however, in which the transition does not lead from solitude to sermon, but leads from the solitude of the question to the solitude of the fullness, from the solitude of the abyss to the solitude of the sea. That is the hidden life.

I believe that this man is tempted as the others are. Like the others, he does not enter Nirvana, but neither does he go to men: he enters the concealment. The concealment will bear his children. 'He who knows his brightness and veils himself in his darkness'—thus Lao-tzu describes it.

What is the sermon to this man? 'Heaven does not speak and yet knows how to find answer.' What is manhood to him? 'He who lives his manhood yet holds to his womanhood, he is the river-bed of all the world.'

This man does not talk to himself and he does not talk to men; but into the concealment. Although he is not himself on the way to men, his word is still necessarily on the way to parable; he is not in transition, but his word remains the word of transition: the image. His speech is not a complete speech of parable like that of Buddha or Jesus, but a speech of images. It resembles a youth who has not yet become detached from the unity like a man, but is no longer tied to the unity like a child. But that would be a youth such as we glimpse, say, in the poems of Hölderlin—who does not have the striving beyond the self of dream and of tragedy; but only the visionary fullness of youth, turned into the unconditional and the eternal where the dream has become mantic and tragedy mystery.

Concealment is the history of Lao-tzu's speech. No matter how mythicized the Sermon of Benares and the Sermon on the Mount may be, that a great truth lies at the base of each myth is unmistakable. In Lao-tzu's life there is nothing corresponding. In his words, in his writings, one marks throughout that his utterances are not at all what we call speech, but only like the soughing of the sea out of its fullness when it is swept by a light wind. In the scanty reports of the historian, this too is communicated or represented. Lao-tzu enters his final concealment; he leaves the country in which he dwelt. He reaches the boundary station. The chief of the boundary station says to him, 'I see that you are entering into the concealment. Would you yet write a book for me before you go?' Thereupon Lao-tzu wrote a book in two sections, that is the *Book of the Tao and of Virtue* in a little over five thousand words. Then he departed. And immediately afterwards the report concludes with the words that I have cited earlier, 'No one knows where he finished his life.' Information or symbol, all the same: this is the truth about Lao-tzu's speech. 'Those who know it do not say it; those who say it do not know it,' it is stated in his book. His speech is just like the soughing of the sea out of its fullness.

The teaching of Lao-tzu is full of images but without parables, provided that we are thinking of the complete parable that develops from the image to narrative. Thus he committed it to the ages. Centuries passed over it, then the teaching came to one who —like all great poets, certainly gathering into himself much folk lore—composed its parable. This man is called Chuang-tzu.

The parable of the Tao-teaching, therefore, is not, like that in the teaching of Jesus and of Buddha, the direct word of fulfilment spoken by the central man. It is, rather, the poetry of one to whom the teaching was delivered when it had already reached its fulfilment.

The manifestation of the Tao-teaching is split into the first word, which stands closer to the naked unity than any other word of the human world, and in the second word, in which the unity wears a richer and more delicate drapery than in any other word of the teaching, and can properly be compared only to the great poems of mankind.

Only the two together give us the completed shape of the teaching in its purest fulfilment; as it proclaims Tao, 'the path,' the ground and meaning of the unified life, as the ground and meaning of all.

5

Chuang-tzu lived in the second half of the fourth and the first half of the third centuries before Christ, hence about two hundred and fifty years after Lao-tzu.* But while Paul, that other apostle who did not know his master in the flesh, dissolved his teaching of the unity of the genuine life and perverted it into an eternal antagonism between spirit and nature—that one could not overcome but only escape—Chuang-tzu was a faithful messenger of the teaching: its messenger to the world. That he composed its parable is not to be understood as if he had 'explained' it through things or 'applied' it to things. Rather, the parable bears the unity of the teaching into all the world so that, as it before enclosed it in itself, the All now appears full of it, and no thing is so insignificant that the teaching refuses to fill it. He who does not zealously spread the teaching, but reveals it in its essence, bestows on each the possibility of also discovering and animating the teaching in himself.

* I cannot agree with the late-dating of Lao-tzu that is recently gaining ground.

Such an apostleship is silent and solitary, as the master-hood that it serves was silent and solitary. It no longer lives in the concealment, yet it is not bound to men by any duty nor by any aim. History imparts to us almost nothing else concerning Chuang-tzu's life than this, that he was poor and the offices that were offered him were declined with the words, 'I shall never accept an office. Thus I shall remain free to follow myself.' The same attitude appears in the reports of his life scattered in his books, clearly penned by the hand of a disciple. And nothing else is signified by the report of his death. He forbade that a funeral should be given him, 'With earth and heaven for my coffin and grave, with the sun and the moon for my two round holy images, with the stars for my burial jewellery, with all creation for my funeral procession—is not all ready to hand? What could you still add to it?'

It is not surprising that the conditioned world rose against him. His age, which stood under the domination of the Confucian wisdom of the moral ordering of life according to duty and aim, called Chuang-tzu a good-for-nothing. In parables, such as that of the useless tree, he gave his answer to the age. Men do not know the use of the useless. What they call the aimless is the aim of the Tao.

He opposed public opinion, which was the law of his age not in reference to any particular content but in its basic spirit. He who flatters his princes or his parents, he said, he who agrees with them blindly and praises them without merit, is called by the crowd unfilial and faithless. But the man who flatters the crowd is not criticized, he who blindly agrees with it, praises it without cause, he who adjusts his attitude and his expression so as to win favour. Chuang-tzu knew the vanity of the crowd and declared it; he knew that only he wins it who subjugates it. 'One man steals a purse and is punished. Another steals a state and becomes a prince.' And he also knew that the teaching of the Tao could never subjugate the crowd. For the teaching brings nothing to men; rather, it says to each one that he will have unity if he discovers it in himself and brings it to life. So it is with men: 'All strive to comprehend what they do not yet know, none strives to comprehend what he knows.' What is great is inaccessible to the crowd because it is simple. Great music, said Chuang-tzu, is not appreciated, but over street songs the populace rejoice. Noble words are not heard while common words predominate; two little earthen bells drown out the peal of the great bell. 'Thus the world goes astray; I know the right path, but how can I conduct men to it?'

Thus his apostleship spent itself in parable that was not zealous, but rested in itself, visible and yet hidden. The world, says Chuang-tzu, stands opposed to the path, and the path stands opposed to the world; the path cannot recognize the world, and the world cannot recognize the path—'Therefore the virtue of the wise is hidden, even when they do not dwell in the mountains and in the forest; hidden even when they hide nothing.' Thus the apostleship of Chuang-tzu found its issue in that in which the masterhood of Lao-tzu had run its course: in the concealment.

6

'Tao' means the way, the path; but since it also has the meaning of 'speech,' the term is at times rendered by 'logos.' For Lao-tzu and his disciples, wherever it is developed figuratively, the first of these meanings is implied. Yet its connotation is related to that of the Heracleitian logos. Both transpose a dynamic principle of human life into the transcendent, though basically they mean nothing other than human life itself, which is the bearer of all transcendence. I shall here set forth this meaning for the Tao.*

In the West, Tao has usually been understood as an attempt to explain the world; the explanation of the world that one glimpses therein always coincides in a remarkable way with the current philosophy of the age. Thus Tao first passes for nature, after that reason, and recently it is held to be nothing but energy. In contrast to these interpretations, it must be pointed out that Tao generally means no explanation of the world; it implies that only

* Citations without special marking are taken from Chuang-tzu, those with (L) from Lao-tzu.

the whole meaning of being rests in the unity of the genuine life, that it is experienced nowhere else, that it is just this unity which is grasped as the absolute. If one wishes to look away from the unity of the genuine life and seek what underlies it, then nothing is left over but the unknowable, of which nothing further can be said than that it is the unknowable. Unity is the only way to realize it and to experience it in its reality. The unknowable is naturally neither nature nor reason nor energy, but just the unknowable which no image reaches because 'the images are in it.' But what is experienced is again neither nature nor reason nor energy, but the unity of the path, the unity of the genuine human way that rediscovers the united in the world and in each thing: the path as the unity of the world, as the unity of each thing.

But the unknowableness of the Tao cannot be understood as one speaks of the unknowableness of some principle of a religious or philosophical explanation of the world, in order to say nevertheless something further about it. Even what the word 'Tao' expresses does not express the unknowable; 'the name that can be named is not the eternal name' (L). If one does not regard Tao as the necessary whose reality is experienced in unified life but as something separate, then one finds nothing to regard: 'Tao can have no existence.' It cannot be investigated nor demonstrated. Not only can no truth be stated concerning it, but it cannot be a subject of a statement at all. What is said concerning it is neither true nor false. 'How can Tao be so obscured that something "true" or something "false" appears in it? . . . Tao is obscured because we cannot grasp it.' When it appears, therefore, that Tao is more present in one time than in another, this is no reality, but only like the sinking and ascending of the tones in music, 'it belongs to the playing.' We cannot discover it in any being. If we seek it in heaven and earth, in space and in time, then it is not there; rather, heaven and earth, space and time, are grounded in it alone. And nonetheless 'it can be found through seeking' (L): in unified life. There it is not recognized and known, but possessed, lived, and acted.

'Only he who reaches it in silence and fulfils it with his being has it,' state the books of Lieh-tzu. And he does not have it as his own but as the meaning of the world. Out of his unity he beholds unity in the world: the unity of the masculine and the feminine elements that do not exist for themselves but only for each other, the unity of the opposites that do not exist for themselves but only through each other, the unity of the things that do not exist for themselves but only with one another. This unity is the Tao in the world. When, in a conversation related by Chuang-tzu, Lao-tzu says to Khung-tzu, 'That heaven is high, that the earth is broad, that sun and moon revolve, that the things grow, that is their Tao,' this statement is only fully comprehensible through an old verse that Lao-tzu quotes in his book. It runs:

> *Heaven obtained unity and thereby radiance,*
> *Earth unity and thereby rest and repose,*
> *The spirit unity and thereby understanding,*
> *The brooks unity and thereby full banks,*
> *All beings unity and thereby life,*
> *Prince and king unity in order to give the world*
>   *the right measure.*

Thus the unity of each thing determines in itself the manner and nature of this thing; that is, the Tao of the thing, this thing's path and wholeness. 'No thing can beget Tao, and yet each thing has Tao in itself and begets it ever anew.' That means each thing reveals the Tao through the way of its existence, through its life; for Tao is unity in change, the unity that verifies itself not only in the manifoldness of things but also in the successive moments in the life of each thing. The perfect revelation of Tao, therefore, is not the man who goes his way without alteration, but the man who combines the maximum of change with the purest unity.

There are two types of life. The one is mere thoughtless living, using life up until its extinction; the other is the eternal change and its unity in spirit. He who does not allow himself to be consumed in his life, but incessantly renews himself and just through that affirms his self in change—which is not, indeed, a static being but just the way, Tao—he attains the eternal change and self-affirmation. For, here as always in the Tao-teaching, consciousness effects being, spirit effects reality. And as in the connection of the life-moments of a thing, so in the connection of the life-moments of the world, Tao verifies itself—in the coming and going of all things, in the unity of their eternal changes. Thus it says in the Books of Lieh-tzu: 'What has no origin and continually engenders is Tao. From life to life, therefore, although ending, not decaying, that is eternity . . . what has an origin and continually dies is likewise Tao. From death to death, therefore, although never ending, yet decaying, that also is eternity.' Tao is unloosing, it is transition to new shape, it is a moment of sleep and contemplation between two world lives. All is becoming and change in the 'great house' of eternity. As in the existence of things, separation and gathering, change and unity, succeed each other, so in the existence of the world life and death follow each other, together verifying Tao as the unity in change. This eternal Tao, which is the denial of all illusory being, is also called non-being. Birth is not beginning, death is not an end, existence in space and time is without limit and cessation, birth and death are only entrance and exit through 'the invisible gate of heaven that is called non-being. This is the dwelling-place of the perfected man.'

Here, too, the perfected man, the unified one, is described as he who directly experiences Tao. He beholds the unity in the world. But that is not to be understood as if the world were a closed thing outside of him whose unity he penetrates. Rather the unity of the world is only the reflection of his unity; for the world is nothing alien, but one with the unified man. 'Heaven and earth and I came together into existence, and I and all things are one.' But since the unity of the world only exists for the perfected man, it is, in truth, his unity that sets unity in the world. That also proceeds from the nature of the Tao as it appears in things. Tao is the path of things, their manner, their peculiar order, their unity; but as such it exists in things only potentially; it first becomes active in its contact with others: 'If there were metal and stone without Tao, there would be no sound. They have the power of sound, but it does not come out of them if they are not struck. Thus it is with all things.'

Consciousness, however, never characterizes a receiving but a giving: 'Tao is conveyed but not received.' As the Tao of things only becomes living and manifest through their contact with other things, so the Tao of the world only becomes living and manifest through its unconscious contact with the conscious being of the unified man. This is expressed by Chuang-tzu through the statement that the perfected man reconciles and brings into accord the two primal elements of nature, the positive and the negative, yang and yin, which the primal unity of being tore asunder. And in the 'Book of Purity and Rest,' a late Taoist tract that appears in this point to rest on a tradition all too narrowly comprehended, it says, 'When man persists in purity and rest, heaven and earth return'; that is, to unity, to undivided existence, to Tao. In the late, degenerated literature, the unified man is still understood as the giving. We may say: the unified man is for the Tao-teaching the creating man; for all creating, from the point of view of this teaching, means nothing other than to call forth the Tao of the world, the Tao of things, to make the latent unity living and manifest.

We shall try to sum it up:

Tao in itself is the unrecognizable, the unknowable. 'The true Tao does not explain itself.' It cannot be represented: it cannot be thought, it has no image, no word, no measure. 'The right measure of the Tao is its self' (L).

Tao appears in the becoming of the world as the original undivided state, as the primal existence from which all elements sprang, as 'mother of all beings' (L), as the 'spirit of the valley' that bears everything. 'The spirit of the valley is deathless; it is called the deep feminine. The deep feminine portal is called the roots of heaven and of earth' (L).

Tao appears in the being of the world as the constant undividedness: as the united transformation of the world, as its order. 'It has its movement and its truth, but it has neither action nor shape.' It is 'eternally without action and yet without non-action' (L). It 'perseveres and does not change' (L).

Tao appears in things as the personal undividedness: as each thing's particular manner and power. There is nothing in which the whole Tao is not present as this thing's self. Here, too, Tao is eternally without action and yet without non-action. The self of things has its life in the way in which things answer things.

Tao appears in men as purposeful undividedness: as the unifying force that overcomes all straying away from the ground of life, as the completing force that heals all that is sundered and broken, as the atoning force that delivers from all division. 'He who is in sin, Tao can atone for him' (L).

As purposeful undividedness Tao has its own fulfilment as its goal. It wills to realize itself. In men Tao can become pure unity as it cannot in the realm of things. He in whom Tao becomes pure unity is the perfected man. In him Tao no longer appears but is.

The perfected man is self-enclosed, secure, united out of Tao, unifying the world, a creator, 'God's companion': the companion of all-creating eternity. The perfected man possesses eternity. Only the perfected man possesses eternity. The spirit wanders through things until it blooms to eternity in the perfected man.

It is this that is signified by the word of Lao-tzu: 'Ascend the height of renunciation, embrace the abyss of rest. The numberless beings all arise. Therein I recognize their return. When the being unfolds itself, in the unfolding each returns to his root. To have returned to the root means to rest. To rest means to have fulfilled one's destiny. To have fulfilled one's destiny means to be eternal.'

Tao realizes itself in the genuine life of the perfected man. In his pure unity it grows out of appearance to direct reality. The unknowable and the unified human life, the first and the last, touch one another. In the perfected man Tao returns to itself from its world wandering through the manifestation. It becomes fulfilment.

7

But what is the unified human life in its relation to things? How does the perfected man live in the world? What shape does knowledge assume in him, the coming of things to man? What shape action, the coming of man to the things?

The Teaching of the Tao

The teaching of the Tao answers this question with a vigorous denial of all that men call knowledge and action.

What men call knowledge rests on the sundering of the senses and the powers of the mind. What they call action rests on the sundering of intentions and deeds. Each sense receives something different, each mental power elaborates it differently, they all stagger through one another in infinity: that is what men call knowledge. Each purpose tugs at the structure, each act interferes with the order, they all are entangled in infinity: that is what men call action.

What is called knowledge by men is no knowledge. In order to demonstrate this, Chuang-tzu assembles almost all the reasons that the human mind has ever devised for putting itself in question.

There is no perception, since things incessantly change.

There is no knowledge in space because only relative and not absolute extension is accessible to us. All greatness exists only in relation—'under heaven there is nothing that is greater than the point of a blade of grass.' We cannot swing out of our own measure. The cricket does not understand the flight of the giant bird.

There is no knowledge in time because duration exists for us only relatively. 'No being attains a higher age than a child that dies in the cradle.' We cannot swing out of our own measure. A morning mushroom knows not the alternation of day and night, a butterfly chrysalis knows not the alternation of spring and fall.

There is no certainty of life; for we have no criterion by which we could decide what is the real and determining life, waking or dream. Each state holds itself to be the real.

There is no certainty of values; for we have no measure of right by which we could decide what is beautiful and what is ugly, what is good and what is evil. Each being calls itself good and its opposite evil.

There is no truth in concepts, for all speech is inadequate.

All this signified only one thing for Chuang-tzu: that what men call knowledge is no knowledge. In separation there is no knowledge. Only the undivided man knows; for only in him in whom there is no division is there no separation from the world, and only he who is not separated from the world can know it. Not in the dialectic of subject and object, but only in the unity with the all is knowledge possible. Unity is knowledge.

This knowledge is not put in question by anything, for it embraces the whole. It overcomes relation in the unconditionality of the all-embracing. It receives each pair of opposites as a polarity without wishing to eliminate their oppositeness, and it includes all polarities in its unity; it 'reconciles in its light the yes with the no.'

This knowledge is without passion and seeking. It rests in itself. 'It is not by going out of the door that one knows the world; it is not by gazing through the window that one sees the way of heaven' (L). It is without the mania for knowledge. It has things, it does not know them. It does not take place through senses and mental powers, but through the wholeness of the being. It lets the senses continue, but only like children at play; for all that they bring to it is only a varicoloured, glittering, uncertain reflection of its own truth. It lets the mental powers continue, but only as dancers who make its music into images, unfaithful and unsteady and rich in shapes, after the manner of dancers. The 'organ playing of heaven,' the playing of unity on the manifoldness of our nature ('as the wind plays on the openings of the trees'), becomes here the organ-playing of the soul.

This knowledge is not knowing but being. Because it possesses things in its unity, it never stands over against them; and when it regards them, it regards them from the inside out, each thing from itself outward; but not from its appearance, rather from the essence of this thing, from the unity of this thing that it possesses in its own unity. This knowledge is each thing that it regards, and thus it lifts each thing that it regards out of appearance into being.

This knowledge embraces all things in its being; that is, in its love. It is the all-embracing love that overcomes all opposites.

This knowledge is the deed. The deed is the eternal measure of right, the eternal criterion, the absolute, the speechless, the unchangeable. The knowledge of the perfected man is not in his thinking but in his action.

What is called action by men is no action.

It is not an effecting of the whole being but single intentions groping their way in the web of the Tao, the interference of single actions in the manner and order of things. It is entangled in aims.

In so far as they approve of it, men call it virtue. What is called virtue by men is no virtue. It exhausts itself in 'love of mankind' and 'righteousness.'

What men call love of mankind and righteousness has nothing in common with the love of the perfected man.

It is perverted because it comes forward as an ought, as the subject of a command. But love cannot be commanded. Commanded love works only evil and harm; it stands in contradiction to the natural goodness of the human heart; it troubles its purity and disturbs its immediacy. Therefore, those who preach thus pass their days in complaining about the wickedness of the world. They injure the wholeness and truthfulness of things and awaken doubt and division. Intentional love of mankind and intentional righteousness are not grounded in the nature of man; they are superfluous and burdensome like surplus fingers or other protuberances. Therefore, Lao-tzu says to Khung-tzu, 'As horseflies keep one awake the whole night, so this talk of love of mankind and righteousness plagues me. Strive to bring the world back to its original simplicity.'

But in still another sense 'love of mankind and righteousness' have nothing in common with the love of the perfected man. They rest upon a man's standing opposite the other men and then treating them 'lovingly' and 'justly.' But the love of the perfected man, for which each man can strive, rests upon unity with all things. Therefore Lao-tzu says to Khung-tzu, 'For the perfected men of ancient times, love of mankind was only a station and righteousness only an inn on the way to the kingdom of the undivided, where they nourish themselves in the fields of equanimity and dwell in the gardens of duty-lessness.'

As the true knowledge, seen from the standpoint of human speech, is called by Lao-tzu 'not-knowing' ('He who is illumined in Tao is like full night'), so the true action, the action of the perfected man, is called by him 'non-action.' 'The perfected man performs the non-action' (L). 'The rest of the wise man is not what the world calls rest: it is the work of his inner deed.'

This action, the 'non-action,' is an effecting of the whole being. To interfere with the life of things means to harm both them and oneself. But to rest means to effect, to purify one's own soul means to purify the world, to collect oneself means to be helpful, to surrender oneself to Tao means to renew creation. He who imposes himself has the small, manifest might; he who does not impose himself has the great, secret might. He who 'does nothing' effects. He who is in complete harmony is surrounded by the receiving love of the world. 'He is unmoved like a corpse whereas his dragon-power reveals itself all around; he is in deep silence, whereas his thunder voice resounds; and the powers of heaven answer each movement of his will, and under the flexible influence of his non-action all things ripen and flourish.'

This action, the 'non-action,' is an effecting out of gathered unity. In ever new parable Chuang-tzu says that each does right who gathers himself to unity in his act. The will of him who is concentrated into one becomes pure power, pure effecting; for when there is no division in the willing person, there is no longer any division between him and what is willed—being; what is willed becomes being. The nobility of a being lies in its ability to concentrate itself into one. For the sake of this unity Lao-tzu says, 'He who has the fullness of virtue in himself is like a new-born child.' The unified man is like a child that screams the whole day and is not hoarse, out of the harmony of his forces, keeps his fists shut the whole day out of concentrated virtue, stares the whole day at *one* thing out of undivided attention, that moves, rests, relieves himself without knowing it, and lives beyond all distress in a heavenly light.

This action, the 'non-action,' stands in harmony with the nature and destiny of all things, with Tao. 'The perfected man, like heaven and earth, has no love of mankind.' He does not stand opposite the creature but embraces it. Therefore his love is wholly free and unlimited, does not depend upon the conduct of men and knows no choice; it is the *unconditioned* love. 'Good men—I treat them well, men who are not good—I also treat them well: virtue is good. True men—I deal with them truly, men who are not true—I also deal with them truly: virtue is true' (L). And because he has no 'love of mankind,' the perfected man does not interfere in the life of beings, he does not impose himself on them, but he 'helps all beings to their freedom' (L): through his unity he leads them, too, to unity, he liberates their nature and their destiny, he releases Tao in them.

As natural virtue, the virtue of each thing, consists of its 'non-being,' in that it rests in its limits, in its primary condition, so the highest virtue, the virtue of the perfected man consists of its 'non-action,' in his effecting out of undivided, opposite-less, enclosed unity. 'He closes his exits, fastens his doors, he breaks his edges, scatters abroad his fullness, makes mild his brilliance, becomes one with his dust. That means deep self-unification' (L).

8

Unity alone is true power. Therefore the unified man is the true ruler.

The relation of the ruler to his kingdom is the highest proclamation of the Tao in the life together of beings.

The kingdom, the community of beings, is not something artificial and arbitrary, but something inborn and self-determining. 'The kingdom is a spiritual instrument and cannot be made. He who makes it destroys it' (L).

Therefore what is called ruling by man is no ruling but a destroying. He who interferes with the natural life of the kingdom, he who wants to lead, master, and determine it from the outside, he annihilates it, he loses it. He who guards and unfolds the natural life of the kingdom, he who does not impose upon it command and compulsion, but submerges himself in it, listens to its secret message, and brings it to light and to work, he rules it in truth. He performs the non-action; he does not interfere, but guards and unfolds what wills to become. In the need and drive of the kingdom the will of the Tao reveals itself to him. He joins his own will to it so that he may become an instrument of the Tao, and all things change of themselves. He knows no violence, and yet all beings follow the gesture of his hand. He uses neither reward nor punishment, and yet what he wants to happen happens. 'I am without action,' speaks the perfected man, 'and the people change of themselves; I love rest, and the people become righteous of themselves; I am without industry, and the people become rich of themselves; I am without desires, and the people become simple of themselves' (L).

To rule means to become a part of the natural order of appearances. But only he can do that who has found unity, and out of it beheld the unity of each thing in itself and the unity of things with one another. He who becomes free of the distinctions and joins himself to the infinite, he who restores both the things and himself to the primal existence, he who liberates and brings to unity both himself and the world, he who redeems both from the slavery of violence and bustle—he rules the world.

The kingdom has degenerated; it has declined to the act of violence of government. It must be liberated from it. That is the goal of the true ruler.

What is the act of violence of government? The compulsion of false might. 'The more prohibitions and restraints the kingdom has, so much the more impoverished the people; the more arms the people have, so much the more will the land be disquieted; the more artificiality and cunning the people have, so much the more monstrous things arise; the more laws and ordinances are proclaimed, so much the more robbers and thieves are there' (L). The government is the parasite that takes away from the people its life strength. 'The people are hungry because the government consumes too many taxes. Therefore they are hungry. The people are hard to rule because the government is all too interfering. Therefore they are hard to rule. The people are heedless of death because they long in vain for fullness of life. Therefore they are heedless of death' (L). The true ruler liberates the people from the violent acts of government because in place of might he allows the 'non-action' to govern. He exercises his transforming influence on all beings, and yet they know nothing of it, for he influences them in agreement with their primal nature. He causes men and things to be cheerful of themselves. He takes all their suffering on himself. 'To bear the country's need and pain, that is to be the kingdom's king' (L).

In the degenerated kingdom no one is granted the privilege of conducting his affairs according to his own insight, but each stands under the dominion of the multitude. The true ruler liberates the individual from this dominion; he makes the crowd no longer a crowd, and allows everyone freely to administer his own affairs and the community the common affairs. But he does all this in the manner of non-action, and the people does not notice that it has a ruler. It says, 'We have become so of ourselves.'

The true ruler stands as the perfected man beyond love of mankind and righteousness. Certainly the wise prince is to be praised who gives to each his own and is just; still more highly to be praised is the virtuous one who stands in community with all and practises love; but the only one who can fulfil on earth the kingdom, the spiritual vessel, is the spiritual prince who creates perfection: unity with heaven and earth, freedom from all ties that conflict with the Tao, deliverance of things to their primal nature, to their virtue.

The true ruler is Tao's executor on earth. Therefore it says, 'Tao is great, heaven is great, the earth is great, the king also is great' (L).

9

I have not considered the Tao-teaching in its 'development' but in its unity. The teaching does not develop, it cannot develop after it has found its fulfilment in the central human life. Instead it becomes a rule, like the teaching of the Buddha, if the apostle who receives it (never directly) from the hands of the fulfilling man is an organizer like Asoka; or it becomes dialectic, like the teaching of Jesus, if this man is a man of action like Paul; or it becomes poetry, like the teaching of the Tao, if the propagator is a poet like Chuang-tzu. Chuang-tzu was a poet. He did not 'develop'* the teaching as it had been given in the words of Lao-tzu, but he shapes it into poetry and into philosophy; for he was a poet of ideas, like Plato.

Chuang-tzu shows many resemblances to Greek philosophers in other respects. He has been compared with Heracleitus; and, in fact, there are words of Heracleitus that could not be associated with any other philosophy with the same justification as with the Tao-teaching: words such as that of the unknowable logos that yet works in all, of the unity that is at once nameless and named, of its manifestation as the eternal order in the world, of the eternal transformation from totality to unity and from unity to totality, of the harmony of opposites, of the relation between waking and dream in the existence of the individual, of that between life and death in the existence of the world. Further, Chuang-tzu may perhaps be compared with the total shape of Greek philosophy that transferred the teaching from the sphere of genuine life into the sphere of the explanation of the world, into an ideological structure, thereby, to be sure, creating something wholly individual and powerful in itself.

It is tempting to compare Chaung-tzu also with Western poets, for which purpose even isolated motifs offer themselves in a strange correspondence. One might proceed from outward to ever more inward affinities: one would begin by placing the story of the skull next to Hamlet's speech in the churchyard, then juxtapose Chuang-tzu's story of silence and the narrative in *The Little Flowers of St. Francis* of Brother Ægidus' meeting with Louis of France, in order, finally, to rediscover in the conversation of eternal dying Goethe's holy longing of 'Die and become' ('*Stirb und werde*') in more austere, more thought-like counterpart. But all this can only be a transition to an acceptance in which one no longer attempts to enregister Chuang-tzu in a category, but receives him in his whole real existence without comparison and co-ordination; him, that is, his work—the parable.

* The teaching that I have presented last, that of the kingdom, is already well established in Lao-tzu, even in the stamp of the words.

To the Contemporary

(Autumn, 1914)

POWER, invading power of the contemporary!
I sat once in the steel-blue solitude of the evening. Then
I opened the window and you came flying in, looking like
a moon-coloured bird laden with the fearful and the sweet. I felt:
in this moment. The ages unfold in the unfathomable, but you laid
the space, the earth-space of this moment, upon my breast like
a skein of wool, and I breathed the dreams of far-distant beings.
Impulses of unknown creatures gathered in my throat, and the
elements of many souls mixed in my blood. The present entered
into me like a music composed of tension, impulse and rapture
of the living; and withstanding the infinity of this moment, I did
not know whether I ruled it or it ruled me; I knew only that it
was bound, bound into corporal music. But I knew more as,
recollecting myself in the depths, I bid you go, power of the
contemporary, and you rose away like a moon-coloured bird,
with unburdened wings. Then I closed my window and felt the
clock-stroke 'All Time' go through my heart. Now they were
again with me, Lao-tzu the Old and the golden Plato, and with
them, kindred to them, the whole present. As in The Crucifixion
of Fra Angelico, the believers of many ages are present at the
event, and the strength of their togetherness removes the scene
from the flow of time, so whenever the ages unite the timeless is
always near.

But now—now you break in my window, now you fall upon
me, robber-eagle, destiny, invading power of the contemporary.
The centuries flee before your roaring, and you hurl the earth-
space of this moment like a firebrand upon my breast. Out of
your firebrand, happenings pour into my blood, shrapnel wounds

59

and tetanus, screams and death-rattle, and the smile of the mouth above the crushed body. Where will this be bound into music, where, where, in what heritage of æons? Where dwells its atonement, where sleeps its song, where does the secret of the master conceal itself? How can I withstand the infinity of this moment?

But never again, O moment, O instorming power of the contemporary, never will I bid you go. You shall stay with me and no one will efface you. Rather shall I be prey and fuel to your fire all the moments of my life. Out of your fire light is born, and nowhere does it flash except out of your fire. I am consumed in you, but I am consumed into light.

Shall I ever forget the bliss of that clock-stroke? But I do not long for it again, now that your raging has visited me, you fatal one! Let the timeless be near where the ages unite; I have found what is greater in the inexorable truth of the moment, which commands to work for tomorrow.

These wounds and these cries which you have brought to me, power of the contemporary, these wounds give forth light, these cries preach, and the confused destiny helps the struggling eternity.

Dimensions of Dialogue

Drama and Theatre

(A Fragment, 1925)

DRAMA, regarded as a species of poetry, is something entirely different from the drama of theatre. It represents the rising to artistic independence of an element that was only tolerated with reluctance by the epic: dialogue. In the narrative only as much space falls to the lot of conversation as it needs in order to carry the action and move it forward; in drama conversation carries all action.

When we read a drama, really read it, we may take scenario and stage directions (whose epic protuberance in our time belongs to the signs of the dissolution of form) as only clarification of the dialogue; otherwise we lose our way in a jumble of perceptions. Regarded as a species of poetry, drama is therefore the formation of the *word* as something that moves *between beings*, the mystery of word and answer. Essential to it is the fact of the *tension* between word and answer; the fact, namely, that two men never mean the same things by the words that they use; that there is, therefore, no pure reply; that at each point of the conversation, therefore, understanding and misunderstanding are interwoven; from which comes then the interplay of openness and closedness, expression and reserve.

Thus through the mere fact, given form by dialogue, of the *difference* between men there already exists, before any actual action, that dramatic entanglement which, woven with the unfathomableness of destiny, appears as 'tragedy,' the same entanglement which drawn into the all-too-clear world of caprice and accident makes for 'comedy.' How both, the tragic and the comic, can unite in pure actionless dialogue has been shown to us by Plato in whose works his master and the many-named sophist

63

confront each other like two types of the Attic theatre: the ironic man (*Eiron*), who does not say what he knows, and the boaster (*Alazon*), who says what he does not know—and what we finally experience is the fate of spirit in the world. With the mere antagonistic existence of the persons that proclaims itself dialogically, the dramatic is essentially present; all action can only unfold it.

If the play as poetry is thus grounded in the fact that man seeks to communicate to men through speaking, and across all barriers of individuation actually succeeds in communication, if only in tension, the play as a theatre production belongs to a more natural level. It originates in the elemental impulse to leap through transformation over the abyss between I and Thou that is bridged through speech—the belief of primitive man that if he assumes the aspect and gestures of another being, an animal, a hero, a demon, he can become this other being. This is no mere belief, but rather an experience. The Australians whose tribe had the kangaroo as the totem animal, the Thracian who danced the satyr in the suite of Dionysus, had a bodily certainty of identity with the represented being. This certainty is not 'acted,' still it is a play, for it disappears as soon as masks and attitudes are stripped off. But even if it lasted until the body swooned, till the extinction of consciousness, it would still be, with each repetition, more distinguishable, more arbitrary, more acted.

None the less, this is not yet a play. The play comes into being with the appearance of spectators. This appearance is not to be understood as something that took place all at once and unequivocally, but as the result of a long development, or rather entanglement. Each transformation play took place originally; indeed, not for its own sake but for the magical aim of achieving in the received form what the community needed. One celebrated the marriage and copulation of the God of Heaven with the Earth Mother because this action signified, effected, included the pouring forth of rain into the womb of the fields. If now 'Spectators' were admitted to the sacred celebration, they thereby participated in the power and the awe of the event, in the certainty of faith in its magic on whose success their happiness, at times their lives, depended. So the actors did not yet know themselves as 'looked at.' They were players but not players of a spectacle; they played to benefit the staring crowd but not to please them. They were 'in a state of innocence,' just like the man who loves according to his impulse and not according to the image he produces in the eyes of others. (It should be mentioned here that on the basis of this distinction between direct men and indirect men, the two basically different types of acting are to be distinguished.) This changes in the same degree in which belief dissolves. The spectator to whom the action that he beholds is no longer a reality penetrating his life and helping to determine his fate and the actor who is no longer overcome by the transformation but is familiar with it and knows how to make use of it mutually correspond. This actor knows himself looked at, looked at without awe and without shame; he plays without awe and without shame, as a show. The magical belief can, of course, clarify into a belief in the importance of the play for salvation, and thereby preserve its might or some part of it. In the theatre of Æschylus there still held sway, over the orchestra as well as over the tiers, something of the consecration of the Eleusinian dromena. What took place on the stage—gestures and speech, and the chorus' singing and marching—was not an illusory imitation of something that had once happened or even a delusive production of something imaginary, but a sacred reality that *concerned* the reality of the life of each of the watching and listening audience, concerned it in a way that could not be defined or represented, yet with primal power. Awe and shame were still present, therefore, both to the beholders and to those beheld.

With this example of Greek tragedy, I have already anticipated. Here both principles are already joined, the spiritual principle of dialogue and the natural one of mimic transformation-play that relate to each other as love to sex, that need each other, as love needs sex in order to obtain body, and sex needs love in order to attain spirit. But one must understand, indeed, that though love certainly appears later in the history of man, it cannot be derived from sex. In the truth of being love is the cosmic and eternal power to which sex is sent as a sign and a means it employs in order that out of it love may be reborn on earth. This is the way of the spirit in all things. Therefore, too, the theatre needs the drama more than drama needs the theatre. The drama that cannot become embodied in a theatre exists disincarnate in lonely spirit. But the theatre that is not obedient to drama bears the curse of soullessness that, for all its luxuriant variegation, it can hardly stifle for the hour's duration of its magic show. An age of unperformed drama can be an heroic Eiron, yet an age in which the self-glorious theatre treats all drama as material and occasion for its phantasmagoria is a pitiful Alazon. In order that a faithless public, which allows 'diversions' to be set before it because it fears concentration, be redeemed from its fear to awe and elevated to belief in the reality of the spirit, great work, great education, great teaching are necessary.

The theatre can take part in this work first of all through submitting itself to the command of the *word*. The word that convulses through the whole body of the speaker, the word that serves all gestures in order that all the plasticity of the stage constructs and reconstructs itself as a frame, the stern over-againstness of I and Thou, overarched by the wonder of speech, that governs all the play of transformation, weaving the mystery of the spirit into every element—it alone can determine the legitimate relation between drama and theatre.

The Space Problem of the Stage*

(1913)

THE genuine feeling of art, like all complete feelings, is a polar one. It transposes us into the midst of a world which we are incapable of entering. Living so enclosed by it that it appears that nothing could separate us from it, penetrated and confirmed by it, we still recognize it as the forever remote distance. This world is reality, unified and certain as no natural world can be; it alone is finished reality. We abandon ourselves to it and breathe in its sphere. Yet it is also image: its essence is withdrawn from and inaccessible to us. Out of this polarity of familiarity and strangeness, total enjoyment, and total renunciation, comes the pathos of the genuine feeling of art.

This holds true in the experience of the scenic event if we stand at once inextricably within the event and detached outside it: carried away by the unconditioned that happens before us yet persisting in the order of the conditioned that is the law of our existence; overpowered and yet observing; both abandoned and preserved. But we stand thus not as cleavage, not as contradiction, but as the polar unity of feeling. This polar unity has nothing to do with the popular distinction between 'appearance' and 'reality'; one can only correctly call that appearance which is not genuine art; the scenic event that is genuine art is reality, if anything is reality. We are encompassed by it; yet it is an image: we cannot enter into it.

I shall consider here only *one* element of scenic experience, but an essential one: the sense of space. If the scenic experience is genuine and sufficient, we are aware that we cannot enter into the space of the theatre although we live in it in our experiencing.

* Written for experiments of the Hellerau theatre in which I participated.

The stage may begin a few steps in front of us; we could take these few steps, but we know that nothing would be accomplished thereby. Our feet can certainly tread the boards of the stage, but we cannot set foot on the space of the stage. Because this space is of another species than ours, because it is created and fulfilled by a life of another density than ours, because our dimensions do not hold good for it. To possess this knowledge as feeling is the core of the genuine scenic experience.

The arch enemy of this knowledge is the modern stage; it strives to annihilate it or to devastate it. To annihilate it: when with its 'advanced' technique it exerts itself to create the illusion that the space of the stage is of the same kind as ours; to devastate this knowledge when it imitates the forms that in purer times spontaneously arose out of the spirit, and that now, robbed of the life that generated and filled them, debase the theatre into a curiosity. In both ways the modern stage has succeeded in thoroughly depraving the space sense of the spectator, his sense of distance.

The ancient stage is illuminated under the same optic conditions as the space of the spectator; but it is thoroughly separated from it through the cultic character that dwells in and shapes it. As ancient tragedy was born out of sacrifice that was first perceived as vision by the optically oriented Greeks—in opposition to the Asians for whom sacrifice is never an object—so the ancient stage is born out of the festive procession whose content is the sacramental destiny, offering, and deliverance of the god, the demon or the hero, and which forms itself in the rhythm of a fourfold movement: battle, suffering, lament and revelation. This festive procession is, whatever mythical or historical event it may actually be celebrating at the moment, never merely memory. Rather it is a life co-ordinated with that event, ever newly born and acting out of itself; for, to the Greek, the demon and his destiny is not a product of completed antiquity but of all time. This festive procession is the visible principle out of whose unfolding the space of the ancient stage was formed, from the edge of the orchestra to the back wall of the set. The spectator, blown upon by the breath of the chorus, is irresistibly carried away by it through awe before the drama that sacramentally and genuinely *takes place* in this space before him wherein he cannot enter.

This sublime actuality is foreign to the medieval stage. Here the decisive does not happen, rather it has happened—the sacrifice has been made. Here the unique happening can now only be portrayed. The stage of the mystery play is no altar, it is a showboard. Here the event becomes play; its consecration is that of repetition and its strength that of presentation. But in order that it can become play, the play must be transformed in its essence; as the essence of sacrifice is transformed in Greek tragedy. In its elemental meaning the play does not exist for any spectator; it is not defined by any process of perceiving, but solely by the agitation of the players and the rule that rhythmically restrains it. But now it is recast in all its moments by the meaningful effect that is intended, without, however, a new creative law being born as at that time when sacrifice joined itself to the tragic festive procession. As long as the play is bound to the traditional matter of the historical-religious occurrence that it represents, it receives its law from it. But the play looses itself from the occurrence. The bond can no longer be genuine since the religious can only prove itself as form-creating if the free might of working actuality is opened to it. The drama detaches itself from its source and wins its abysmal freedom, that of the detached play. The universal spectacle that is only meant to be observed gives itself its own law. As on the stage of the mystery the space of the scene was shaped by the bound play, so on Shakespeare's stage it was shaped by the autonomous play. There the booths on the free square, the action proceeding from one to another like stations of Calvary, erected for the play and after the play torn down; here the permanent set with its bare or tapestried walls, in the centre the balcony supported by pillars and fitted with steps, capable of signifying all places, awaiting the orders that the prologue or the play-bill announces with the name of the town; booths and sets living by grace of the play that exercises its transforming power on bare boards and has its greatness in transformation. (We cannot ascribe this to imperfect technique; imperfect technique is never anything but parallel manifestation.) And the spectator crowding the boards or even seated on the edge of the stage, none the less finds before him its inaccessible space because this is not the space in which he can move, but a space created, shaped, and fulfilled by the play—through the ingenuity of the consistently space-creating playwright, the skill of the experienced space-executing players, and his, the spectator's, faculty of imagination that adapts him to it.

In the place of the world-renewing sacrifice and the world-embracing play, our age, which is unacquainted with either, is not able to establish any new spirit out of which drama might be realized anew in the people. The space of the modern stage is not shaped by a principle of life and of art, but is constructed through a particularizing creation of illusion and reproducing archaism.

The illusion-stage aspires to overcome the spectator's sense of distance—the strongest motive of artistic theatrical effect—and to convert its space into one altogether continuous with his.

In all ages the creation of illusion undoubtedly belonged in some degree to the elements of scenic representation, and the Greek stage already had its rotating wing-pillars. But this art of illusion did not aim to engender the appearance that the space of the scenic event was constituted like the spectator's, but to make its own space clear by referring to places and changes of place in their actual contextual relations; the coulisse was a painted play-bill. Seen from the standpoint of the means, this art of illusion did not work through particulars but through wholes; in opposition to our space of details it set a space of significant totalities; it did not allow the impression of a locally-determined space to form out of fragments, but awakened it through a few simple, representative, symbolically valid unities of form or colour. But the theatre of our day is not at all satisfied with two- and three-dimensional details. It wants to convert its space into a 'real' one and so rob the experience of the scenic occurrence of its necessary polarity: the genuine sense of distance as well as the genuine relation that is only possible through activity. In contrast to this, the modern stage allows the spectator to gaze in passive and unimaginative astonishment at the perfected technique of its 'scenic design.'

Out of the longing for the restoration of the stage that functioned as a totality and of the sense of distance, there have grown a few synthetically archaic experiments that have attempted to depict the stages of an earlier age, the ancient or the medieval or the Elizabethan, and have copied their forms; as if these stages could endure without the living principle that once dwelled in and animated them. In fact, the result has been that the sense of distance has either not been produced at all or only as an artificial and indirect one, the 'cultivated' sense of distance of those who observe out of curiosity. Hardly anything else is gained thereby than that the museum character of our time has now found a worthy representation in this province, too.

Another form of reaction is represented by the attempt to shape what is, certainly, another kind of space, but one whose principle is taken from the world of painting or of decoration. This effect, too, must remain unfruitful; for instead of bringing the sense of distance into the scenic experience, it brings in an alien art that dissipates the experience.

Whether in our time a new spirit will come to life capable of generating a new scenic principle, we contemporaries cannot tell. Even if we think that we foresee such a spirit, we cannot presume to be at once those who live it and those who know it, at once to receive the new and to define it. All we can do is to work from the place and moment where we are, and to hope that our work, if it succeeds in being true to our intention, will not remain unblessed by the spirit. There is no point, therefore, in devising a new space-shaping principle. What matters is discovering a solution, one corresponding to the forms of our life and making meaningful use of our techniques, a solution to the problem of a space that fulfils the basic demand that drama makes of the stage. This demand is for a space that is at once unified and changeable. If it succeeds, we may expect of it that it will again guarantee to the scenic experience its full polarity—relation and distance. For only that space can endure uniformly in the midst of transmutations which is self-enclosed, which is different from ours in its nature, which announces its nature to us so clearly and cogently that, throughout all the streams of relation, we experience it as inaccessibly over against us. And it can only be changeable in the midst of unity if its metamorphoses are supplemented by the activity of our perception, if this active relationship—the only genuine one—is not crippled, as it is on the modern stage, but awakened and nourished.

That a space that remains unified in change can only be created through the institution of simple, homogeneous forms that work as a totality must be clear to everyone who is not misled by the 'riches' of the modern stage. The only element that can invest a unitarily constituted stage with changeableness is light, a fact that cannot remain hidden from a time in which Rembrandt's spirit speaks to the spirit as never earlier. Out of the meeting of both kinds of knowledge has arisen the partial experiments which the projected theatre performances in Hellerau will attempt to present.

Tessenow's Great Hall has simple and significant proportions that awaken the impression of essential life. Architectonically the hall is a unity; the public does not sit in dividing darkness but in the common light, and the stage is separated from it not through its construction but solely through what is done with it. The stage is nothing else than what is done with it. But all that is done with it is strictly and clearly unified in itself, strictly and clearly separated from the audience through the way in which it takes place; this stage does not set before us a space that is essentially like our own but one that is essentially different, it is the space of drama. This space is technically constructed out of two elements: the substrata underlying the transformations and the changing agent. The substrata are a few simple grey planes and paths of material that border and articulate the stage. The agent is the diffuse light that does not stream forth sporadically, like the usual spot-light, but spreads uniformly over great surfaces through great periods of time. Through the variability of the lighting, the substrata can be conducted through all grades of materiality. The material can appear now soft, now hard, now flat, now round. With its change changes the image of the space that alters the light from a narrow one to one that opens into the infinite, from one clear in all points to one mysteriously vibrating, from one signifying only itself to one intimating the unnamable. But it is itself something unnamable, this space. It is shaped by a principle whose name we do not yet know and of which we know only a symbol drawn from the senses: the creative light.

Goethe's Concept of Humanity[*]

(1949)

SINCE I am unable to attend the Goethe Convocation in person, I should like to contribute to its proceedings from afar by outlining some basic features of Goethe's concept of humanity.

In the retrospective view of his old age, Goethe saw the meaning and significance of his writings in the 'triumph of the purely human.' The expiation of all human failings by 'pure humanity' was, he then proclaimed, the message of his *Iphigenie*. But already at the age of thirty-four, in his last letter to Lavater, having painfully realized 'how far we have drifted apart,' but still addressing himself to the friend 'so that we may come in touch once again,' he had written: 'Let me partake of the purely human side of your doings and your being.'

We know what this means. Little more than two years before, Goethe had addressed his friend as 'you most human man,' and described 'the human quality' manifested in his published letters as 'most amiable.' But that same Lavater who, when associating with writers, was the most tolerant and gentle of creatures, was likely on other occasions, as a teacher and preacher of his religion, to practise the most rigid intolerance. His advice to a young man on leaving home was 'not to trust, nor even consort with, a man who was not a Christian.' So Goethe, who described himself as a 'convinced non-Christian,' found it more and more difficult to bear with him, and eventually pleaded: 'Let me hear your human voice, so that we may remain linked on this side, since it is impossible on the other side.' But it seems that Lavater, though he may

* Read by Ernst Simon at the Goethe Bicentennial Convocation at Aspen, Colorado, in June–July 1949.

have tried to effect a separation of the two 'sides,' was not, or was no longer, able to do so; the 'pact of peace and toleration' which Goethe proposed to him did not materialize. Lavater could not admit that 'there are many recipes in our Father's pharmacy.'

It was Goethe, however, who broke off their correspondence and declared, barely three years later, that for him Lavater no longer existed. Lavater had put up with the fact that Goethe had opposed to his faith, 'as a firm unshakable rock of humanity,' his own faith, the faith of those 'who devote themselves to the study of any truth revealed by man and to man and who, as sons of God, worship Him in themselves and all His children.' He, the intolerant, had continued their debate even after Goethe had discovered in the Gospel 'blasphemies against the great God and his revelation in nature.' Goethe, for his part, had soon found it impossible to continue a friendship with one 'in whom supreme human understanding and crudest superstition' were linked 'by a most subtle and indissoluble tie.'

The appeal contained in his last letter—that Lavater should speak to him only of the purely human side of his nature—already betrays a certain estrangement. A few years later, Goethe is 'rid for ever of both hate and love.' Lavater, still undeterred, dares to preface a tract entitled 'Nathanael' with a dedication 'to a Nathanael whose hour is not yet come.' Goethe cannot bring himself to answer. But among his notes on the Italian journey there is one which says: 'Your sermon is addressed to the wrong man. I am not a Nathanael, and as for the Nathanaels among my people, I will fool them myself; I will tell them stories myself, according as it suits me or as need arises. So begone, sophist, or there'll be blows.' Lavater later declared that he had never met a man 'both so tolerant and so intolerant' as Goethe.

What is that 'purely human' to which Lavater, the 'most human man,' is asked to confine himself in his dealings with Goethe if he wishes to preserve their friendship?

Lavater, when associating with writers, was not only 'tolerant and gentle,' but, above all, of a spontaneity ('*Glut und Ingrimm*,' Goethe called it) which won him the heart of the young Goethe, whose enthusiasm was kindled by everything spontaneous. In his own writings, however, Lavater was completely lacking in genuine spontaneity and therefore bound to irritate a reader who, also as a reader, was a genius. Yet Goethe's criticism was not primarily concerned with this; on some of Lavater's writings he bestows a praise which we, who have no patience with such 'troubled emotionalism,' find rather odd. What he avows, both to himself and to his problematical friend, to be unbearable is Lavater's persistent attempt to convince him of his supposed 'spontaneous experience of Christ' ('*ummittelbares Christusgefühl*').

The intensity of his missionary zeal may have had something to do with the doubtful character of this aspect of Lavater's spontaneity. 'You are right,' he once wrote to Goethe with disarming candour; 'so long as I am not as certain of His existence as I am of yours, anything I may predicate about Him is nothing but self-worship . . . I should almost say, spiritual onanism.' Significantly enough, this image recurs in Lavater's letters almost a year later. But now it no longer applies to his own behaviour but to the religion 'of most people,' which he asserts to be mere emotionalism ('*Schwärmerei*'), that is, the 'illusion of being touched by another creature while they are touching themselves.' He had 'intimate experiences,' but they were not sufficient, under self-scrutiny, to assure him of the real presence of Him to whom he attempted to convert others. We may suppose that, unconsciously, the *élan* of his proselytizing efforts was primarily intended to quell a sense of insufficiency in his own heart. As for Goethe, it is obvious that these psychological antics could only be distasteful to him. That is why he attempted to lead this straying 'most human man' back to pure humanity, i.e., to rid him of an adventitious, not a purely human element.

Needless to say, his criticism was not aimed at Lavater's Christianity as such, but at the violent manner in which he asserted it. 'The moment I cease being a Christian,' he wrote to Goethe, 'I am an atheist. . . . If Jesus Christ is no longer my God, I have no God at all.' Or even more pointedly: 'I have no God but Jesus Christ. . . . His Father . . . exists for me only in Him . . . would exist for me nowhere if He did not exist for me in Him.'

76

This convulsively maintained alternative not only repelled Goethe, but shocked and offended his relationship to Divine Being. Since his early days, he had been concerned with his relationship to Divine Being. Not always, it is true, but again and again—and we know that 'again and again' was the keynote of his life. He had been concerned, not as *a* man but as *Man*, with maintaining a relationship to Divine Being—not merely intellectually, as a relationship to something intellectually comprehensible, but in his own life, as a relationship to the Supremely Alive, i.e., to Divine Being. This attitude alone seemed to him capable of producing that pure humanity, expiating all human failings, whose triumph he regarded, at the end of his career, as the main theme of his life's work. He felt entitled to demand this 'purely human' attitude also from his friends, and the continuance of his friendship, by virtue not of his will but of his nature, became dependent on the fulfilment of this demand.

The meaning of the operative phrase 'as Man'—which, it is true, was not coined by Goethe but by me as his commentator—will perhaps be best understood by reference to a passage written over ten years before Goethe's breach with Lavater, that most noteworthy passage of *The Sorrows of Werther* in which Werther, five weeks before his suicide, asks the friend to whom he is writing to let him 'suffer to the end' ('*ausdulden*'). He speaks as one who stands outside 'religion,' by which he means not the belief in God but Christianity, and that not in a general sense, but as the condition of a man certain of being redeemed by the Mediator. He does not question the divinity of Christ; he calls Him not only the Son of God but 'God from Heaven,' and even, using an Old Testament appellation of the Father, Him 'who stretches out the heavens like a curtain.' The only idea he rejects, because his 'heart' bids him reject it, is that he should be one of those whom the Father, in the language of the Gospel of St. John, has given to the Son: 'What if the Father wants—as my heart tells me he does—to keep me for Himself?' But he who is thus retained by the Father is destined to be crucified by the world, i.e. to suffer, in his own actual life, not by way of imitation of Christ, what the Son of God has suffered. His is 'the human lot of having to bear one's full measure of suffering.' He has to drain, with lips that are nothing but human, the cup which 'was too bitter for the human lips of the God from Heaven.' And when at last he, too, asks the Father why He has forsaken him, then the voice in which he is speaking is 'that of creature, thrown back entirely upon himself, deprived of his self, and sinking into abysmal depths.'

Here Goethe, whom we are inclined to regard as representing the euphoria of an age prior to its death throes, anticipates what our own time has defined as 'thrownness' (*Geworfenheit*). In this context, he refers to man as 'creature,' for in this supreme agony man, stripped of all the prerogatives of creatorial subjectivity, experiences himself as a creature. It is obvious, however, that Goethe does not mean here a mere creature-among-creatures, he means that individual in which the creature 'man' has found his fulfilment. The true essence of humanity reveals itself, not in the species but in the person of him whom Goethe calls '*der edle Mensch.*' We know this term from the writings of Meister Eckhart. And Eckhart says of his *homo nobilis* that he is 'the only-begotten Son of God, whom the Father procreates eternally.'

Werther's bold words about his relationship to the Father indicate how far Goethe, already at this early stage, was prepared to go in this direction, and how far he was able to go without transgressing the borderline which separated him from a mystical, timeless view of Being. From here, 'man' in Goethe's highest use of the term, man as embodying pure humanity ('*der Menschen-Mensch,*' as Lavater called Goethe), appears as the human person who has passed the *ausdulden* stage and emerged from the subsequent, purgatory-like process of purification ('Infinite purification is proceeding in me,' Goethe wrote to Lavater). This is the exemplary fulfilment of '*stirb und werde.*' 'The whole trick,' Goethe wrote with the gentle irony of the sexagenarian, 'consists in abandoning our existence in order that we may exist.'

This is how real existence is achieved. It is the existence of the individual, viewed in a perspective already approaching that of Kierkegaard, and yet essentially different from it. It may also be called the existence of the 'personality,' provided Goethe's understanding of the term is retained. What is now usually associated with this term—namely, distinctiveness and compact-ness—will then appear as its mere factual content as distinct from its true essence. No doubt the true human person is again and again required to detach and shut himself off from others—Lavater found Goethe 'more self-contained' at their last meeting—but this attitude is alien to his innermost being. The attitude congenial to him is openness to the world; he craves the company of other human beings; such frustrations as he experiences in this sphere are the appointed lot of the personality amid his fellow-men. Goethe's *edler Mensch* achieves true humanity ('that which distinguishes us from all other beings known to us') only by being 'helpful and kind.' Only through him, within the sphere of his helpfulness and kindness, can man's acts of discerning, choosing, and judging become real human acts, which lend perpetuity to the moment and accomplish the impossible, the freedom of decision within the framework of immutable laws. This is why he alone, as Man in the highest sense of the word, as an image of those beings whose existence we can only surmise, can reward the good and punish the wicked.

The poem expressing these ideas, entitled 'The Divine' ('*Das Göttliche*'), was written at the time of the Lavater controversy. Goethe's *edler Mensch* is permitted to distinguish and decide be-tween good and evil men, but he does not presume, as Lavater so violently did, to proclaim his relationship to Divine Being—irrespective of whether it is based on something common to him-self and a community, or whether it concerns nobody but him-self—as the only legitimate one, in the face of which all others must be rejected. Any genuine life-relationship to Divine Being—i.e., any such relationship effected with a man's whole being—is a human truth, and man has no other truth. To realize this does not mean to relativize truth. The ultimate truth is one, but it is given to man only as it enters, reflected as in a prism, into the true life-relationships of the human persons. We have it, and yet have it not, in its multicoloured reflection. 'The True, which is identical with the Divine, can never be perceived by us directly; we only contemplate it in its reflection, in the example, the sym-bol.' Human truth is not conformity between a thing thought and the thing as being; it is participation in Being. It cannot claim universal validity, but it is lived, and it can be lived exemplary, symbolically. Beyond acts of discerning, choosing, and judging, beyond acts of rewarding and punishing, we contemplate a pure humanity which expiates all human failings.

Is there a prospect of mankind's becoming a humanity? In the same year in which the poem '*Das Göttliche*' was written, Goethe, who was fully aware of the questionableness of all 'aristocracies' in history, declared in a letter to Lavater that if he were to speak in public, he would speak in favour of what in his opinion was the aristocracy instituted by God. He saw no other prospect of mankind's becoming a humanity than through an association of truly human persons, which would irradiate and comprehend all others. We may suppose that this achievement was to have been the subject of the third part of the *Wilhelm Meister* trilogy, the '*Meisterjahre*.' Thus, in this respect even Goethe's almost inconceivably vast lifework has remained fragmentary. But his 'triumph of the purely human' bears a message, both exhorting and encouraging, to our time, although, or precisely because, it is so evidently remote from a mankind-humanity.

Bergson's Concept of Intuition[*]

(1943)

DESCARTES understood by intuition 'the conception of a pure and attentive spirit'; only through such intuition can 'the first principles' be known. Spinoza defined what he called 'clear knowledge' as knowledge that did not arise through rational conviction but through a 'feeling and enjoying of the object itself.' The pure and attentive spirit that Descartes prescribed for the act of intuition, accordingly, shall so turn itself towards an object that it is not merely acquainted with it intellectually but also feels and enjoys it directly. Here Bergson begins when he calls intuition the sympathy through which one transposes oneself into the interior of an object. Goethe, in particular, has expressed such an intuition in his relationship to men; it was natural for him to place himself in the situations of others, to feel each special kind of human existence. Balzac describes it still more exactly: 'With me,' he says, 'observation had become intuitive; it gave me the capacity *de vivre de la vie de l'individu*, which manifested itself by allowing me to put myself in his place.'

An intuition so understood does not enable one to think away the enduring duality between the beholder and what is beheld. The beholder transposes himself into the station of the beheld, and experiences its particular life, its sensations and impulses from within. That he can do so is explicable through a deep community between the two, as Goethe has, in fact, explained it in connection with the viewing of nature. The fact of duality is not weakened thereby; on the contrary, it is just this cleavage of the primal community that lays the foundation for the act of

---

[*] The concluding section of an essay published in 1943 as an introduction to the Hebrew translation of Bergson.

intuition in its specific nature. The intuitive way of knowing is based, like every act of knowing, on the undiminished persistence of the dual presence of observer and observed.

Bergson, like Schelling, wants to abolish this duality, but not, as he did, through the I's comprehending itself as such, but rather through our plunging into the immediate process of the experienced happening, there 'where we no longer see ourselves act, but where we act.' That still reminds us, at first, of Schelling for whom the question is one of 'at once producing and contemplating certain actions of the spirit so that the producing of the object and the contemplation itself are absolutely one.' This brings to mind Bergson's formula, according to which the act of knowledge coincides with the act that produces reality.

Although the essential task of intuitive metaphysics for Bergson is to know the spirit, he does not mean by 'action' a specific activity of the spirit but the action of man in general. In an experience permeated by reflection, man sees himself act, that is, the duality of observer and observed has entered into the person himself. The task is to find one's way back from there to the original unity and to do so knowingly. But therein lies a contradiction. That unity consists in just this fact that man acts originally without knowing that he acts. Not merely when he 'sees himself act,' but with every act of knowledge, even the 'intuitive,' he influences the course of the action and impairs its unity, provided that he actually achieves the knowledge at the same time as he executes the action. If he does not do this, if in the moment in which he knows, the decisive action is already gone by, then he knows only something past and remembered; his knowing relates to an 'object,' but not to the happening itself. Bergson holds that the difficult undertaking can succeed through a powerful, in fact, a 'violent' exertion. But every violence of this sort is bound to influence and alter the constitution of the happening in tempo, rhythm, intensity—in the whole structure of its process. Such attempts certainly yield remarkable and stimulating aspects of reality that can lead to significant insights; but an absolute knowledge, such as Bergson has in mind, cannot be reached by this method.

The basic problem of the contradiction between being and knowing becomes clearest in its vital character when we consider our relations to other living beings, in particular to our fellow-men. We live in contact with them, and in this contact we perceive many things about them. But the being that is perceived, that is 'known,' is not identical with the existing being, with whom I have contact. It is not identical and cannot become identical with him. That intuition by virtue of which we 'transpose ourselves into the interior of the other' may diminish the difference, but it cannot abolish it. The tension between the image of the person whom we have in mind in our contact and the actual existing person is in no way, however, to be understood merely negatively. This tension makes an essential contribution to the proper dynamic of life between man and man. As in conversation the tension between the meaning that a word used in it has for me and the meaning that it has for my companion can prove fruitful and lead to a deeper personal agreement, so out of the tension between the image of the person and the existing person a genuine understanding can spring forth; a fruitful meeting between two men issues directly into a break-through from image to being. The Thou whom I thus meet is no longer a sum of conceptions nor an object of knowledge, but a substance experienced in giving and receiving. Of course, the moment I seek to utilize for purposes of knowledge the nearness and familiarity thus gained, I have surrendered the dimension of I-Thou, and, without having gained an adequate knowledge, have lost contact with the substance.

For the understanding of philosophical intuition, Bergson has repeatedly referred to the intuition of the artist; though this applies only to the individual, his aim is to extend this intuition to life in general. The great painter notes in nature aspects that have never been noticed before, and he lays his vision before us; so the philosopher can directly observe life itself and make it visible, too. Bergson believes at the same time that, if it succeeds, this philosophical vision will constitute absolute knowledge, and that it will set a single philosophy in the place of the contending systems.

This claim is so alien, indeed so repugnant, to the nature of art and its distinctive intuition that the comparison forfeits the very core of its validity. Certainly each great painter is a discoverer. But he is just the discoverer of an 'aspect'; that is, of a view of the world in which a certain manner of seeing manifests itself that is peculiar to him, this painter. This aspect is, of course, something that would not have become visible unless his eyes had beheld it. But it is not something that existed in itself outside these eyes; it is a reality of relation, the product of a meeting. The painter lives in the immeasurable multiplicity and diversity of these aspects, to none of which, nor to all of them taken together, can the character of an absolute perception be ascribed. The situation is not essentially different with regard to philosophy.

Something further must still be said. When we regard the arts together, we mark that the decisive event that engenders the work of art is not the perception of a being but the vital contact with the being, an ever-renewed vital contact with it in which the experience of the senses only fits in as a factor. Of course one cannot say of this contact that it is reflected or displayed in the work: waves proceed from it that are converted in production, powers are put in motion by it through whose transformation the work arises. The artist does not hold a fragment of being up to the light; he receives from his contact with being and brings forth what has never before existed. It is essentially the same with the genuine philosopher, only here a great consciousness is at work that wills to bring forth nothing less than a symbol of the whole.

Bergson attempts to bridge the cleft between being and knowing through showing intuition as developing out of instinct. In its relation to the environment and to itself, the life principle has split into instinct and intellect. But the intellect offers us only an image of the world elaborated under the influence of utilitarian aims, and instinct offers no image at all. Only when the intellect liberates itself from the mastery of utilitarian aims and elevates itself to the longing for more adequate knowledge will it find the way to it. But then that way is not one the intellect itself can follow. The task devolves upon it of making instinct self conscious, of bringing it to the point where it 'internalizes itself in knowledge instead of externalizing itself in action'; where it 'reflects on its objects and expands it into the indeterminate'; and also where it reflects on itself.

But what, then, is instinct? Bergson says it is knowledge at a distance; namely, knowledge grounded in 'sympathy,' in direct participation in an alien life. By this, however, the essence of the instincts that propound to us such riddles is not grasped. Let us consider a typical case adduced by Bergson, the well-known one of the wasp and the cricket. One species of wasp paralyses the caterpillar of the cricket (in whose body it wants to lay its eggs) exactly on the three nerve centres that its three pairs of feet set in motion. The wasp, says Bergson, knows that the caterpillar has three nerve centres, or, at least, it acts as if it knew. But that is just the question: does it really 'know' or does it merely act as a knowing animal would act? We cannot, of course, know whether and to what extent the wasp knows. But if we choose to presume knowledge in order to understand the action, we shall in no case be justified in concluding that it 'knows' in any manner of knowing that might develop into intuition. It is, says Bergson, a *'connaissance implicite'*; it is a *'connaissance innée,'* and, to be sure, one that is *'virtuelle ou inconsciente.'* But then it would only be an awareness, an acquaintance, but not a knowing, not an act of knowledge accomplished by this being. However this being attains this acquaintance, it is in any case not through its having known. Between the wasp and his victim, says Bergson, there exists a sympathy in the etymological sense of the word, a suffering-with or feeling-with that therefore gives the wasp intelligence, 'as though from within,' about the vulnerability of the caterpillar. The two animals do not confront each other as two organisms, but as two centres of activity within the life-system.

'The instinctive knowledge which one species has, to an important degree, of another species has its roots in the unity of life itself which, to use the expression of an ancient philosopher,* is a whole sympathetic to itself.' So says Bergson. But if this is life, life is still not a whole that knows itself. Knowing is rather

* Bergson has in mind a saying of the Stoic Chrysippos about the cosmos.

allotted to individuation. Life can know itself only through the act of knowledge of living individuals, that is, in limitation and variety. Beyond this there exists the contact, the living connection between living beings, that can also express itself in the fact that one of them can by his actions directly adapt himself to and become a part of the nature and manner of existence of another (even if at times just in order to paralyse the other for his own purposes). But this can only remind us of how two muscles work together in an organism or a muscle with an intestine, but not of how my eye observes my hand. The powers active in instinct, the energies excited through vital contact, we can make serviceable to our intuition, as the artist does. But no way leads from instinct to intuition. Intellect operates where we know in order to act with some purpose, and are thus divided between the two activities; instinct rules where we act purposefully without requiring knowledge; intuition where our whole being becomes one in the act of knowing. The intellect, which divides the self, holds us apart from the world that it assists us in utilizing. Instinct joins us to the world, but not as persons. Intuition, through vision, binds us as persons with the world which is over against us, binds us to it without being able to make us one with it, through a vision that cannot be absolute. This vision is a limited one, like all our perceptions, our universal-human ones and our personal ones. Yet it affords us a glimpse in unspeakable intimacy into hidden depths. Bergson has raised a claim for intuition that cannot be due it or any mortal knowledge whatever. But it remains his great service that he, as no other thinker of our day, has directed our attention to intuition.

Franz Rosenzweig[*]

(1930)

THE catastrophes of historical reality are often at the same time crises of the human relation to reality. Of the special manner in which our time has experienced this crisis, I know of no greater or clearer example than that of Franz Rosenzweig. His crisis can be conceived, in its literary aspect, as the way from one book to another, from *Hegel and the State* substantially written before the First World War, completed in 1919 and published in 1920) to *The Star of Redemption* (substantially written at the front during the war, completed in 1919 and published in 1921). The two books can scarcely be compared. *Hegel and the State* is a monograph which makes a significant contribution to the history of philosophy; 'The Star of Redemption' is a secular system—not a 'system of philosophy,' as Rosenzweig himself later thought, but the systematic testimony of a meeting—a contemporary meeting—between philosophy and theology. But as a measuring rod whereby his way, our own way, is to be read they belong together.

Rosenzweig's teacher, Friedrich Meinecke, to whom *Hegel and the State* is dedicated, wrote, in a memorial essay, to the effect that *The Star of Redemption* must be understood as a flight from

[*] Franz Rosenzweig (1886–1929), a great German Jewish philosopher and theologian who was a close friend of Martin Buber's and who together with Buber translated the Hebrew Bible into German. Rosenzweig's central work, *The Star of Redemption*, is still untranslated, but some idea can be obtained of it from Nahum N. Glatzer, *Franz Rosenzweig: His Life and Thought* (New York: Schocken Books, 1953), and Franz Rosenzweig, *Understanding the Sick and the Healthy* (New York: The Noonday Press, 1953). See also Maurice Friedman, 'Franz Rosenzweig and Martin Buber,' *Congress Weekly*, Vol. 23, No. 31 (November 26, 1956), pp. 14–16.

German-Protestant spirituality into the author's hereditary Jewish spirituality. That is a far-reaching error. In reality, it is not a question of the passage from one historical province to another, but of the passage from a world where the historical absorbs all that is ontic, into one in which the historical itself (historical not in any dialectic sense but in the contingent) gains ontic character. It is a question thus of the passage from a philosophizing in the post-Hegelian sense to an 'existential' philosophizing. This existential philosophy is ultimately not to be comprehended as a mere philosophizing about concrete existence, but, over and above that, as one that avails itself of the philosopher's concrete existence, not merely representing and proclaiming itself in it, therefore, but verifying itself in reality. I speak intentionally of a philosophizing and not of a philosophy. For *The Star* itself admits*—at least concerning its second part, though it may well apply to the whole—that the science it pursues is that of theology. But this theology is just a philosophizing one.† It proceeds from 'facts,' from which alone it can proceed and whose centre is revelation; but it does not treat these facts as the content of dogma but as objects of thought. Since it joins with the world of revelation-less 'pre-world'—by no means intended as merely a world of antiquity—basically it need exclude nothing, as is a matter of course in genuine philosophizing. Through rediscovering the fundamental identity of revelation with speech, it acquires an eminently philosophical method, authorized by its theological centre, indeed quite properly 'covered' by it: the method of the philosophy of language.

Such crisis of the human relation to reality shatters our familiar manner of orienting ourselves, and compels us to withstand, with our knowledge and our lives, a reality stripped of orientation, a reality that threatens us with the horror of meaninglessness. Like lesser convulsions, such a crisis summons individual spheres of the spirit to attempt to master the new chaos, an attempt that

* Vol. II, p. 67, of the second edition of *Der Stern der Erlösung* (1930); Part II, p. 67, of the third edition (Verlag Lambert Schneider, Heidelberg, 1954).

† 'Philosophy desires today, in order to become free from aphorisms, hence just for the sake of its scientific character, that "theologians" philosophize' (*Ibid.*, II, 24).

necessarily leads to the uncovering of the problem peculiar to each individual sphere. But it is also this basic crisis that confronts with one another the spheres that have been shaken up in such problematic fashion. It enables these spheres to recognize one another—at first, certainly, as limited by one another, but then as also addressed and claimed by one another. Out of this encounter finally, as an especial good fortune of the spirit, an existential co-operation in the task of mastery can arise, a self-verifying thinking with one another and serving one another that stands firm in knowledge and life. Rosenzweig's *Star of Redemption* represents such good fortune in the interchange between philosophy and theology in our time.

If the fundamental problem of theology is that of the reciprocity between God and the human person, in the meeting of theology with philosophy the disquieting and inflaming problem for the former must be philosophy's proclamation that there exists a third entity, the world, and not, indeed, as a Kierkegaardian springboard, but as reality in the highest positive sense. For philosophy, on the other hand, there remains, naturally, the vexation and sting of the resistance of theology to every attempt to replace the absolute concreteness of God and the relative concreteness of the human person by conceptual images that allow themselves to be subsumed in the category of the 'universal' (the might of theology, in fact, rests before all else on the seriousness with which it ever again affirms the incomprehensible concreteness of these, its two incomprehensible forms, as the themes reserved to it and not to be torn away from it by any metaphysics and any psychology). Rosenzweig's system is constructed on the recognition of these three: God, man, world. He shows them in the first part of the book in isolation as not being reducible to one another in order to 'narrate'* their relations in the

---

* 'A narrating philosophy was foretold by Schelling in his fragments of genius, "The Ages." The second part seeks to give this' (Rosenzweig, 'Das neue Denken. Einige nachträgliche Bemerkugen zum "Stern der Erlösung," in Rosenzweig's *Zweistromland, Kleinere Schriften zur Religion und Philosophie*, Berlin, 1926). Most of 'The New Thinking' is printed in translation in Nahum N. Glatzer, *Franz Rosenzweig: His Life and Thought* (New York: Schocken Books, 1953), pp. 190–208.

second, and in the third to indicate the life lived in the light of what has been illuminated in this way. Theology and philosophy have combined here through the very fact of their being provoked, and have thereby achieved the possibility of a co-operation that is faithful to the truth.

This is a co-operation that exceeds a mere helping each other. It does not begin where thought builds and forms; it takes its beginning where thought is born. It is not established in order to express something; rather, it is not established in order . . . , but it has come into being because. . . . It is situation, destiny, necessity, and therefore it is fruitful. 'The divine truth conceals itself from him who only reaches for it with one hand, no matter whether this reaching hand is the objectivity of philosophy that floats above the things, imagining itself to be suppositionless, or the experience-proud blindness of theology, shutting itself away from the world. It must be supplicated with both hands. He who implores it with the double prayer of the believer and the unbeliever, to him it will not deny itself.'*

We can now discern why this meeting starts from Jewish theology (I do not say 'takes place within Jewish theology' since the real way in which Christian theology is included in the third part is very significant). The new meeting between theology and philosophy must remain a mere dispute, the less a theology is able, in its special presuppositions, to recognize the 'world' as reality in the highest positive sense. Catholic theology succeeds for that reason in attaining a firmer and more inclusive togetherness than Protestant theology, which had to obtain the single co-operation with philosophy which it undertook—that of German idealism—by a renunciation of its own character as theology. After it had recollected its character, Protestant theology was no longer disposed to make this renunciation; thus it can hardly envisage anything other than a dialogue that elucidates and strengthens the proper boundary-attitude. But Jewish theology can reach a still stronger and more comprehensive togetherness than the Catholic, because it recognizes no incarnation and cannot, therefore, fuse the two divine acts of revelation to man and redemption of the

* *Ibid.*, III, 47.

world; redemption for it is just the redemption of the *world* in that highest real and positive sense. Thereby it became possible for Jewish theology to conclude that genuine alliance with philosophy which has received a powerful literary testimony in *The Star of Redemption*.

In this connection one naturally recalls a related and yet very different book, Hermann Cohen's masterly legacy—admired and praised by Rosenzweig—*The Religion of Reason from the Sources of Judaism*. But this work, in which Cohen reacted to the modern crisis of the human relation to reality and in which he advanced from the idealism of his system to the existentialism of 'correlation,' is consciously religious philosophy, the philosophy of the Jewish religion. Rosenzweig, in contrast, rightly stresses the fact that in *The Star* the word 'religion' does not appear. Rosenzweig is not discoursing about views of God, man, and world, he is speaking directly about God, man, and world; indeed, one might even dispense with this 'about' and say that he speaks between them as an interpreter speaks. Cohen's book discusses a religious doctrine; Rosenzweig's, on the basis of a belief, discusses all things and in such a way that one feels he serves the things that he discusses. The religious reality of Judaism has entered into both works, but in *The Religion of Reason* it appears as a systematic setting forth of principles, in *The Star of Redemption* as a life-process.

The architectonic of *The Star* is of a purity and legitimacy of correspondences such as I have not found in any other writing of our time, and it is a dynamic one. As the three 'substances' of which it speaks—God, man, world—can only be understood in their relations—creation, revelation, redemption—so these must not be frozen into principles; they must remain in the 'entirely real' time, they must be narrated. And where this takes place (in the second part), and where history itself, therefore, appears in its ontic character, in the believing sense of happenings under revelation and between creation and redemption, still there is no 'Judaism.' It first appears in the third part, where the 'eternal life' is represented by it, as the 'eternal way' by Christianity. But here also what is dealt with is not its creed and views but its life.

Now history renews itself in the constant, lived recurrence, in the commemoration days of the festal year. Here, too, the entirely real time holds sway.

This candour in the face of the spirit which does not wish to philosophize by grace of the spirit, but by grace of Him by whose grace the spirit is, this insatiability that refuses to be put off with spiritually-formed 'essences' but dares to seek out the reality itself concealed by these 'essences,' this rebellious courage, awakened in the crisis, for life 'in the Face,' makes Rosenzweig's book a work both of the future and for the future. Over the first, the philosophical part, he set the words 'in philosophos'; over the second, the theological part, 'in theologos'; but over the third, which receives the harvest of the first two, 'in tyrannos.' He fights 'with both hands' against a tyranny for the liberation of reality, the *whole* reality. He does not 'flee,' but stands firm just there where he, the Jew, stands. Only now is existential thinking present.

This standing firm where one stands must not be understood as a renunciation of the approach to truth, but as the opening out moment by moment of the one approach that exists; for it exists at every moment when a person really stands there where he stands. 'But we know,' it is said in *The Star*,★ 'that it is the essence of truth to be someone's share and that a truth that did not belong to anyone would be no truth; but the "whole" truth is only truth because it is God's.' But we can only have a share in the truth if each of us verifies it in his here and now—existing just there and just therein. 'The truth, too, must be verified and just in the manner in which one commonly denies it; namely, through letting the "whole" truth alone and none the less recognizing the share in it that one holds to as the eternal truth. It must happen thus because here it is a question of the eternal.† Because it is a question of the eternal, there is no other means of obtaining truth than the lived hour. The realization of truth depends ever and again upon the verifying power of a life-reality. The crisis of the human relation to reality can only be overcome through realization.

★ *Ibid.*, III, 201. † *Ibid.*, III, 172.

Healing through Meeting*

(1951)

A MAN who follows an 'intellectual profession' must pause time after time in the midst of his activity as he becomes aware of the paradox he is pursuing. Each of these professions stands, indeed, on paradoxical ground. When he pauses, something important has already happened. But this happening only becomes significant if he does not content himself with taking such fleeting upheavals of a well-ordered world into the register of the memory. Again and again, not too long after the completion of the thus interrupted activity, he must occupy himself, in strenuous yet dispassionate reflection, with the actual problematic to which he has been referred. With the involvement of his living and suffering person, he must push forward to greater and still greater clarity of that paradox. Thus a spiritual destiny, with its peculiar fruitfulness, comes into being and grows —hesitating, groping, while groping wrestling, slowly overcoming, in overcoming succumbing, in succumbing illuminating. Such was the destiny of Hans Trüb.

But the particular profession that is in question here is the most paradoxical of all; indeed, it juts forth out of the sphere of the intellectual professions not less than do these ordered intellectual activities, taken together out of the totality of the professions. Certainly the lawyer, the teacher, the priest, no less the doctor of the body, each comes also to feel, as far as conscience genuinely infuses his vocation, what it means to be concerned with the needs and anxieties of men, and not merely, like the pursuer of a 'non-

* Introduction to Hans Trüb's posthumous book, *Heilung aus der Beregnung. Eine Aueinandersetzung mit der Psychologie C. G. Jungs,* ed. by Ernst Michel and Arie Sborowitz (Stuttgart: Ernst Klett Verlag, 1952).

intellectual' profession, with the satisfaction of their wants. But this man here, the 'psychotherapist,' whose task is to be the watcher and healer of sick souls, again and again confronts the naked abyss of man, man's abysmal lability. This troublesome appendage had been thrown into the bargain when that process unknown to nature was acquired, which may be characterized in the specific sense as the psychic.* The psychotherapist meets the situation, moreover, not like the priest, who is armed with sacred possessions of divine grace and holy word, but as a mere person equipped only with the tradition of his science and the theory of his school. It is understandable enough that he strives to objectivize the abyss that approaches him and to convert the raging 'nothing-else-than-process' into a thing that can, in some degree, be handled. Here the concept of the unconscious, manifoldly elaborated by the schools, affords him invaluable help. The sphere in which this renowned concept possesses reality is located, according to my understanding, beneath the level where human existence is split into physical and psychical phenomena. But each of the contents of this sphere can in any moment enter into the dimension of the introspective, and thereby be explained and dealt with as belonging to the psychic province.

On this paradoxical foundation, laid with great wisdom and art, the psychotherapist now practises with skill and also with success; generally, too, with the assistance of the patient, whom the tranquillizing, orienting, and to some extent integrating procedure for the most part pleases. Until, in certain cases, a therapist is terrified by what he is doing because he begins to suspect that, at least in such cases, but finally, perhaps, in all, something entirely other is demanded of him. Something incompatible with the economics of his profession, dangerously threatening, indeed, to his regulated practice of it. What is demanded of him is that he draw the particular case out of the correct methodological objectification and himself step forth out of the role of professional superiority, achieved and guaranteed by long training and practice, into the elementary situation between one who calls and one

* By this nothing else is meant than the series of phenomena that opens itself to the introspective activity.

who is called. The abyss does not call to his confidently functioning security of action, but to the abyss, that is to the self of the
doctor, that selfhood that is hidden under the structures erected
through training and practice, that is itself encompassed by chaos,
itself familiar with demons, but is graced with the humble power
of wrestling and overcoming, and is ready to wrestle and overcome thus ever anew. Through his hearing of this call there erupts
in the most exposed of the intellectual professions the crisis of its
paradox. The psychotherapist, just when and because he is a
doctor, will return from the crisis to his habitual method, but as a
changed person in a changed situation. He returns to it as one to
whom the necessity of genuine personal meetings in the abyss of
human existence between the one in need of help and the helper
has been revealed. He returns to a modified methodic in which, on
the basis of the experiences gained in such meetings, the unex-
pected, which contradicts the prevailing theories and demands his
ever-renewed personal involvement, also finds its place.

An example, sketched only in general outline, may serve here
for clarification of what has been set forth and show something
further concerning it.

A man saddles himself with guilt towards another and represses
his knowledge of it. Guilt, this fundamental life occurrence, is
only rarely discussed in the psycho-analytic literature, and then
generally only in terms of its subjective side, and not within the
circumference of the ontic reality between man and man; that is,
only its psychological projection and its elimination through the
act of repression appear to be relevant here. But if one recognizes
the ontic, in fact, suprapersonal ontic character of guilt, if one
recognizes, therefore, that guilt is not hidden away inside the
human person, but that the human person stands, in the most real
way, in the guilt that envelops him, then it also becomes clear
that to understand the suppression of the knowledge of guilt as
a merely psychological phenomenon will not suffice. It hinders
the guilty man, in fact, from accomplishing the reconciliation
whose ontic nature has, to be sure, been rather obscured by some
discussions of moral philosophy and moral theology. It hinders
him from thereby influencing the suprapersonal facts of the case

through setting right the disturbance engendered in the human constellations—a setting right of which the 'purification' of the soul is only the accompanying manifestation within the person. Reconciliation cannot take place merely in relation to the man towards whom one has become guilty (and who is perhaps dead), but in relation to all and each, according to the path of his individual life, according to his surroundings and his circumstances. What matters is only that, starting with the fact of guilt, that life be lived as a reconciling, a 'making good.'

Let us assume that the man who has repressed his knowledge of guilt falls into a neurosis. He now comes to the psychotherapist for healing. The therapist draws what is especially favoured by him within the all-containing microcosmos of the patient— Oedipus complex or inferiority feeling or collective archetype— from the unconscious into the conscious, and then treats it according to the rules of his wisdom and art; guilt remains foreign to him or uninteresting. In one case, of which I am thinking in particular, a woman took another woman's husband, later suffered the same loss herself, then 'crept away into her soul,' only to be visited and unsettled by vagrant pains. The analyst (a well-know disciple of Freud) succeeded so thoroughly in 'healing' that the pain fully ceased, the patient 'came forth out of the soul' and lived her life to the end amid an abundance of agreeable and, to her mind, friendly social relationships: that incessant and highly painful reminder of the unreconciled, the disturbed relation-to-being that must be set right, was eradicated. I call this successful cure the exchange of hearts. The artificial heart, functioning entirely satisfactorily, no longer feels pain; only one of flesh and blood can do that.*

To the psychotherapist who has passed through this crisis of the paradox of his vocation, such 'healing' is barred. In a decisive hour, together with the patient entrusted to and trusting in him, he has left the closed room of psychological treatment in which

* For a more detailed discussion of this particular example (the case of 'Melanie') and an extensive discussion of ontic, or "existential," guilt, see Martin Buber, "Guilt and Guilt-Feelings," trans. by Maurice S. Friedman, *Psychiatry*, XX, No. 2 (May 1957), pp. 114–129.

the analyst rules by means of his systematic and methodological superiority and has stepped forth with him into the air of the world where self is exposed to self. There, in the closed room where one probed and treated the isolated psyche according to the inclination of the self-encapsulated patient, the patient was referred to ever-deeper levels of his inwardness as to his proper world; here outside, in the immediacy of one human standing over against another, the encapsulation must and can be broken through, and a transformed, healed relationship must and can be opened to the person who is sick in his relations to otherness—to the world of the other which he cannot remove into his soul. A soul is never sick alone, but always a between-ness also, a situation between it and another existing being. The psychotherapist who has passed through the crisis may now dare to touch on this.

This way of frightened pause, of unfrightened reflection, of personal involvement, of rejection of security, of unreserved stepping into relationship, of the bursting of psychologism, this way of vision and of risk is that which Hans Trüb trod. After repeated wrestlings with the word for the unfamiliar, he has set forth his findings ever more maturely, ever more adequately, until its maturest and most adequate expression in this work, which he was not able to finish. His foot can no longer push on, but the path is broken. Surely there will not be wanting men like him—awake and daring, hazarding the economics of the vocation, not sparing and not withholding themselves, risking themselves—men who will find his path and extend it further.

Education and World-View*

(1935)

WE who work in so-called adult education again and again encounter opposition by groups with one world-view (*Weltanschauung*) or another to the general' studies there pursued. These critics declare, first, that the selection of what their adherents ought to know cannot legitimately be made by any other criterion than that of the purpose that defines their group since only from here can the educator decide what one needs to know in order to contribute to carrying out this purpose. Second, they declare that in general each group has to take care of its total educational activity in its own house; for only among the like-minded is that discipline and energy possible on which it depends. The only rational reason for meeting with other groups, according to them, is to 'come to terms' with them, not in order to learn together with them anything that passes as common—what must therefore, they think, be empty or at least poor, in world-view.

The points are made especially concerning the young, of course. But basically they apply to all people no matter how old, in so far as they still possess youth and are thus still educable. In this age, indeed, many who before seemed wholly crystallized have obtained a second youth, a crisis youth; they have been stirred up and loosened, have become again soft earth.

It must be said, to begin with, that to me this attitude of the groups holding world-views is quite understandable. Direct

* An address given at the *Freien Jüdischen Lehrhaus* in Frankfurt-am-Main and stemming from the adult education work that the author carried on in this and other centres throughout Germany to give the Jewish people, and especially the youth, a steadfast position in their fight against Hitler's will to crush the Jews.

action rules the hour, and one has no time to lose. No wonder that the opinion has arisen that an unpolitical education weakens the impetus and that the general spirit diverts from the goal that is always just a particular goal and as such opposed to the other goals.

This attitude will only do in the foreground, however, where things are seen as on a canvas; it will no longer do when one moves into the third dimension and experiences what 'hides behind.'

Nothing can be undertaken with any of the current educational concepts; they do not suffice. The educational concept that is really true to its age and adequate to it must be founded on the insight that in order to arrive somewhere it is not enough to *go towards* something; one must also *proceed from* something. And the fact is that the 'towards what' can be set by us, by our goal-defining 'world-view,' but not the 'from where.' It is not given us to set this; what we pretend to prepare thus soon proves itself to be deceptive artifice. The place which one can actually proceed from—not merely persuade oneself that one does so, but really take one's start from—must be something other than a standpoint or an individual station. It must be a real and primal ground: a primal reality that does not abandon me on the way to my goal. Although I myself have chosen it for myself, it guides me so that in proceeding I do not confound it with another and thus miss it; it stands by me. It must be one that has produced me and one that is ready, if I entrust myself to it, to bear me, to guard me, to educate me. To it, to my origin, to its educative forces, the work of education will provide the full access that has been lost or diminished, or it will give its forces access to me.

We cannot dispose of these forces, we can only lead to them—to these particular, original forces, which are not ethnic, however, any more than they are religious, but both in one and more and other. But with the insight into the particularity of the educative forces nothing is said about the educative material. The realm from which this is to be drawn is no special one; basically it includes everything. But what is taken from it at any particular time is not determined by any universal principles; what is decisive here is our present situation. It alone furnishes the criterion for selection: what the man who shall withstand this situation, what our growing generation needs in order to withstand it, that and nothing else is the educative material of our hour. Here the universal and the particular properly unite and mix.

The education that is being discussed here has to do with the 'world,' whose manifold aspects are the 'world-views.' There are, indeed, not merely the different conceptions of a nationality in whose sign and about whose truth the groups within the people contend. There is also the actual nation itself that they all mean and that none of them comprises: it enters into all of them, mirrors and refracts itself in each—yet belongs to none. The work of education points to the real unity that is hidden behind the multiplicity of aspects. It does not presume to replace the world-views by the world; it cannot supplant them and should not want to. It knows that one cannot have a world as one has a world-view; but it also knows that for the formation of the person and, accordingly, for the formation of the great community growing out of persons and their relations, everything depends upon how far one actually has to do with the world that the world-views interpret.

But can one then guide men to a world? No one can show others a reality except as it presents itself to him, necessarily, therefore as an aspect! Is it then possible to teach without any world-view? And if it were possible, would it be desirable?

No, it is not possible, and no, it would not be desirable. But for him who is teaching as for him who is learning, the question is whether his world-view furthers his living relationship to the world that is 'viewed' or obstructs it. The facts are there; it is a question of whether I strive to grasp them as faithfully as I can. My world-view can help me in this if it keeps my love for this 'world' so awake and strong that I do not grow tired of perceiving what is to be perceived. Let us assume I am discussing a text from our literature. It has been interpreted countless times and in countless ways. I know that no interpretation, including my own, coincides with the original meaning of the text. I know that my interpreting, like everyone else's, is conditioned through my being. But if I attend as faithfully as I can to what it contains of word and texture, of sound and rhythmic structure, of open and hidden connections, my interpretation will not have been made in vain—I find something, I have found something. And if I show what I have found, I guide him who lets himself be guided to the reality of the text. To him whom I teach I make visible the working forces of the text that I have experienced.

It is just the same with an historical manifestation. Its first chronicler, certainly, may already have coloured it through his world-view, at least through the selection of what is communicated; but what of it? Fired by my world-view to know this manifestation, I labour honestly over the penetration of the material, over the vision of what is concealed 'behind it.' Somewhere, I know not where, my lack of bias in perceiving may be interspersed with the bias instilled by my world-view, and this bias may fashion the material perceived. Into the result that I carry home reality is chemically mingled. You cannot extract it, to be sure, but it is there and is effective. My faithfulness is not in vain if only I set out to experience whatever I can experience. The facts are there, the faithfulness to them is there; the faithfulness is conditioned, like everything human, and, like everything human, of essential importance. It is not granted us to possess the truth; but he who believes in it and serves it has a share in building its kingdom. The ideological factor in what each individual calls truth cannot be extracted; but what he can do is to put a stop in his own spirit to the politization of truth, the utilitarizing of truth, the unbelieving identification of truth and suitability. Relativizing rules in me as death rules in me; but unlike death, I can ever again set limits to it; up to here and no farther!

The education here being discussed sets groups with different world-views before the face of the whole. Since this whole is not a detachable object, however, but is the life that they bear in common, these groups cannot stand in separate bands and contemplate it. They must have to do with one another in this experienced communality. Only in lived togetherness, indeed, do they really come to sense the power of the whole.

The modern group wants to 'make its way,' it wants to become the whole. But the whole is not made, it grows. He who tries to force it loses it while he appears to be winning it, he who gives himself to it grows with it. Only in the wholeness that has *grown* is the elementary (i.e. the free) productivity of a people authenticated, only in reference to this wholeness is it possible.

The work of education unites the participating groups, through access to the educative forces and through common service to the facts, into a model of the great community. This community is no union of the like-minded, but a genuine living together of men of similar or of complementary natures but of differing minds. Community is the overcoming of *otherness* in living unity.

The question is not one of exercising 'tolerance,' but of making present the roots of community and its ramifications, of so experiencing and living in the trunk (here the often questionable metaphor is rightfully used), that one also experiences, as truly as one's own, where and how the *other* boughs branch off and shoot up. It is not a question of a formal apparent understanding on a minimal basis, but of an awareness from the other side of the other's real relation to the truth. What is called for is not 'neutrality' but solidarity, a living answering for one another—and mutuality, living reciprocity; not effacing the boundaries between the groups, circles, and parties, but communal recognition of the common reality and communal testing of the common responsibility.

Vital dissociation is the sickness of the peoples of our age, and this sickness is only apparently healed through crowding men together. Here, nothing can help other than men from different circles of opinion honestly having to do with one another in a common opening out of common ground. This is the object of the pedagogy, the andragogy of our educational work.

But this pedagogy does not merely set groups with different world-views in direct relation to one another; it also gives to each individual group what it needs for its own world-view and what it cannot give itself.

In so far as it steps out of the realm of thinking and planning into the realm of human living, each world-view joins itself to a peculiar problematic, including an entirely new question of truth that has not and could not have been posed before. It is the problematic of what I might call the dialectical inner line.

So long as a world-view soars in the heights of pure thought and unconditioned will, it looks smooth and joint-less; as soon as it sets foot on the earth of our life, it receives a crack, a hardly noticeable, yet most important crack through its middle.

We now find ourselves in the sphere of the concrete, personal life. Each group has, in fact, what it gladly forgets—its concreteness, the concrete trial that determines the future: in the lives of the persons who belong to it.

Here in this sphere distinction and decision take place within the world-view.

The distinction proceeds from a double question: Upon what does your world-view stand? And: what are you undertaking with your world-view? Upon what it stands means, on what manner and what density of personal experience, of living awareness of things and of one's own person. To be attached to a group with a world-view can mean a genuine choice or an awkward groping, as in blind-man's buff.

The ground on which a world-view rests, the roots that it has—air-roots or earth-roots—decide what nourishing reality will flow to it, decide its reality content, and from this the reliability of its working.

And the second—what one undertakes with his world-view—means, whether one only fights for and 'carries into effect' one's world-view or also lives and authenticates it as well as one can at any particular time (as well as one can; for there is a seemingly magnificent either/or that is essentially nothing else than flight, evasion). The truth of a world-view is not proved in the clouds but in lived life.

In the uniform marching line of the group today there is no distinguishing any more between one person's step which is the expression of his direction-moved existence and another person's step which is nothing else than an eloquent gesture. And yet this distinction, which cuts straight across each group, is more important than that between groups and groups. For only those who realize with their life-substance will establish new, viable reality. Success may depend upon the impetus of the troop, but upon the genuineness of the individuals depends what this success will announce in the depths of the future: genuine victory or its counterfeit. The work of education has a twofold influence upon the adherents of the world-views: a founding one and a postulating one. First, it helps each to take its root in the soil of its world through enabling him to experience this world widely and densely. It provides him access to it, exposes him to the action of its working forces. And, secondly, it educates in each his 'world-view-conscience' that examines ever anew his authentication of his world-view and opposes to the absence of any obligation to put his world-view into effect the obligation of the thousand small realizations of it.

Certainly what one believes is important, but still more important is how one believes it. This 'how' is no æsthetic nor even an ethical category. It is a question of reality in the most exact sense, of the whole reality, in relation to which the categories of the æsthetic and the ethical are only abstractions. Does a world-view dwell in the head or in the whole man? Does it live only in the hours of proclamation or also in the silent private periods of his life? Does he use it or does he give himself to it? That is the distinction between men of genuine conviction and the men of fictitious conviction—between the conviction that is so fully realized that it enters entirely into reality and the conviction that is facilely effectuated and effectuated until nothing is left of it. It is a question of the existential responsibility of the person for having a world-view; this my group cannot take from me, it may not.

Let no one call this 'individualism'! It does, indeed, concern persons, but not for the sake of the persons; it concerns them for the sake of the future. Whether in the realm of any particular world-view the men of genuine conviction or the men of fictitious conviction will be dominant, whether the decisions that are to be made are made from the standpoint of the existential responsibility or not, what takes place in the internal front dividing truth and falsehood that extends straight across all world-views—upon these questions still more depends than upon whether any particular world-view is 'victorious' or not. Upon such questions depends whether the historically recorded victory is a genuine victory and not perhaps a catastrophe. How far the future community will correspond to the desired image depends essentially upon the life-attitude of present-day persons—not only of those who lead but of each individual in the ranks. The goal does not stand fast and wait. He who takes a road that in its nature does not already represent the nature of the goal will miss the goal, no matter how fixedly he holds it in sight. The goal that he reaches will resemble the road he has reached it by.

We live—one must say it ever again—in a time in which the great dreams, the great hopes of mankind, have one after another been fulfilled as the caricature of themselves. What is the cause of this massive experience? I know of none save the power of fictitious conviction. This power I call the uneducated quality of the man of this age. Opposed to it stands the education that is true to its age and adjusts to it, the education that leads man to a lived connection with his world and enables him to ascend from there to faithfulness, to standing the test, to authenticating, to responsibility, to decision, to realization.

The education I mean is a guiding towards reality and realization. That man alone is qualified to teach who knows how to distinguish between appearance and reality, between seeming realization and genuine realization, who rejects appearance and chooses and grasps reality, no matter what world-view he chooses. This education educates the adherents of all world-views to genuineness and to truth. It educates each of them to take his world-view seriously: to start from the genuineness of its ground and to move towards the truth of its goal.

3

Politics, Community, and Peace

What is to be Done?

(1919)

IF you mean by this question, 'What is one to do?'—there is no
answer. *One* is not to do anything. *One* cannot help himself,
with *one* there is nothing to begin, with *one* it is all over. He
who contents himself with explaining or discussing or asking
what *one* is to do talks and lives in a vacuum.

But he who poses the question with the earnestness of his soul
on his lips and means, 'What have I to do?'—he is taken by the
hand by comrades he does not know but whom he will soon
become familiar with, and they answer (he listens to their wonderful reply and marvels when only this follows):

'You shall not withhold yourself.'

The old eternal answer! But its truth is once again new and intact.

The questioner regards the truth and his astonishment becomes
fruitful. He nods. And as soon as he nods, he feels on the palms of
his hands the blood-warmth of togetherness. It speaks for him,
but it seems to him as if he himself spoke:

'You shall not withhold yourself.

'You, imprisoned in the shells in which society, state, church,
school, economy, public opinion, and your own pride have
stuck you, indirect one among indirect ones, break through your
shells, become direct; man, have contact with men!

'Ancient rot and mould is between man and man. Forms born
of meaning degenerate into convention, respect into mistrust,
modesty in communicating into stingy taciturnity. Now and
then men grope towards one another in anxious delirium—and
miss one another, for the heap of rot is between them. Clear it
away, you and you and you! Establish directness, formed out of
meaning, respectful, modest directness between men!

'You shall not withhold yourself.

'Solitary one, two solitudes are interwoven in your life. Only one shall you root out: shutting oneself up, withdrawing into oneself, standing apart—the solitude of the men incapable of community. The other you shall now really establish and consolidate—the necessary ever-again-becoming-solitary of the strong. In order to gather new strength, the strong man must from time to time call home his forces into a solitude where he rests in the community of the things that have been and those that will come, and is nourished by them, so that he may go forth with new strength to the community of those who now exist.

'To it you shall learn to go forth—go forth and not withhold yourself.

'You shall help. Each man you meet needs help, each needs *your* help. That is the thousandfold happening of each moment, that the need of help and the capacity to help make way for one another so that each not only does not know about the other but does not even know about himself. It is the nature of man to leave equally unnoticed the innermost need and the innermost gift of his own soul, although at times, too, a deep hour reminds him of them. You shall awaken in the other the need of help, in yourself the capacity to help. Even when you yourself are in need—and you are—you can help others and, in so doing, help yourself.

'He who calls forth the helping word in himself, experiences the word. He who offers support strengthens the support in himself. He who bestows comfort deepens the comfort in himself. He who effects salvation, to him salvation is disclosed.'

The voices of the unknown, the familiar become silent. The questioner reflects on what has been said. But soon they begin again, transformed, beyond him.

'And you:

'You who are shut in in the fortress of your spirit, who admit no one who does not know the password, enthroned in withholding, and you who exchange the sign of recognition with the fellow-conspirators of the secret alliance, you who walk in withholding, the time has come when you must forget word and sign—or be submerged! For not otherwise will you find the new word and sign that will bind the coming torrent.

'The torrent that with facile words you call "the crowd."

'Who has made the crowd so great? He who hates it and he who despises it, he who is horrified by it, he who is disgusted by it, each indeed who says, "the crowd!"—all of them have made it so great that it now wants to surge up to your spiritual fortresses and your secret alliances.

'But now is the time, and now is still the time for the work of conquering.

'Make the crowd no longer a crowd!

'Out of forlorn and impotent men, out of men who have attacked one another through forlornness and impotence, the shapeless thing has come into being—deliver man from it, shape the shapeless to community! Break the withholding, throw yourselves into the surging waves, reach for and grasp hands, lift, help, lead, authenticate spirit and alliance in the trial of the abyss, make the crowd no longer a crowd!

'Some say civilization must be preserved through "subduing." There is no civilization to preserve. And there is no longer a subduing! But what may ascend out of the flood will be decided by whether you throw yourselves into it as seeds of true community.

'No longer through exclusion but only inclusion can the kingdom be established. When it no longer horrifies you and no longer disgusts you, when you redeem the crowd into men and strike even the heart of the crude, the greedy, the stingy with your love, then and then alone is there present, in the midst of the end, the new beginning.

'You hesitate, you doubt—you know from history that each unchaining is answered by new chaining? You do not yet understand, then, that history no longer holds. But the day is not far off when the well-informed security will be pulverized in the souls. Recognize this before it is too late!'

Again the voices become silent. But now they do not begin again. Silently the world waits for the spirit.

Three Theses of a Religious Socialism

(1928)

Any socialism whose limits are narrower than God and man is too narrow for us.

LEONHARD RAGAZ.

I

R ELIGIOUS socialism cannot mean the joining of religion and socialism in such a manner that each of the constituents could achieve, apart from the other, independence if not fulfilment; it cannot mean merely that the two have concluded an agreement to unite their autonomies in a common being and working. Religious socialism can only mean that religion and socialism are essentially directed to each other, that each of them needs the covenant with the other for the fulfilment of its own essence. *Religio*, that is the human person's binding of himself to God, can only attain its full reality in the will for a community of the human race, out of which alone God can prepare His kingdom. *Socialitas*, that is mankind's becoming a fellowship, man's becoming a fellow to man, cannot develop otherwise than out of a common relation to the divine centre, even if this be again and still nameless. Unity with God and community among the creatures belong together. Religion without socialism is disembodied spirit, therefore not genuine spirit; socialism without religion is body emptied of spirit, hence also not genuine body. But—socialism without religion does not hear the divine address, it does not aim at a response, still it happens that it responds; religion without socialism hears the call but does not respond.

2

All 'religious' forms, institutions, and societies are real or fictitious according to whether they serve as expression, as shape and bearer of real *religio*—a real self-binding of the human person to God—or merely exist alongside it, or even conceal the flight from actual *religio* which comprises the concrete response and responsibility of the human person in the here and now. So, too, all 'socialist' tendencies, programmes, and parties are real or fictitious according to whether they serve as strength, direction, and instrument of real *socialitas*—mankind's really becoming a fellowship—or only exist alongside its development, or even conceal the flight from real *socialitas*, which comprises the immediate living with and for one another of men in the here and now. At present the prevailing religious forms, institutions, and societies have entered into the realm of the fictitious; the prevailing socialist tendencies, programmes, and parties have not yet emerged from the fictitious. Today appearance is currently opposed to appearance. But within the hidden sphere of the future the meeting has begun to take place.

3

The point where religion and socialism can meet each other in the truth is the concrete personal life. As the truth of religion consists not of dogma or prescribed ritual but means standing and withstanding in the abyss of the real reciprocal relation with the mystery of God, so socialism in its truth is not doctrine and tactics but standing and withstanding in the abyss of the real reciprocal relation with the mystery of man. As it is presumption to 'believe' in something without—however inadequately—living that in which one believes, so it is presumption to wish to 'accomplish' something without—however inadequately—living what one wants to accomplish. As the 'there' refuses to give itself to us when the 'here' is not devoted to it, so the 'then' must refuse when the 'now' does not authenticate it. Religion must know that it is the everyday that sanctifies or desecrates devotion. And socialism must know that the decision as to how similar or dissimilar the end which is attained will be to the end which was previously cherished is dependent upon how similar or dissimilar to the set goal are the means whereby it is pursued. Religious socialism means that man in the concreteness of his personal life takes seriously the fundamentals of this life; the fact that God is, that the world is, and that he, this human person, stands before God and in the world.

Recollection of a Death

(1929)

WHEN Gustav Landauer* delivered a memorial address for Karl Liebknecht and Rosa Luxemburg in Munich on February 6, 1919, he spoke, to begin with, of social democracy. 'Does it not have a Janus head?' he asked.† 'Is it not true that every daring man of the spirit is drawn to her as the representative of socialism, of justice—repelled by her as a church of bondage, of bureaucracy, of military spirit . . .?' But this concept of the military spirit evoked in him another train of thought. 'Oh,' he cried, 'there is a martial spirit that is still living that can also move our hearts. . . . Listen!' And he read a poem of the Hungarian lyric poet Petöfi (fallen July 31, 1849) in the translation (first published in 1899) by Hedwig Lachmann—Gustav Landauer's wife—who died in February 1918. It begins:

> *A gentle feeling of anxiety troubles me:*
> *I would not die on a soft pillow—*
> *I will not welter in anguish on the cushion,*
> *Will not slowly droop, melt,*
> *Like the candle that one forgets in the room,*
> *Like the flower that a worm eats away*

And further on it reads:

> *If once a spirit drunk with freedom*
> *Tears the enslaved peoples from their slumber,*

---

* Gustav Landauer (1868–1919), a German socialist and man of letters who was a close friend of Martin Buber's and had a considerable effect on his religious socialism. See Buber's chapter on Landauer in Martin Buber, *Paths in Utopia* (London: Routledge & Kegan Paul, 1949), Chap. VI, pp. 46–57. (Ed.)

† The quotations are from Landauer's handwritten draft of the talk.

They rub the sleep out of their eyes
And write 'world freedom!' on their flag
And on the common battle-field,
With flaming face and blood-red flag
They march against the tyrants,
And the blaring battle trumpets
Resound far off—
Then I will fall!

'He died,' Landauer commented, 'as he had wished to; he fell in the fight for freedom—his corpse was not found. Thus also died Rosa Luxemburg, thus also Liebknecht. . . . And yet—how different was this battle! In the street fight of the licentious, anti-revolutionary soldiery, led by professional non-commissioned officers and officers of the General Staff, Karl Liebknecht and Rosa Luxemburg were taken prisoner; in prison they were cowardly murdered by a dishonourable belligerent, the lone, the defenceless, by superior numbers.'

Three months later, on the second of May, Gustav Landauer was murdered by the same 'licentious anti-revolutionary soldiery.'

But what is a licentious soldiery and what is a revolution? A licentious soldiery consists of men who are called soldiers, and a revolution is made up of men who call themselves revolutionaries. What binds together the one group as the other is the actual situation.

The actual situation of the soldier is that he 'combats' what is designated as 'hostile'—no matter whether the 'enemy' is an 'external' or 'internal' one. He must, therefore, 'disable' him, as well as he can and in so far as he is commanded to do by any means he is ordered to use, from robbing him of his freedom to destroying him. The situation can correspond with a conviction: the belief that what has been designated as 'hostile' is really 'hostile,' not merely in the sense that it stands opposite threatening death, but hostile to his very being, his life ground, his highest value, and that, if it is not destroyed, would destroy this highest value. But instead of such belief there also exists doubt, uncertainty, hesitation in all degrees up to the antithetical conviction: that what stands opposite him is not at all inimical. And this conviction can also, gradually or suddenly, break forth in the midst of that full belief that this is 'the enemy.' These men are still joined together as 'compulsory' soldiers but not as 'willing' ones. Probably all of them do not want the situation itself, to be sure, but in their own bearing in this situation—how far the individual wills or does not will his own bearing, 'what he must do' —therein lies his own personal stake within the common camp. And only when the question arises of what 'must' means! Through the centre of the 'licentious soldiery,' through the heart of the soldier, runs the true front.

The situation of the revolutionary resembles that of the soldier in that it also contains the enemy and struggles against it. As to the difference in the situations, one might point out that the revolutionary himself chooses his enemy. But how few really 'recognize' him, how often is he not here too merely 'designated,' knowingly or unknowingly, by speakers and books, by experience of childhood and youth, by deprivations and disappointments! Of course, the tension does not exist between situation and conviction, between having to and wanting to. But still more important is the fact that for the revolutionary the actual fighting is not the situation itself but only an accompaniment; what is at stake here is not, as with the soldier, the battle, but the *revolvere*, the revolution, and the battle only signifies the setting aside of hindrances. In order that the new or changed institutions that are envisaged can come (which those also have in mind who strive for nothing else than the 'fruitful freedom'), those in power, who defend the old institutions, must be conquered.

That means that the revolutionary stands, according to the situation, in the tension between goal and way, and within its responsibility, neither of which the soldier knows. His personal statement is not, 'I must here use force, but I do not want to do so'; but, 'I have taken it on myself to use as much force as is necessary in order that the revolution be accomplished, but alas for me and for it if more force is used than is necessary!' The personal responsibility of the soldiers stems from principle; he can carry the contradiction out to its logical conclusions in his soul, reaching perhaps a decision to allow himself to be killed rather than to kill; even if he does not follow this conclusion in practice, he at least achieves the fundamental formulation of it. But the personal responsibility of the revolutionary is, according to its nature, one of demarcation. The watchword of his spirit is 'Up to here,' and for that 'Up to here' there is no fast rule, each moment presenting it with ever new face.

The revolutionary lives on the knife's edge. The question that harasses him is, in fact, not merely the moral or religious one of whether he may kill; his quandary has nothing at all to do, as has at times been said, with 'selling his soul to the devil' in order to bring the revolution to victory. His entanglement in the situation is here just the tension between end and means. I cannot conceive anything real corresponding to the saying that the end 'sanctifies' the means; but I mean something which is real in the highest sense of the term when I say that the means profane, actually make meaningless, the end, that is, its realization! What is realized is the farther from the goal that was set the more out of accord with it is the method by which it was realized. The 'ensuring' of the revolution may only drain its heart's blood. The responsibility which results from these presuppositions must penetrate most deeply in the leader who is summoned to make the watchword of the spirit into the watchword of the event. But none of those who are led can neglect responsibility save by flight from self-recollection, that is, by the atrophy of the spirit within. Here again the true front runs through the centre.

The recollection of the death of Gustav Landauer always evokes two other recollections in me.

The first stems from the fall of 1919. I journeyed in the early morning from Munich to a city on the lower part of the Inn river. Although I reached the railway-station on time, all the carriages were so crowded that it appeared impossible to find a seat. Still I looked for one and finally came to a halt in one carriage; people made room for me in a friendly manner so far as they could. Only men were there, almost all of them in field-grey uniform.* There was loud, confused interchange of voices. Suddenly I was surprised to hear the name Landauer, and I sought to get a look at the speaker. A soldier, a man of middle age with reddish beard, was remarking to his neighbour, 'No, that was not so with Landauer. Landauer wanted the right thing; if he had only been one of us.'

The other recollection is earlier but belongs to the same year. About two weeks after Landauer's memorial address on Karl Liebknecht and Rosa Luxemburg I was with him, and several other revolutionary leaders in a hall of the Diet building in Munich. Landauer had proposed the subject of discussion—it was the terror. But he himself hardly joined in; he appeared dispirited and nearly exhausted—a year before his wife had succumbed to a fatal illness, and now he relived her death in his heart. The discussion was conducted for the most part between me and a Spartacus leader, who later became well known in the second communist revolutionary government in Munich that replaced the first, socialist government of Landauer and his comrades. The man walked with clanking spurs through the room; he had been a German officer in the war. I declined to do what many apparently had expected of me—to talk of the moral problem; but I set forth what I thought about the relation between end and means. I documented my view from historical and contemporary experience. The Spartacus leader did not go into that matter. He, too, sought to document his apology for the terror by examples. 'Dzertshinsky,' he said, 'the head of the Cheka, could sign a hundred death sentences a day, but with an entirely clean soul.' 'That is, in fact, just the worst of all,' I answered. 'This "clean" soul you do not allow any splashes of blood to fall on! It is not a question of "souls" but of responsibility.' My opponent regarded me with unperturbed superiority. Landauer, who sat next to me, laid his hand on mine. His whole arm trembled.

The true front runs through the licentious soldiery, the true front runs through the revolution, the true front runs through

* The uniform of the German soldier in the First World War.

the heart of the soldier, the true front runs through the heart of the revolutionary. The true front runs through each party and through each adherent of a party, through each group and through each member of a group. On the true front each fights against his fellows and against himself, and only through the decisions of these battles is he given full power for other decisions. Those are the men of whom it is said that they have weakened the battle strength; those are the men who keep alive the truth of the battle.

Landauer fought in the revolution against the revolution for the sake of the revolution. The revolution will not thank him for it. But those will thank him for it who have fought as he fought and perhaps some day those will thank him for whose sake he fought.

China and Us*

(1928)

I<small>T</small> happens from time to time that a call comes to Europe from the East to make common cause with Asia. I recall a remark of Tagore's. He said, approximately, 'Indeed, why do you do all this here in Europe? Why do you have all this bustle, all this industrialization, all this ballast? All of this is really quite unnecessary. Cast off all this and let us, West and East, contemplate truth in common!' That was said in a heartfelt manner. But it seemed to me removed from the reality of the hour in which we live. I pictured to myself a man who proposed to erect a great symbol on a mountain peak that had not yet been conquered and who climbed up the mountain burdened with this symbol. If someone should now call to him, 'Why all the trouble? Just throw away that heavy thing, then you will ascend much more easily!' then the man would rightly answer, 'I intend either to ascend with this symbol or to fall headlong with it.'

It is this burden that the West is called upon to master. Upon the real mastering of it depends whether this epoch will fulfil its meaning or not. Stripping off this burden and going back behind all this industrializing and technicizing and mechanizing, we would no longer proceed on the way at all; we would, in general, no longer have a way. It is not so, therefore, that we could give up all of this in order now, together with the Oriental, to seek and contemplate what is common to both. Rather we can only come together with them, taking with us this our task, with its problematic, its element of disintegration, which we experience today and of which we can reduce nothing. We must take it

* Address at the fall, 1928, conference of the China Institute, Frankfurt-am-Main, Germany.

121

upon us as it is, bear it as it is, overcome it as it is. If we pass through our task thus, then we may hope to meet an Asia advancing to meet us. May it be spared our road! But when I consider the development of Japan—yes, even the development of India—I doubt whether it can be spared it.

But within this problematic, can the contact with Asia none the less have some significance for us? Do we still have something to take, to receive, from Asia? Understand me rightly, not in the intellectual manner that was customary in the eighteenth century, when one superficially appropriated any sort of external product of Chinese art or wisdom. Not, for example, in the way in which the secret of the Chinese art of engraving was elaborated into the in part very charming *chinoiserie*. Nor in the way in which one took hold of Confucian wisdom, not according to its concrete original contents, but only just as something universally noble and valuable, without perceiving that such receiving is a sin against the spirit, that real receiving can only take place as the receiving of a living reality with the forces of one's own life. I do not mean this. But the question is, is there something that we can receive from living Chinese reality, from the real life powers of its customs, its education, its culture, and if so what?

It does not seem to me now that there is anything that we can take over in this sense from the Confucian culture.

I shall advance only two of the reasons for my view. One concerns the most important foundation of this culture: its ancestor cult. That is, of course, a concept by which one usually understands things of very different natures. An ancestor cult exists among the so-called primitives, from dread before the continuing, horrifying, sinister presence of the dead, whom one wishes to propitiate. Another ancestor cult exists in which the ancestors migrate into a higher sphere of existence, becoming demons, heroes, gods—detached from, and incapable of being touched by, the vicissitudes of earthly life. They are, thereby, only an object of veneration for the later human generations, but not a living relationship. The Chinese ancestor cult is of an entirely different nature. It signifies an attitude of the receiving principle; it means that the generation that lives after receives from the dead. This ancestor cult is thus only possible in a culture where familiarity with the dead prevails. I mean familiarity, therefore neither horror nor distant veneration, but natural intercourse without any uncanniness, such as the Chinese tales again and again tell of, most clearly in the stories of love relationships with the dead. Here is nothing of the horror of the medieval incubus; one has intercourse, as on the same plane, with the spirits of the dead who have entered into our life. This case of intercourse with the dead goes together with the Chinese type of ancestor cult. The generation that lives after receives from the generation that we call the past. And thereby the seed of the custom, the formation is ever again planted in the growing generation—not as something that is only held fast, only continued, only preserved, but as something that engenders and whose engendering is reborn in the new generation, seemingly this same custom and yet formed anew, grown anew.

That is something that must certainly remain alien to the West. The foundations of this ancestor cult are not given in the West. An organic relation between the dead and the living, as in the Chinese culture, is not present in the West, and is, it seems to me, not possible. And that is one reason why I doubt that such a connection of the generations, such a belief of the new in the old that is for it precisely *not* the old, could grow here. It might certainly be necessary for us; for we have entered into a crisis not merely of the individual institutions, but of our institutions in general. But I do not see how we could take over what offers itself here.

The second reason is that culture is always connected with an image and, in fact, with a universally-valid image. There exist, indeed, not merely universally-valid concepts, as philosophy teaches, but also universally-valid images. The ages that possess real culture are ages where a universally-valid image of man stands above the heads of men. Looking upward to these images that are invisible and yet living in the imagination of all individuals constitutes the life of culture; the imitation of them out of the material of the person is the educating, the forming of man. Now, however, the East Asian image is a different species from that of the Occident. The universally-valid image of man in China is the original man, the 'pure man of yore.' Erected on the ancestor cult of China, this image is a monument of the trust in the original state, in that which must ever again be reborn, ever again formed anew. This trust in the primal being is missing in the Western man and cannot be acquired by him. Even Christianity was not able to alter this situation, although it did, in fact, transmit to the West the Oriental teaching of the paradisaical primal state of mankind. Of the Biblical story of the first man, only the Fall is present in a living way in the reality of the personal life of Christian Western man, not the life before the Fall. The trust in the original being of the human substance is lacking, and I do not believe that it is to be won on the paths of the historical culture visible to us. (You understand that I do not speak of other paths. We speak of the relations of cultures to each other; we speak of the historical, not of the superhistorical that may ever again burst through and transform the historical.) These are two of the reasons that make me doubt whether we can absorb into our life something of the great connection of China, its continuity, something of that warranting of the institutional principle that the Chinese culture offers.

But there is still something that we can receive and actually from the standpoint of the progress of our history, of our experiences in this world hour. That is not, to be sure, something of the great structure of the Confucian culture; it is something revolutionary, protestant, though basically, of course, ancient. I believe that we can receive from China in a living manner something of the Taoist teaching of 'non-action,' the teaching of Lao-tzu. And for the reason that—bearing our burden on our way—we have learned something analogous, only negatively—on the reverse side, so to speak. We have begun to learn, namely, that success is of no consequence. We have begun to doubt the significance of historical success, i.e. the validity of the man who sets an end for himself, carries this end into effect, accumulates the necessary means of power and succeeds with these means of power: the typical modern Western man. I say, we begin to doubt the content of existence of this man. And there we come into contact with something genuine and deeply Chinese, though not, to be sure, Confucian: with the teaching that genuine effecting is not interfering, not giving vent to power, but remaining within one's self. This is the powerful existence that does not yield historical success, i.e. the success that can be exploited and registered in this hour, but only yields that effecting that at first appears insignificant, indeed invisible, yet endures across generations and there at times becomes perceptible in another form. At the core of each historical success hides the turning away from what the man who accomplished it really had in mind. Not realization, but the hidden non-realization that has been disguised or masked just through success is the essence of historical success. Opposed to it stands the changing of men that takes place in the absence of success, the changing of men through the fact that one effects without interfering. It is, I believe, in the commencing knowledge of this action without doing, action through non-action, of this powerfulness of existence, that we can have contact with the great wisdom of China. With us this knowledge does not originate as wisdom but as foolishness. We have obtained a taste of it in the bitterest manner; indeed, in a downright foolish manner. But there where we stand or there where we shall soon stand, we shall directly touch upon the reality for which Lao-tzu spoke.

Gandhi, Politics, and Us

(1930)

The Question of Success

WHILE Gandhi lay in prison, shortly after he had received far-reaching plenary powers from the Congress of Ahmedabad (December 1921), and then issued the ultimatum to the viceroy (February 1922), but a few days afterwards, upon the outbreak of the riots of Chauri Chaura, withdrew it, a high British official expressed himself in the following manner: 'He thoroughly frightened us. His programme filled our prisons—but one cannot for ever lock up and lock up, especially when it is a matter of a people of three hundred and nineteen millions. And if they had gone a step further and had refused to pay taxes—who knows where that would have led! What Gandhi undertook was the most powerful of all experiments that the history of the world has known and only fell a little short of succeeding. *But in him the insight into human passions was lacking.*'

That opinion was falsely formulated. What Gandhi 'lacked' was not insight into human passions but the readiness to exploit them. Both the actual insight and the lack of readiness are clearly expressed in the withdrawal of the ultimatum. The outbreak of riots he called a warning of God 'that there does not yet exist in India that truthful and non-violent atmosphere that alone can justify mass disobedience.' The final judgment of the British official does not mean basically that political success is not possible without an insight into human passions, but that political success is not possible without exploitation of human passions. That certainly is not true. But from this starting-point we must

126

inquire further concerning Gandhi's relation to political success.

When, not ten days after the withdrawal, Gandhi's position met strong opposition at the conference of the All-India Committee in Delhi and 'in order to avoid a painful discussion,' he had to renounce having the designations 'truthful' and 'non-violent' included in the programmatic resolution, he wrote that he had wanted, now as so often before, to remain in a small minority: 'I know that the only thing that the government fears is this monstrous majority that I appear to command. They do not know that I fear it still more than they do themselves. I am literally sick over it. I would feel myself on surer ground if I were spit upon by them.' And further, 'If I also, perhaps, stood before the prospect of finding myself in a minority of *one* voice, I humbly believe that I would have the courage to remain in such a hopeless minority. This is for me the only truthful position.' That is unquestionably the statement of a truthful man, and I know of nothing in modern Western public life to put by its side, unless it were, for all the difference in its source, the words of the American Thoreau in his classical treatise on the duty of civil disobedience.

But can this also be regarded as the statement of a political man, that is, a man who undertakes to influence the formation of institutions and their operation? In other words: is the statement of Gandhi's that we have quoted a declaration against lies in politics or is it a declaration against politics? Can a political action change institutions, that is a political success, without a majority or a revolutionary-minority mass following, whether by dictation or voluntary assent? Is the aphorism of Schiller and Ibsen concerning the strong man who is most powerful alone or the man who stands alone being the strongest man in the world, not merely morally true, hence true on the plane of personal authentication, but also politically true, that is true on the plane of social realization? Can this solitary man be politically effective otherwise than by masses 'following' him, compelled by his charisma?

But it is just this following without inner transformation that fails to satisfy Gandhi, as shown by his words about his 'fear.'

'In the Ramayana,' he writes, 'we see that when all was ready for Rama's coronation, Rama was exiled into the wild woods.' Now in the Indian epic, after Rama had long refused to accept the rule because the time of the exile first had to be fulfilled, he was finally consecrated king. But that no longer implies a political hope, nothing directly to be realized in the public sphere through public activities, but only a religious one. This hope is not for an ostensible 'following,' but only for their conversion.

In the memorable paper, 'Neither a Saint nor a Politician,' Gandhi elucidates his position, 'I seem to take part in politics, but this is only because politics today strangles us like the coils of a serpent out of which one cannot slip whatever one tries. I desire, therefore, to wrestle with the serpent.' And further, 'I have experimented with myself and with my friends in order to introduce religion into politics.' Our question once again changes its form; it now reads: Does religion allow itself to be introduced into politics in such a way that a political success can be obtained?

Religion means goal and way, politics implies end and means. The political end is recognizable by the fact that it may be attained—in success—and its attainment is historically recorded. The religious goal remains, even in man's highest experiences of the mortal way, that which simply provides direction; it never enters into historical consummation. The history of the created world, as the religions believing in history acknowledge it, and the history of the human person, as all religions, even those that do not believe in history, acknowledge it, is what takes place on the journey from origin to perfection, and this is registered by other signs than that of success. 'The Word' is victorious, but otherwise than its bearers hoped for. The Word is not victorious in its purity, but in its corruption; it bears its fruit in the *corruptio seminis*. Here no success is experienced and recorded; where something of the kind appears in the history of religion, it is no longer religion that prevails, but politics of religion, that is, the opposite of what Gandhi proclaimed: the introduction of politics into religion.

Once again, then: Can political success be attained through religious deed?

That Gandhi's own attitude is religious in the most genuine sense remains beyond doubt. But already when he speaks of 'experimenting with friends' the painful question concerning the views of many of these friends obtrudes. Some of his closest followers have declared before the court of justice that, as long as Gandhi proclaims the watchword of non-violence, they will steadfastly hold to it, yet if another word came from his mouth, then they would certainly follow that one; not to mention the broad circle of the movement. 'I see,' wrote Gandhi after the day of Delhi, 'that this our non-violence is only skin-deep. . . . This non-violence appears to me to originate simply in our helplessness. . . . Can genuine voluntary non-violence arise out of this apparently compulsory non-violence of the weak?' These are words that even to-day, despite Gandhi's great educational effect, retain much of their validity.

So far as Gandhi acts politically, so far as he takes part in passing parliamentary resolutions, he does not introduce religion into politics, but allies his religion with the politics of others. He cannot wrestle uninterruptedly with the serpent; he must at times get along with it because he is directed to work in the kingdom of the serpent that he set out to destroy. He refuses to exploit human passions, but he is chained as political actor to the 'political,' to *untransformed* men. The serpent is, indeed, not only powerful outside, but also within, in the souls of those who long for political success. The way in which Gandhi again and again exercises self-criticism, going into heavy mortification and purification when the inner serpent shows itself too powerful in the movement, is worthy of the purest admiration. But we do not follow him in this; we know that if we consider the *tragic* character of his greatness, that it is not the tragedy of an inner contradiction, but that of the contradiction between the unconditionality of a spirit and the conditionality of a situation, to which situation, precisely, the masses of his followers, even of the youth belong. This is the tragedy that resists all superficial optimistic attempts to bring about a settlement; the situation will certainly be mastered, but only in the way in which at the close of a Greek tragedy, a theophany (the so-called *deus ex machina*, in truth *ex gratia*) resolves the insoluble fate. But that is the very soft, very slow, very roundabout, not at all 'successful' step of the deity through history.

In September 1920 Gandhi said and wrote that if the Indian people showed discipline, self-denial, readiness to sacrifice, capacity for order, confidence and courage, then Swaraj—Indian independence—would be attained in a year. Three months later, asked by the correspondent from *The Times* what he meant by that, he explained that the British people would recognize the strength of the Indian public opinion and at the same time the dreadful injustice that had been done to India in their name, and would forthwith offer a constitution 'that will correspond exactly to the wishes of the Indian people.' Gandhi ended the conversation with a variation on the prophetic word, 'The lion will then rest by the lamb.' One could not express more clearly the *religious* character of that expectation; but if it is taken seriously, the presupposition that Gandhi sets for it implies not merely an attitude of the people but an inner transformation. Gandhi unmistakably rejects the 'political,' the untransformed, the men who are not changing themselves. 'If India,' he once wrote later, 'wants to become free, it can only do so with God's help. God loves the truthful and the non-violent.' But God's love is not measured by success. How God's love works is His affair. One may be certain of the truthfulness and non-violence of the love of God, but not of the attainment of Swaraj in one year. 'In one year' is a political word; the religious watchword must read: Some time, perhaps today, perhaps in a century. In religious reality there is no stipulation of time, and victory comes, at times, just when one no longer expects it.

In the last part of the year of expectation, Gandhi wrote that the 'miracle' of so rapid an attainment of Swaraj must be 'preceded by a miraculous *conversion* of India to the teaching of non-violence, at least in its limited purpose; that is, as an indispensable precondition for securing India's freedom.' But does that not mean conversion to a religious teaching, 'at least' in its political form? In religious teaching non-violence remains the way to the goal, even when it rejects it as means to an end. It must, of course, be sufficient for Gandhi as *political actor*, if the masses accept the right attitude, but conversion means the turning of the being, an innermost change of heart.

Certainly, when a religious man, one who is serious about his religiousness in any situation whatever, functions in the political sphere, religion is introduced into politics. But the way to the religious goal is essentially dissimilar in its conduct of the path, its perspective, its manner of going, its tempo, and, lastly, in the unforseeableness of attainment and political success. The holy cause of 'introducing' the religious reality into politics runs the danger, therefore, that the categories will mingle, that the goal will become an end, the way a means; that man, instead of treading in the path taken by that step of God through history, will run blindly over it. If religion is threatened at one pole by the ice of isolation in which it forfeits a tie with the communal-building human share in the coming of the kingdom, here it is threatened by evaporation in the rapid fire of political activity. Only in the great *polis* of God will religion and politics be blended into a life of world community, in an eternity wherein neither religion nor politics will any longer exist.

The most natural of all questions, the question concerning success, is religion's ordeal by fire. If religion withdraws from the sphere where this question is asked, it evades its task, despite all hosts and sacraments of incarnation; and if it sinks into that sphere, then it has lost its soul. Gandhi, as no other man of our age, shows us the difficulty of the situation, the depth of its problematic, the manifoldness of the battle fronts, the potency of the contradiction, which is encompassed by paradox and must be endured in every hour.

As I write this, the Mahatma has set out on his march—a far-reaching symbolical counterpart of the flight of the aged Tolstoy. Manifestly this is no political journey, but a pilgrimage, a pilgrimage with political intent. But beneath the political aspect, probably hidden from the consciousness of most of those who accompany him, abides the religious, where the refusal to pay a tax no longer signifies an instrument in the fight against the British regime, but the recourse of the man whom in this world hour it avails to experience factually and through the devotion of self *how much* is Cæsar's.

I do not believe that the independence of India stands at the end of this pilgrimage. But I believe that this pilgrimage will essentially co-determine the nature of the man in an independent India, whenever and however that independence is attained. What would Swaraj amount to if it implied only a transformation of institutions and not a transformation of men also!

Gandhi's Work and an Indian Politics

But if we wish to understand Gandhi's place not only in the history of religiousness and its consequences there but also in that of politics, we must consider the Indian ideal of independence on the basis of its actual and possible contents. This can be most clearly seen, it seems to me, if we compare the programme of the Mahatma with that of his opponent, the great patriot Chitta Ranjan Das.

While Gandhi sat in prison—on December 26, 1922—Das opened the All-India Congress in Gaya with a speech in which, beginning with an homage to the Mahatma, he formulated three postulates.

The first, a tactical one, opposed to the non-co-operation of Gandhi the demand for an 'inner' boycott of the British councils into which one should let oneself be delegated and the activities of which one should obstruct. This demand does not leave the province of non-violence; but seeks to give it, instead of a passive content, a direct and active one, one, certainly, whose consequences might possibly be hazardous to the preservation of non-violence.

The second, extra-political plan projected, in opposition to Gandhi, who would only let India proceed through its own efforts, the programme of an Asiatic federation to arouse India and in which India would work. To appreciate this idea, one must realize that in India it means something entirely different from what it would mean in, say, Russia or Japan. Here again non-violence is adhered to; an Asiatic League is intended which will give the West notice of co-operation and declare itself independent. The possible effects on the preservation of non-violence are here, of course, still more hazardous than in the first proposal.

The third and most important constructive programme concerns the inner structure of an independent India. Swaraj, Das explains, can become neither a parliamentary nor a bureaucratic government. To replace the British bureaucracy by an Indian one would be futile. Rather the basic form of the old Indian village community must be recovered. A system of relatively autonomous small communities has to be erected which will be joined to larger, likewise autonomous, communities; these in their turn will be so grouped as to form a unifying central power of predominantly consultative character which would have to exercise authority only in exceptional cases.

This third proposal, which I have felt to be a brotherly response out of Asia to related ideas of a European circle, represents in my eyes a high pinnacle of *political* man. What is expressed here is the presentiment of the overcoming, through politics itself, of that political degeneration that calls itself politics in modern state centralism; it is an aspiration to a genuine communal life that will reduce the apparatus of the state to the technically necessary minimum.

At the beginning of February 1924 the sick Gandhi was released from prison. In May he openly declared himself against the first of the three designs of Das, that of obstructionist parliamentarianism; in July against the second, that of an Asiatic federation; and at the same time against the third, against the innermost programme. In opposition to this he stated that Swaraj is nothing else than that constitution of India the people might desire at a particular moment. Such a statement is a purely political, democratic-political one, which appears to me, for all that, far poorer in its political substance and content and in political autochthony than Das' basic revolutionary idea.

In November Gandhi concluded the well-known compromises with the Swarajists led by Das that meant a personal but not an essential victory by Gandhi. In June of the following year Das died. Since then there has been no thought of a further development and execution of his programme.

About the tactical controversy I cannot judge. Das' Asiatic scheme is of unmistakable political greatness. I have already said that the dangers both proposals threatened to the cause of non-violence cannot be overlooked. Yet from the standpoint of this cause there is nothing decisive against it. But what concerns us here is the constructive postulate.

Gandhi did not, indeed, strive for just any kind of free India, but for a genuinely Indian society, in which the essence of the people that is to be found in individual souls, teachings, and holy books should acquire body. But such an India cannot be constructed out of amorphous swarms of individuals, held together only by the state; it must be formed out of naturally linked smaller and larger communities, each possessing an autonomy as extensive as possible, where what prevails is no longer the artificial state, which disregards all human reality, but the concrete counselling of one another, deciding with one another, acting with one another in the concrete public sphere; communities in whose structure the people will for the first time constitute itself as such politically. Gandhi has not recognized that here there was a political vision that supplemented his own religious one; he has not admitted that it is of fundamental importance for the Indian cause, too, to ascertain in a practical political sense how much is 'Cæsar's' —that is, how much belongs to the concentration of power in general—and how much 'God's'—that is, politically formulated, how much belongs to the human people living communally in creaturely immediacy.

Gandhi, of course, believes that he is able to secure to the coming Indian society the purity and uniqueness that will preserve it from 'civilization.' Already in 1909 he wrote home from South Africa that there is no insurmountable barrier between East and West. There is no such thing as Western civilization, there is just modern civilization which is a purely materialistic one; it, not England, governs India. If the British regime were replaced by an Indian one that was grounded in modern culture, India would be no better off. East and West, so Gandhi says, could only really meet when the West had thrown modern civilization almost entirely overboard. If the East were to accept modern civilization, the meeting would be only apparent, signifying but an armed truce 'such as that between Germany and England, in which both nations live in the hall of death in order not to be devoured by the other.' But the way in which Gandhi declares in this, in so many respects clear-sighted, letter that he wishes to protect India, would scarcely preserve the country from the process of industrialization taking place before our eyes. The spinning-wheel, honoured as a symbol even by sympathetic textile manufacturers, cannot, in fact, be preserved in any realistic way.

'Modern civilization' is a destiny for mankind which embraces both its highest task and its decisive test. All attempts at reduction, even the most exalted, evade this test.

Modern civilization in its fundamental nature is not 'material.' It necessarily appears so only because and in so far as it displays still unconquered material, material not yet permeated by spirit. The problem, in India as everywhere, is one of rescuing and disclosing a human substance, which is equal to animating this civilization, and which, incarnating the spirit, authenticates itself in it, with it, and through it. The task is, therefore, to shape out of the rescued souls men who will hold their ground. This is Mahatma Gandhi's great work in India; it is not to be accomplished in the tempo of political undertakings and success, but in that of the step of God.

Should Politics then be Pursued?

The modern Occident rests upon the sanctioned duality of politics and religion. One need only listen to how the politician speaks the word 'ethics' and the theologian the word 'action.' Politics is unenlightened but powerful; religion (in its broadest sense, the superstructure of sacred 'values') is the object of all shades of feelings of sacredness but it is not binding.

Through his attempt 'to introduce religion into politics' Gandhi has entered the ranks of those who strive to overcome the still continually growing duality of politics and religion. The tragedy he has thereby entered is that peculiar to the prophetic man. This tragedy must be recognized and honoured.

Emil Roniger says in the Foreword to *Gandhi's Time of Suffering*, a book edited by him (in German): 'Life allows itself to be permeated by religion—politics does not. A life that was to be permeated by religion would no longer know politics. Only the permeation of life with the yeast of the religious can one day deliver us from the serpent of politics that holds us ensnared with its cold coils.' But that means virtually to abandon public life to damnation here and now, to separate the private and the public phases of life, to confirm the spirit in its very incapacity in our time for being translated into conduct, for being made public. This incapacity hinders the development of a new community structure; it deprives mankind, before the decisive test, of the powers that it needs to meet it. Jesus could content himself with the bidding to give the distant Roman emperor just that which was 'his,' and so to demarcate the limits of the kingdom proper from the state centralism which did not make itself really felt then since it had not absorbed the life of the city-dweller, far less that of the Palestinian in general. The prophets of Israel had to oppose the king in Jerusalem, as the protector of injustice in the land, with the firebrands of religio-political words.

One should, I believe, neither seek politics nor avoid it, one should be neither political nor non-political on principle. Public life is a sphere of life; in its laws and forms it is, in our time, just as deformed as our civilization in general; today one calls that deformity politics as one calls the deformity of working-life technique. But neither is deformed in its essence; public life, like work, is redeemable.

States and parties have successfully endeavoured to conceal the reality of the public situations through fictions and political fabrications. These fabrications must be torn off the current situation, which demands that one enter into it and exercise responsibility in it and for it. States and the parties have further successfully contrived to hinder the formation of unions and, finally, the comprehensive union of those men who have *real* convictions (convictions to be realized in one's life), and who could therefore co-operate in real responsibility, to hinder this by illusory unions. In these a minority of men of genuine convictions is coupled with a majority of men of fictitious convictions, ostensibly with the same aim, but one which they do not intend to realize in personal life; thereby the minority is rendered innocuous. He who will remain obedient to the spirit *in* politics may not forget in any situation that what matters is the coming into being of those genuine unions and finally of that union of man. Nor may he forget that, if his work is to be done in public life, it must be accomplished not above the fray but in it. He has a task to perform within his party if he knows himself strong and free enough to fight *in it* against the lies of party structures. Even if he succumbs, he has done work that will continue to have effect.

The real evil in politics is the 'political means' prevailing there as elsewhere: to win over other men through imposing views on them. But in public life (as elsewhere) it is possible and necessary to employ religious instead of political means; to win others through helping them to open out. He who attempts this may appear weak in the midst of the political tumult. But through working on the kingdom of man, he works on the kingdom of God.

We can only work on the kingdom of God through working on all the spheres of man that are allotted to us. There is no universally valid choice of means to serve the purpose. One cannot say, we must work here and not there, this leads to the goal and that does not. We cannot prepare the messianic world, we can only prepare for it. There is no legitimately messianic, no legitimately messianically-intended, politics. But that does not imply that the political sphere may be excluded from the hallowing of all things. The political 'serpent' is not essentially evil, it is itself only misled; it, too, ultimately wants to be redeemed. It does not avail to strike at it, it does not avail to turn away from it. It belongs with the creaturely world: we must have to do with it, without inflexible principles, in naked responsibility.

There, too, we can learn from Gandhi; there, too, we cannot simply follow in his steps.

The West cannot and may not abandon 'modern civilization,'

the East will not be able to shun it. But just the work of mastering these materials, of humanizing this materiality, the hallowing of this world, our own world, will lead the two hemispheres together through establishing here and there the covenant of men faithful to the Great Reality. The flaming sword of the cherubim circling the entrance of the Garden of Eden prohibits the way back. But it illumines the way forward.

A Letter to Gandhi*

(1939)

MAHATMA GANDHI,

Let the Nazis, the lords of the ice-inferno, affix my name to a cunningly constructed scarecrow; this is the logical outcome of their own nature and the nature of their relations to me. But you, the man of goodwill, do you not know that you must see him whom you address, in his place and circumstance, in the throes of his destiny?

Jews are being persecuted, robbed, maltreated, tortured, murdered. And you, Mahatma Gandhi, say that their position in the country where they suffer all this is an exact parallel to the position of Indians in South Africa at the time when you inaugurated your famous 'Strength of Truth' or 'Soul Force' (*satyagraha*) campaign. There, you say, the Indians occupied precisely the same place, and the persecution there also had a religious tinge. There also the constitution denied equality of rights to the white and the black races including the Asians; there also the Indians were assigned to ghettoes, and the other disqualifications were, at all events, almost of the same type as those of the Jews in Germany. . . In the first of your speeches with which I am acquainted, that of 1896, you quoted two particular incidents . . . first, that a band of Europeans had set fire to an Indian village

---

* On November 26, 1938, Gandhi published a statement in his paper, the *Harijan*, in which he suggested that the Jews in Germany use *satyagraha*, or soulforce, as the most effective reply to Nazi atrocities, and at the same time criticized Zionism and the Jewish settlement in Palestine as unjust to the Arabs who possessed the land. To this statement Martin Buber and Judah Magnes wrote public replies. For the complete text of Gandhi's statement and of Buber's reply (of which this selection represents about half), see Martin Buber and Judah Magnes, *Two Letters to Gandhi* (Jerusalem: Reuben Mass, 1939).

shop causing some damage; and second, that another band had thrown burning rockets into an urban shop. If I oppose to this the thousands on thousands of Jewish shops, destroyed and burnt-out, you will perhaps answer that the difference is only one of quantity and that the proceedings were almost of the same type. But, Mahatma, are you not aware of the burning of synagogues and scrolls of the Torah? Do you know nothing of all the sacred property of the community—in part of great antiquity, that has been destroyed in the flames? I am not aware that Boers and Englishmen in South Africa ever injured anything sacred to the Indians. I find further only one other concrete complaint quoted in that speech, namely, that three Indian school-teachers, who were found walking in the streets after 9 p.m., contrary to orders, were arrested and only acquitted later on. . . . Now, do you know or *do you not* know, Mahatma, what a concentration camp is like and what goes on there? Do you know of the torments in the concentration camp, of its methods of slow and quick slaughter? I cannot assume that you know of this; for then this tragi-comic utterance 'almost of the same type' could scarcely have crossed your lips. Indians were despised and despicably treated in South Africa, but they were not deprived of rights, they were not outlawed, they were not hostages to induce foreign powers to take the desired attitude towards South Africa. And do you think perhaps that a Jew in Germany could pronounce in public one single sentence of a speech such as yours without being knocked down? Of what significance is it to point to a certain something in common when such differences are overlooked? It does not seem to me convincing when you base your advice to us to practise *satyagraha* in Germany on these similarities of circumstance. In the five years which I myself spent under the present régime, I observed many instances of genuine *satyagraha* among the Jews, instances showing a strength of spirit wherein there was no question of bartering their rights or of being bowed down, and where neither force nor cunning was used to escape the consequences of their behaviour. Such actions, however, apparently exerted not the slightest influence on their opponents. All honour, indeed, to those who displayed such strength of soul! But I cannot recognize herein a maxim for the general behaviour of German Jews which might seem suited to exert an influence on the oppressed or on the world. An effective stand may be taken in the form of non-violence against unfeeling human beings in the hope of gradually bringing them thereby to their senses; but a diabolic universal steam-roller cannot thus be withstood. There is a certain situation in which from the '*satyagraha*' of the strength of the spirit no '*satyagraha*' of the power of truth can result. '*Satyagraha*' means testimony. Testimony without acknowledgment, ineffective, unobserved martyrdom, a martyrdom cast to the winds—that is the fate of innumerable Jews in Germany. God alone accepts their testimony, and God 'seals' it, as is said in our prayers. But no maxim for suitable behaviour can be deduced therefrom. Such martyrdom is a deed—but who would venture to demand it? ...

When you were in South Africa, Mahatma, there were living there 150,000 Indians. But in India there were far more than two hundred millions! And this fact nourished the souls of the 150,000, whether they were conscious of it or not: they drew from this source their strength to live and their courage to live. Did you ask then, as you ask the Jews now, whether they want a double home where they can remain at will? You say to the Jews: if Palestine is their home, they must accustom themselves to the idea of being forced to leave the other parts of the world in which they are settled. Did you also say to the Indians in South Africa that if India is their home they must accustom themselves to the idea of being compelled to return to India? Or did you tell them that India was not their home? And if tomorrow—though indeed it is inconceivable that such a thing could come to pass—the hundreds of millions of Indians were to be scattered over the face of the earth; and if the day after tomorrow another nation were to establish itself in India and the Indians were to declare that there was yet room for the establishment of a national home for them, thus giving to their diaspora a strong organic concentration and a living centre; should then a Jewish Gandhi—assuming there could be such—answer them as you answered the Jews, 'This cry for the national home affords a colourable justification for your expulsion'? Or should he teach them, as you teach the Jews: the India of the Vedic conception is not a geographical tract but a symbol in your hearts? A land about which a sacred book speaks to the sons of the land is never merely in their hearts; a land can never become a mere symbol. It is in men's hearts because it is in the world; it is a symbol because it is a reality. Zion is the prophetic image of a promise to mankind, but it would be a vain metaphor if Mount Zion did not actually exist. This land is called 'holy'; but this is not the holiness of an idea, it is the holiness of a piece of earth. That which is merely an idea and nothing more cannot become holy, but a piece of earth can become holy.

Dispersion is bearable, it can even be purposeful, if somewhere there is an ingathering, a growing home centre, a piece of earth from whence the spirit of ingathering may work its way out to all the places of dispersion. When there is this centre, there is also a striving, common life, the life of a community which dares to live today because it hopes to live tomorrow. But when this growing centre, this increasing process of ingathering, is lacking, dispersion becomes dismemberment. On this criterion, the question of our Jewish destiny is indissolubly bound up with the possibility of ingathering, and this with Palestine.

You ask, 'Why should they not, like other nations of the earth, make that country their home where they are born and where they earn their livelihood?' Because their destiny is different from that of all other nations of the earth; it is a destiny which in truth and justice should not be imposed on any nation on earth. For their destiny is dispersion: not the dispersion of a fraction and the preservation of the main substance as in the case of other nations; it is dispersion without the living heart and centre; and every nation has a right to demand the possession of a living heart. It is different because a hundred adopted homes without one original and natural one render a nation sick and miserable. It is different because although the well-being and the achievement of the individual may flourish on stepmother soil, the nation as such must languish.

Decisive for us is not the promise of the Land—but the command, the fulfilment of which is bound up with the land, with the existence of a free Jewish community in this country. For the Bible tells us and our inmost knowledge testifies to it, that once, more than three thousand years ago, our entry into this land was in the consciousness of a mission from above to set up a just way of life through the generations of our people, such a way of life as can be realized not by individuals in the sphere of their private existence but only by a nation in the establishment of its society: communal ownership of the land,* regularly recurrent levelling of social distinctions,† guarantee of the independence of each individual,‡ mutual help,§ a common Sabbath embracing serf and beast as beings with equal claim,‖ a Sabbatical year where, by letting the soil rest, everybody is admitted to the free enjoyment of its fruits.¶ We went into exile with our task unperformed, but the command remained with us, and it has become more urgent than ever. We need our own soil in order to fulfil it; we need the freedom of ordering our own life. . . . It may not be that the soil and the freedom for fulfilment be denied us. . . .

But you say—and I consider it to be the most significant of all the things you tell us—that Palestine belongs to the Arabs and that it is therefore 'wrong and inhuman to impose the Jews on the Arabs.'

I belong to a group of people** who, from the time when Britain conquered Palestine, have not ceased to strive for the concluding of genuine peace between Jew and Arab.

By a genuine peace we inferred and still infer that both peoples should together develop the land without the one imposing his will on the other. In view of the international usages of our generation, this appeared to us to be very difficult but not impossible. We were well aware, and still are, that in this unusual —yes, unexampled—case, it is a question of seeking new ways of understanding and cordial agreement between the two nations.

* Lev. 25:23.   † Lev. 25:13.   ‡ Ex. 21:2.
§ Ex. 23:4 ff.   ‖ Ex. 23 12.   ¶ Lev. 25:5-7.
** A group for Arab-Jewish rapprochement founded by the late Judah Magnes, first president of the Hebrew University, and still existing, in recent years, under the name *Ichud* (Union). Martin Buber is one of its leaders. (Ed.)

Here again we stood and still stand under the sway of a commandment.

We considered it a fundamental point that in this case two vital claims are opposed to each other, two claims of a different nature and a different origin, which cannot be pitted one against the other, and between which no objective decision can be made as to which is just or unjust. We considered and still consider it our duty to understand and to honour the claim which is opposed to ours and to endeavour to reconcile both claims. We cannot renounce the Jewish claim; something even higher than the life of our people is bound up with the land, namely, the work which is their divine mission. But we have been and still are convinced that it must be possible to find some form of agreement between this claim and the other; for we love this land and we believe in its future; and, given that such love and such faith are surely present also on the other side, a union in the common service of the land must be within the range of the possible. Where there is faith and love, a solution may be found even to what appears to be a tragic contradiction. . . .

By what means did the Arabs attain to the right of ownership in Palestine? Surely by conquest and, in fact, a conquest followed by settlement. . . . Settlement by force of conquest justifies for you a right of ownership of Palestine; whereas a settlement such as the Jewish one—the methods of which, though not always doing full justice to Arab ways of life, it is true, were, even in the most objectionable cases, far removed from those of conquest —do not justify, in your opinion, any participation in this right of possession. These are the consequences which result from your statement in the form of an axiom that a land belongs to its population. . . . What if this wandering nation—to whom the land once belonged, likewise on the basis of a settlement by force of conquest, and who were once driven out of it by mere force of domination—should now strive to occupy a free part of the land, or a part that might become free without encroaching on the living room of others, in order at last to acquire again for themselves a *national* home—a home where its people could live *as a nation*? Then you come, Mahatma Gandhi, and help to draw

144

the barriers and to declare 'Hands off! This land does not belong to you!' Instead of helping to establish a genuine peace; giving us what we need without taking from the Arabs what they need, on the basis of a fair adjustment* as to what they would really make use of and what might be admitted to satisfy our requirements! . . .

You once said, Mahatma, that politics enmesh us nowadays as with serpent's coils from which there is no escape however hard one may try. You said you desired, therefore, to wrestle with the serpent. Here is the serpent in the fullness of its power! Jews and Arabs both have a claim to this land, but these claims are in fact reconcilable as long as they are restricted to the measure which life itself allots and as long as they are limited by the desire for conciliation—that is, if they are translated into the language of the needs of living people for themselves and their children. But instead of this they are turned through the serpent's influence into claims of principle and politics, and are represented with all the ruthlessness which politics instils into those that are led by her. Life with all its realities and possibilities disappears, as does the desire for truth and peace: nothing is known and sensed but the political watchword alone. The serpent conquers not only the spirit but also life. Who would wrestle with her?

We began to settle in the land anew, thirty-five years before the 'shadow of the British gun' was cast upon it. We did not seek out this shadow; it appeared and remained here to guard British interests and *not ours*. We do not want force. . . . We have not proclaimed, as you do and did Jesus, the son of our people, the teaching of non-violence. We believe that a man must sometimes use force to save himself or even more his children. But from time immemorial we have proclaimed the teaching of justice and peace; we have taught and we have learned that peace is the aim of all the world and that justice is the way to attain it. Thus we cannot *desire* to use force. No one who counts himself in the ranks of Israel can desire to use force.

* Before partition the author first advocated a bi-national state of Palestine and after partition Israel's entry into a Near East Federation.

145

But, you say, our non-violence is that of the helpless and the weak. This is not in accordance with the true state of affairs. You do not know or you do not consider what strength of soul, what *satyagraha*, has been needed for us to restrain ourselves here after years of ceaseless deeds of blind violence perpetrated against us, our wives and our children, and not to answer with like deeds of blind violence. . . .

You say it is a stigma against us that our ancestors crucified Jesus. I do not know whether that actually happened, but I consider it possible. I consider it just as possible as that the Indian people under different circumstances should condemn you to death. . . . Not infrequently nations swallow up the greatness to which they have given birth. How can one assert, without contradiction, that such action constitutes a stigma! I would not deny, however, that although I should not have been among the crucifiers of Jesus, I should also not have been among his supporters. For I cannot help withstanding evil when I see that it is about to destroy the good. I am forced to withstand the evil in the world just as the evil within myself. I can only strive not to have to do so by force. I do not want force. But if there is no other way of preventing the evil destroying the good, I trust I shall use force and give myself up into God's hands. . . . If I am to confess what is truth to me, I must say: There is nothing better for a man than to deal justly—unless it be to love; we should be able even to fight for justice—but to fight lovingly.

I have been very slow in writing this letter to you, Mahatma. I made repeated pauses—sometimes days elapsing between short paragraphs—in order to test my knowledge and my way of thinking. Day and night I took myself to task, searching whether I had not in any one point overstepped the measure of self-preservation allotted and even prescribed by God to a human community, and whether I had not fallen into the grievous error of collective egoism. Friends and my own conscience have helped to keep me straight whenever danger threatened. Weeks have now passed since then, and the time has come when negotiations are proceeding in the capital of the British Empire on the Jewish-Arab problem—and when, it is said, a decision is to be made.

But the true decision in this matter can only come from within and not from without.

I take the liberty, therefore, of closing this letter without waiting for the result in London.

MARTIN BUBER.

Jerusalem, February 24, 1939

People and Leader*

(1942)

I

'OUR time,' I said in 1927.† 'wishes to be rid of the teacher in every realm. It believes it can manage with the leader alone. That is understandable. In an hour in which an enormous amount depends upon the independence and superiority of the spirit, those "spiritual men" who, without knowing what they are doing, have made the spirit into a clever and obedient little dog that retrieves ideologies for the existing powers that fling words to him, have contributed to the discrediting of the spirit, and of its guiding function in life.

'Other and deeper forces have co-operated in this. The result is not merely what took place even earlier at times—that the official politics of states proclaimed their independence of the spirit. Inner movements and groupings of the life of peoples also declare themselves free from the spirit; indeed, they glimpse their guarantee of success in their independence of it. And they are not entirely wrong. Leading without teaching is successful: one attains something. Only this something that one attains is something entirely different from, and at times a direct caricature of, what one actually wanted to attain. What then? As long as the goal was a pure goal, longing and hope rules; but when in the "attainment" the goal is transformed—what then? Certainly the people that has no leader is unfortunate: but thrice unfortunate is the people whose leader has no teacher.'

* Inessential passages in the essay published in Hebrew at that time have been omitted.

† In one of the addresses published in the author's book *Kampf um Israel* (1933), pp. 150 ff.

What has happened in the world during the last fifteen years has confirmed the truth of my words to a degree that at that time I could barely have had a presentiment of. Successful leading without teaching comes near to destroying all that makes human life seem worth living. Let us consider what the nature of this successful leading is, and especially the nature of its relation to the people led, according to the spontaneous confessions of the leaders.

2

Mussolini, who once characterized fascism as a 'socialismo alla Sorel' (as late as 1934 one of his closest collaborators assured me that his 'chief' was still a syndicalist, and the day would come when he will set to work as such), took a step beyond Sorel's theory of the 'social myth,' as his leading-without-teaching logically led him to do. 'We have,' he says, 'created our myth.' It is not necessary that this myth have a reality content; it will serve as reality itself because it 'is a sting, a hope, faith, courage,' and he adds, 'Our myth is the nation.' Here the myth is only a useful fiction which is 'created'; useful because it works on the masses as desired, as a proclamation to realize the mythical greatness of the nation, but actually to establish permanently the fascist structure (Mussolini, in fact, has himself in a chamber speech defined the revolution as 'the firm will to retain power').

Of course, one might think, a fiction remains useful only so long as the masses do not see through it, for it cannot merely be a matter of having a 'belief' but of having a truth worthy of belief. One wonders that Mussolini publicly performs this unveiling. But he obviously knows his masses. They are masses who have despaired of a truth worthy of belief, because the previous war and what followed it have not only dashed to pieces the current truths but also have driven out the belief in truth in general, the objective trust. The norm, that—in opposition to Mussolini's famous central statement which asserts the contrary—formerly had preceded action, even revolutionary action, has failed; it has been disowned by action and has not taken courage to protest. A new truth worthy of belief has not emerged; so out of despair action is accepted that precedes the norm and determines it. No one could really believe in this norm, but since no one sees any other way to take part in action, everyone lets it be explained by the very norm offered by fascism through the newly created myth of the 'nation' (in 1910 Mussolini had still called the national flag 'a rag worthy to be planted on a dunghill'). Although what he calls a nation is but a sheer fiction, nothing further is necessary than to confound the real nation and the fictitious one. This is made possible because there is the 'leader,' the 'leaders.' If there were not the leader, one would see no way before one; but the leader does, in fact, go in advance, and since one sees him go, one admits as true that he is on a way and one follows after him.

'A sting, a hope, faith, and courage,' says Mussolini. Do the masses really believe? Now, everyone thinks he believes, or lives in any case as if he believed. 'We will believe in it,' said Mussolini in his speech on pragmatism when he was still active in the socialist movement, 'we must believe in it. Faith removes mountains because it confers the illusion that mountains allow themselves to be removed. Illusion is perhaps the unique reality of life.' Do the masses really hope? One masks one's despair as hope and finally lets oneself be deceived by the mask until midnight comes. Is one really courageous? There is nothing left to one but to show courage. This so-called myth is, at any rate, a 'sting.'

3

A decisive difference between fascist and bolshevist totalitarianism is that the latter arises from the tradition of a real idea and in vital relationship to it; bolshevism is established, therefore, on the belief in a truth, whereas fascism in contrast, basically acknowledges nothing but 'the firm will to retain power.' No matter how far bolshevism has removed itself, through its tendency to the accumulation of power, from the life-attitude common to all genuine socialist thinking, it remains bound to an idea as its goal, and the glimpse of this goal is what ultimately holds together its masses. One need only compare a speech of Lenin with one of Mussolini to mark the antithesis of the two kinds of man, the two kinds of existence. Undoubtedly no historical personage distinguishes between his cause and himself. What sets in marked relief the great historical figure is the fact that he believes in his cause and feels himself as empowered by it. In 1921 Mussolini said of Lenin that he was an *artista formidabile* who shaped the human material which in brittleness surpasses ore and marble—an image more characteristic of the æstheticizing speaker than of his subject.

Soon thereafter Mussolini put himself to the test in this 'art.' But he has remained a dilettante; indeed, an unscrupulous and at first successful one. Lenin fashioned because he had a vision; Mussolini undertook time and again to fashion what he had just contrived. Lenin strove for power because he strove to promote his cause as no other could, and because he could only provide it with this service if he ruled. Mussolini wants to rule because he does not want to serve. When he was twenty-seven, he wrote on Stirner's book *The Ego and His Own* that it was 'the gospel of individualism and the greatest poem that has ever been sung to the glorification of the man who has become God.' As dictator he has attained the possibility of playing the role of a man who has become God, and his successful performance satisfied him. 'The idea,' he writes after ten years as dictator, 'incarnates itself in few rather than in one.' But does he really believe in what supposedly incarnates itself in him? To the question whether in the decisive hour in which he marched on Rome he found himself in the mood of the artist commencing his work or of the prophet obeying a summons, he answered, 'The artist.' The question was a literary one, the answer was histrionic. I do not believe, as is related of an authentic Roman, Nero, that Mussolini, in the hour of defeat, will also succeed in feeling like an 'artist.'

4

Certain utterances of Hitler's* allow us to penetrate more deeply into the problem of fascist leadership. They are distin-

* Rauschning's communications are used because these have clearly changed only the style and not the content of what was heard.

guished atmospherically from those of Mussolini we have quoted by the fact that they were intended only for individual intimates, for an inner circle. Mussolini, as we have seen, makes no secret at times of his real private view. After the conquest of Addis Ababa, from the pinnacle, therefore, of his power, he said to a group of farmers, 'I am with you because I know that you are with me.' Hitler certainly says to peasants or workers, 'I am with you as you are with me,' but he would never say 'because.' He expresses his factual relationship to the people like his factual relationship to the cause only when secluded from publicity. In the years of ascent Mussolini found satisfaction in demonstrating the solidity of his power while he publicly unveiled his attitude; Hitler does not ever allow the line between his attitude towards the people and his attitude towards the initiated to be effaced. He is no pathetic cynic, like Mussolini. He is honest before the microphone and honest in intimate conversation, but the contents of the two honesties contradict each other. Moreover, he is no actor like Mussolini; whenever he surrenders to the magic of public or semi-public address, he is a possessed man. Let him explain himself to an intimate, he keeps a requisite distance from this possession and can lay bare motives which he perceives nothing of when the hysterical muse inspires his raging rhetoric. But in this laying bare Hitler has made a weighty contribution to our knowledge of the fascist leadership in its enlarged and revised German edition, an edition that corresponds to the Italian as the real transformation into a demon corresponds to a masterful portrayal of this species of being. When one considers Mussolini, one can be astonished and frightened by what man is; but when one looks at Hitler, one is seized by dizziness.

5

It is the attitude towards the conscience which shows most incisively the relation between leadership divested of teaching and those who are led. From the standpoint of those who are led, Hitler's famous second-in-command, Göring, states the essential. 'I have no conscience,' he says; 'my conscience is called Adolf

Hitler.' By this he wishes to say that since he 'has' Hitler, he is rid of what until then he had called his conscience; he no longer needs it. Hitler stands in its place, his orders govern action. What distinguishes man as man, that he himself may judge concerning what he does and what he leaves undone, has been superseded. One detects in Göring's words the sense of liberation. How burdensome it was, this demanding and accusing voice to which one could not shut one's ears! How simple and comfortable it is to surrender oneself to the leader (*der Führer*) who provides all that is necessary! Thus speak those who are led.

But it must not be thought that Hitler now has conscience for all. That he emphatically rejects. 'Conscience is a Jewish invention,' he scoffs. He is clearly rid of the conscience, too. We cannot know how and when, for he has not, indeed, like those he leads received a Hitler in conscience's stead at a certain moment of his career. Though the conscience of others, he himself has none.

'Conscience,' he says, 'is like circumcision, a mutilation of the human being.' He appears to have restored the mutilated member through becoming the man without conscience, and he has apparently won thereby magic power to restore it in all he leads through becoming the conscience for them all.

That is an occurrence of religious pathos, so to speak, but with a negative signature. Hitler, who once said of National Socialism that it is 'even more than a religion,' seems to feel strongly the religious pathos in it, to be sure as the annihilation of the 'Jewish' Christianity through an anti-Christianity. 'In the place of the vicarious suffering and dying of a divine saviour,' he affirms, 'steps forth the vicarious living and acting of the new lawgiver who releases the mass of believers from the burden of free decision.' Conscience is, of course, no Jewish invention; ever since men have existed there has existed this ever-renewed self-confrontation of the person with the image of what he was destined to be and what he has relinquished, and even the oldest Germans, as we know from the Icelandic sagas, knew how to remonstrate with themselves when they had left their essential predisposition unfulfilled. But it is significant that in our time a man has arisen in whom the tension between what one is and what one should be is dissolved, the man without a conscience, the man without restraint. In his complete and fundamental lack of restraint also lies the secret of Hitler's effectiveness.

'The expression "criminal," ' he declaims, 'stems from a conquered world. Providence has predestined me to be the supreme liberator of mankind. I liberate man from the sordid and degrading self-torment of a chimera called conscience and morals, and from the demands of a freedom and personal independence to which always only a very few can be equal' (more exactly, as we learned from the statement of Göring, only one). 'I must liberate the world from its historic past.' Where have we heard before such lapidary statements? So far as I am aware, nowhere in the Indo-Germanic world. But an exact parallel is found in a peculiarly Jewish eighteenth-century product of disintegration: the pseudo-messiah Jacob Frank. 'I have come,' he said, 'in order to abolish all laws and all doctrines, and my desire is to bring life into the world. . . . You shall rid yourself of all laws and doctrines and follow after me, step by step.'

6

In the world envisaged by Hitler only the leaders are persons. The 'people' stand opposite them as a mass of the spiritually castrated. 'What need have we,' he boasts, 'of the socialization of banks and factories? We socialize men.' Not only what persists of personal substance in people, but also what survives in them of a folk structure has to be eradicated; all independent connection, all independent organization. 'I blend the people,' says Hitler. 'I speak to them as masses!' He blends people into masses. And, in fact, where there is no longer a place for the person, there is also no longer a place for the people.

I shall quote from myself once more. In an essay written in 1936,* I wrote of the individual who simultaneously lives in spirit and with the people: 'At the place where he stands, exalted or insignificant, with the powers he possesses, compressed authority or fading word, he does what he can to make the crowd no

* 'The Question to the Single One' in *Between Man and Man*.

longer a crowd. . . . Even if he has to speak to the crowd, he seeks the person; for only through the person, through the self-authentication of persons, can a people discover and rediscover its truth.' It is necessary to go still a step farther and clearly to state: a people in the real sense of the term exists only when there is throughout, below and above, among those led as among the leaders, the element of the person, the sphere of the person, the freedom and responsibility of the person. The substance of a people and the latent substance of the person are one; where the one is suppressed, the other will be suppressed. The totalitarian mass marks not only the end of personal life, it is also the end of the life of a people.

In order 'to dissolve the order that has rested till now on historical connections,' explains Hitler, he must 'recast into a higher order' the nations as 'the manifest forms of our history.' This higher order is called 'race,' more exactly 'master race.' The racial theory so expressed is by no means founded on a common biological type; Hitler wants to be rid of a theory that aims to link a man to those who look like him. The new racial theory cuts right across what used to be called 'race'; it signifies nothing at all other than 'the new selection.' 'Throughout the whole of Europe and throughout the whole world,' declares Hitler, 'I will set in motion this new selection, as National Socialism has produced it in Germany'—by which, as careful scrutiny shows, not the party but the leadership are meant. In Hitler's image of the future the world of man breaks into two: the race and the mass, the former the 'active,' the latter the 'passive' part of the nations that place themselves without resistance at the disposal of the 'activity' of the 'race' or is compelled by it to serve its activity. We have learned the nature of this activity; it means absence of restraint. The coming élite of mankind, which will then also produce biologically the new master race, is founded on the common absence of restraint.

But what is the goal of this activity? 'There is no firm fixed goal,' answers Hitler. None exists; for there is no truth that one can strive to realize, none which helps the man who acts responsibly. 'There is,' he says, 'no truth, either in the moral or in the scientific sense.' That means there is truth only in the political sense: 'true' designates whatever one currently wants the masses to hold as true in order that the new dominion can accomplish whatever it currently wants to accomplish. Hitler says of it, to be sure, that it is 'responsible to history.' But an actual responsibility before history exists only when there is a goal, not when goals are from time to time staked out by the one who acts. 'Those who are responsible before history,' says Hitler, 'grow ever more visibly into the role of destiny and of an omnipotence already overstepping the earthly limits. . . . The preservation of their power must be for them the highest and single law of their activity.' There is no room here for an actual responsibility before history; this concept is clearly, for Hitler, a last residue of the superseded past.

To believe in nothing except his own power, that is for him the necessary principle of the leader. This rule is to be found again—not, as many think, in Machiavelli, who believes in the state and in power only for the sake of the state—but in Jacob Frank. 'I say to you,' Frank explained to his disciples, 'all leaders must be without belief.' In other words, the leader must not believe in anything other than himself.

Thereby the problematic of this belief is already characterized. For only he can truly believe in himself—not convulsively flog himself to this belief, but believe in certainty and composure— who feels himself with the utmost seriousness to be commissioned and empowered by the Unconditioned. Whoever finds the being of the Unconditioned empty must find his own being necessarily empty, and this emptiness he always experiences when he reflects upon himself. But absence of restraint includes just the natural capacity and perfected skill to avoid this reflection upon oneself. Jacob Frank and Adolf Hitler are pre-eminent examples of the man without restraint and, as it were, without reflection. I say 'as it were,' for probably both have experienced what it is to stand at midnight staring at one's own naked face. But that is a mystery into which no other person can penetrate.

7

Now we must ask what merits historically the name of leadership. By that only responsible leadership towards an envisaged goal can and may be meant. He alone can be called a leader who responsibly leads his group—whether it is a whole people or a band of a few faithful—towards a goal that he sees. Believing vision of the goal is the first requisite, responsible leadership towards it the second. In the case of the first, the question is not one of how the leader names his creed, what he believes in, if only the goal represents for him the unconditioned. In the case of the second, the question does not concern what this man calls the court before which he has to be responsible for his leadership, as long as it is a living court and the responsibility he means is a real responsibility.

But what the leader essentially has to be responsible for is not whether he, and with him the people, do or do not attain the goal he sets at that time, but what in the meantime has become of the people he leads. He who increases the power of his people in ways whereby the people loses its capacity to do the right thing with its power, he who leaves the people powerful but evil, stands before the living court before which he is responsible, with or without foreknowledge, as the corrupter of those he has led.

Ranke says of Machiavelli that he was bold enough to prescribe poison for the desperate condition of his fatherland. But there are poisons which, in order to lead to an apparent healing, deliver the organism to a gradual decomposition. He who administers them is not to be called bold but wanton.

To strive for power for power's sake means to strive for nothing. He who seizes empty power ultimately grasps at emptiness. Will to power because one needs power to realize the truth in which one believes has a constructive strength; will to power as power leads from the self-aggrandizement of the individuals to the self-destruction of the people.

In 1921, a year after the National Socialist Party received its name, Walther Rathenau*—a German statesman and a Jew, whose love for the German people and the German Reich was unrequited—wrote, 'That was a frivolous word in which we have long believed "The Lord God is on the side of the bigger battalions." The true word is that destiny is with the deeper responsibility.' Today, after twenty years, it is not in fascist states alone that many are inclined to the opinion that the bigger battalions need no Lord God. These many are mistaken. Power without genuine responsibility is a dazzling-clothed impotence. The stronger battalions that believe in nothing save the leader are the weaker battalions. Their powerlessness will become manifest in the hour when they must vie with a strength born of belief. Those who depend upon empty power will be dragged down in its collapse.

8

In great epochs of history important work has been done by important persons. In our age powerful transformations are accomplished through individuals who are not equal to the deeds they bring about, who are not the sufficient subject of their acts but through their false bearing cause themselves to be taken for the persons to whom these acts belong. They are, in fact, only the exploiters of a situation. This situation is one of despair in which the man without restraint who arises and cries, 'I will show you a way,' finds a following and attains success. He knows no way, he points to none; he marches without direction and the masses follow. It is easy to understand why the crowd sees in the man who dares to usurp leadership at such a juncture the instrument of history, empowered to change its course. It is also understandable that strength accrues to the man who is thus believed in. But in the core of reality he remains just what he is, and the greater the transformation the world undergoes through him, the greater will be the contradiction between being and appearance.

Another feature of the age can be noted: it leers. There have been epochs in which barbarian hordes inundated civilized lands;

* Walther Rathenau (1876–1922), foreign minister in the Weimar Republic, was assassinated by Nationalist fanatics (Ed.).

but they did not say, like Hitler, 'Yes, we are barbarians! We want to be barbarians!' There have been eras when men ruled with ruthless brutality; but the rulers did not ogle their brutality. Where such leering takes place, degeneration is always in force. An age that stands before the mirror and admires its greatness lacks greatness.

Max Weber has characterized the mystery of the influence of a leader on those he leads as charisma, a gift of grace. But there is a force that I would like to call negative charisma. It is difficult to distinguish it from the positive by its physiognomy. When one examines closely how this negative man 'leads,' one notes that he envisages no goal. The striving for power for power's sake is the characteristic of negative charisma. It has at its disposal all the arts of dissimulation. Only two years before the seizure of power, Mussolini wrote (the article is naturally not included in the collected edition of his writings), 'I proceed from the individual and aim against the state. Down with the state in all its forms, the state of yesterday and of tomorrow!' Yet just before the seizure of power he cried out, 'By what means will fascism become state? We want to become state!' Later he recognized the individual only in so far 'as he is in accord with the state.' Hitler, in whose public utterances the nation is one and all, is, in fact, concerned with a planet-encompassing alliance of the possessors of power to support one another in the preservation of power over the human weal, for the sake of the 'selection of a new ruling class,' which, as he once said, 'has the right to rule on the ground of its superior race.'

'For us,' Hitler once deposed, 'leader and idea are one, and each party comrade has to do what is commanded by the leader, who embodies the idea and alone knows the final goal.' The leader alone knows the goal, but there is no goal. The leader embodies the idea, but there is no idea. The 'superior race' decides, and those who include themselves in it decide who belongs to it—provided that they are in power. But what does that mean concretely? 'There is always,' according to Hitler, 'only the fight of the racially inferior lower stratum against the ruling higher race.' The victorious racially inferior lower stratum proclaims itself the higher race. The superman is he whom no inner restraint hinders from proclaiming, 'I am the superman.'

9

We have already encountered with Mussolini the 'man who has become God'; with Hitler we find him again. 'Man becomes God,' he says, 'that is the simple meaning'—of Nietzsche's superman, 'Man is the becoming God.' The trivial pathos of this motif, which in the ancient Orient and in imperial Rome once belonged to court parlance, Napoleon side-stepped by a witty repartee, 'The place of God the Father?' he said 'Ah, I do not want it—it is a blind alley!'

'In Plato's *Theages*,' said Nietzsche, 'it is written: "Each of us would like to be lord of all men, if possible, and, best of all, God!" In this dialogue, which undoubtedly is not Plato's work, these inexactly quoted words are spoken by a youth who is brought by his father to Socrates as a pupil. Socrates does not contradict the haughty statement, but he instructs the speaker through referring him to the great models, the examples of the noble and distinguished, Themistocles and Pericles, neither of whom could be rightly represented as wanting to become lord of all men, much less God. Nietzsche did not foresee that his idea of the 'becoming God' would be taken possession of not by the type that he called the 'higher man,' but by the lower man who is, to be sure, without restraint, but at times is probably assailed by doubts in his innermost being, and must strive, therefore, to be worshipped in order to be able basically to believe in himself. We already literally find in Nietzsche the 'intention of training a ruling caste—the future masters of the earth'; he did not foresee that it would be the men without restraint—those who drag the masses along with them—who would most readily appropriate this intention. He wanted 'to give back the good conscience' to him whom he praised as the evil man, the man of great passion, the strong man. He did not foresee that he would strengthen the lack of conscience in the type he called the bad man, the abortive, the misshapen, who, as we know from the life of primitive tribes, slips easily into the vocation of the great sorcerer.

Society and the State

(1951)

IN Bertrand Russell's book on *Power*, which appeared late in 1938—the author calls it a 'new social analysis'—power is defined as 'the fundamental concept in social science, in the same sense in which energy is the fundamental concept in physics.' This bold concept on the part of a distinguished logician, which reminds us of Nietzsche's doctrine that he attacked so vigorously, is a typical example of the confusion between the social principle and the political principle even in our time, one hundred years after the rise of scientific sociology. It has long been recognized that all social structures have a certain measure of power, authority, and dominion, without which they could not exist; in none of the non-political structures, however, is this the essential element. But it is inherent in all social structures that men either find themselves already linked with one another in an association based on a common need or a common interest, or that they band themselves together for such a purpose, whether in an existing or a newly-formed society. The primary element must not be superseded by the secondary element—association by subordination, fellowship by domination or, schematically speaking, the horizontal structure by the vertical. The American political scientist, MacIver, has rightly said that 'to identify the social with the political is to be guilty of the grossest of all confusions, which completely bars any understanding of either society or the state.'

The defective differentiation between the social and the political principles, upon which the more or less problematical co-operation of all human group-existence rests, goes back to very ancient times. A classic example of mistaking the one principle for the other, though, to be sure, of a very different kind, is the well-known chapter in the *Politeia*, where Plato begins by tracing the origin of the *polis* directly from the primæval social fact of division of labour, and then, almost imperceptibly, goes on to include among the essential occupations that of the rulers, so that we suddenly find the population split up into two pre-eminently political sections: those who give orders and those who obey them; rulers and ruled; those who possess the instruments of co-ercion and those who are subject to them—all this under the harmless guise of the mere division of labour. We should take careful note of what Plato does here. He has his Socrates set his interlocutors the task of 'seeing with their mind's eye a *polis* in the making.' The readers of this dialogue naturally thought in terms of the contemporary Athens as it had emerged from the reforms of Kleisthenes; in other words, in terms of a society of free citizens who were hardly aware of the difference between the rulers and the ruled because of the constant interchange be-tween the former and the latter within the citizenry, whereby the constituents of today became the representatives of tomorrow; and because, furthermore, the fact that the officials could be elected and dismissed obviated any feeling that an irksome bureaucracy might arise. This community, in which a firm foundation of slavery made it theoretically possible for every citizen to participate in the business of the Council while engaged in his private concerns, could, indeed, be deduced from an evo-lution of the division of labour—an evolution in which the voca-tion of politics was not specialized. However, the class—or rather the caste of the guardians—which Plato introduces into this dis-cussion comes not within the scope of the historical *polis* but of that of his Utopia, where this caste, which has been represented to us as one vocation among others, actually stands in a political relationship to the rest of the community: that of a ruling society over against a society of the ruled. The term 'society' and not a mere 'group' is used here advisedly inasmuch as, in liberating its members from private property and private marriage, Plato raises it above the general community and constitutes it as a separate society.

This confusion of the social principle with the political is typical of by far the greater part of the thinking of ancient times. There is no tendency whatever towards an ideological distinction between political and non-political social structures in most of the ancient empires, obviously because the latter were allowed no independent existence or development of any kind. The one exception in this respect is ancient China, where two civilizations existed side by side: the State-urban civilization, which was centred in the royal court and based on the army, the bureaucracy and the litterati; and the rural civilization, which was based solely on the village community. The former was a political-historical civilization in every respect, while the latter was absolutely unhistorical, being determined solely by the unchanging natural rhythm of the seasons and of the human generations, that is to say, a social civilization in the strictest sense of the term. It was the latter civilization, relatively self-sufficient and enclosed within itself, that served as the foundation for Lao-tse's doctrine. That doctrine interposed between the individual and the state (the single States which together constituted the empire) two purely social structures, namely the home and the community. In the Confucian system, which was rooted in the urban civilization, there remained, however, only one of these two social structures—the home, the family which, contrary to its status in the village, was in its urban form completely integrated into the State.

A similar ideological development took place in classical antiquity, but from very different causes. There—at all events in the *polis* where, in the main, discursive thought was evolved, that is to say, in that of Athens—the well-developed social principle had penetrated so deeply into political life and merged with it so completely that while, on the one hand, the Demos was almost like a social gathering, on the other the family receded into the background of social life, and corporate existence, however firmly entrenched, nowhere attained genuine autonomy. In this connection, as we have already seen in Plato's thinking, no strictly ideological distinction was drawn between the State and the unions, which were not part of the State: The State, the *polis*, so completely coincided with society, or the community, the *koinonia*, that asocial persons, the *dyskoinoetoi*, were regarded as the antithesis of the friends of the State, the *philopolides*, as though it were not possible for a man to be social and yet not political in his thinking. It was only with the decline of the *polis*, when it was fast disintegrating from within and servitude loomed on the historical horizon without, that the thinking finally drew a distinction between the two principles. Two hundred years after Lao-tse, Aristotle interposed the family and the community—by which term he, too, meant primarily the rural community—between the State and the individual; and to the community were joined various kinds of associations. But of the social category, that of the *koinonia*, he had only the most general notion, so that he could describe the State as a certain kind of *koinonia* though, indeed, one transcending and comprehending all the others, while all the others are regarded as mere preliminary stages to this society on the one hand, and mere means towards the ends of the State on the other. Thus, even here, no genuine categorical distinction between the social and the political principle can be drawn; and even though Aristotle in one passage calls man a *zoon koinonikon* and in another a *zoon politikon*, both terms mean the same thing. And though Aristotle explicitly tells us that man was not created solely for the political community but also for the home, he sees in the *polis* the consummation of the *koinonia*, in which—and in which alone—men's co-existence in a community has any purpose and significance. In fact, the *polis* is called the *koinonia* of all the particular *koinonias* within which all families and communities and societies and associations of all kinds band themselves together. Aristotle's idea of the State is identical here with ours of society, that is to say, a unit comprehending all the different associations within a specific national entity. Such an idea of the State bars any approach to a strict and consistent differentiation and separation between the social and the political principles. Incidentally, it is noteworthy that of all the unions which Aristotle recognizes as special forms of the *koinonia*, he attaches significance to the family alone and, unlike Plato, recognizes it as the primæval cell in the process of the division of labour. In his view, the family alone is the foundation of the State, and he does not attach any permanent importance to the rural community, since it is destined to be absorbed in the *polis*, while he considers the associations important only because they have a place within the State. The restrictive process of thought, which was evolved from Lao-tse down to Confucius and from which all social structures that might successfully have resisted absorption by the centralizing State are excluded, here comes to full flower in the thinking of a single philosopher.

The post-Aristotelian thought of ancient times did not remedy this defect in the ideologial approach to the principles in question. Even the apparently more precise Latin idea which, for the 'collectivity' (*koinonia*) substituted 'society' (*societas*), did not serve the purpose. True, in those days there was no such thing as a society of citizens in the modern sense of an all-inclusive society existing side by side with the State and *vis-à-vis* the State; but sociality did exist in all its forms, which manifested itself in all the large and small associations; and the same principle of co-operation predominated in all of them, a principle which enters into all kinds of alliances with the political principle, but nevertheless possesses a specific reality of its own which strives for recognition. Even the *stoa*, which went farthest in this direction, did not explicitly recognize the social principle. In the last days of the *stoa* Marcus Aurelius did, indeed, give the Aristotelian definition a social stamp by saying that 'We are born to co-operate'; but what was not achieved was just that which must be required of any ideological specification if it is to achieve the character of genuine apperception, namely, the search for, description and interpretation of those elements of reality which correspond to the newly-acquired specific idea. The new concept of society loses concreteness because it is deprived of its limitations; this occurs in the most sublime manner in that the ideal of universal humanism is formulated without any indication being given as to how it is to be realized. Whether the Stoic speaks in the new terms of a society of the human race (*societas generis humani*) or in the old terms of a megalopolis, it amounts to the same thing: a high-souled idea emerges to confront reality but cannot find a womb from which to propagate a living creature because it has been stripped of corporeality. Plato's State which, though directed against the *polis*, was nevertheless derived from it, actually was a structure, though it existed only in thought. Zenon's slogan—'Only one way of life and only one political régime'—as proclaimed a century later, was only a fine sentiment; and finally so little remained of it that Cicero could envisage the Roman Empire as the fulfilment of cosmopolitanism. Incidentally, there is no practicable universalism—universalism that is realizable, though with the utmost effort—except that adumbrated by the prophets of Israel, who proposed not to abolish national societies together with their forms of organization, but rather to heal and perfect them, and thereby to pave the way for their amalgamation.

Medieval Christianity adopted the fundamental concept of the Stoic universalism in a Christianized form, in that at one time it designated the unified humanity to be striven for as a *res publica generis humani*, a world State, and at another as an *ecclesia universalis*, a universal church. Nevertheless, the social principle as such is expressed now and then in this connection in a purer form than was ever conceived by the Stoics. Thus, for example, William of Occam, the great fourteenth-century thinker whose theory of intuition gave the *quietus* to scholasticism, said: 'The whole human race is one people; the collectivity of all mortal men is a single community of those who wish for communion with one another.' Every particular association is recognized by him as a part of this community. In general, however, medieval thought did not go beyond Aristotle's amalgamation of the social with the political. The flourishing corporations of the period were, indeed, taken into account in the legal ideology; but no sociological recognition of the non-political associations as such was evolved. On the contrary: there was a growing tendency to include them, in theory, within the State and, in practice, to subject all of them to it; or, as the legal historian Gierke put it: 'Exclusive representation of all community life by the State.'

It was only in the late Renaissance that thinking reached the point of a vigorous stand in defence of the rights of the non-political unions in relation to the State. The most vigorous expression of this point of view is to be found in the book entitled *Politics* by the German jurist Althusius (1603). Even there these bodies do not stand between the individual and the all-inclusive society—this special concept is still lacking—but between the individual and the State as in Aristotle's concept. Hence no difference in kind is recognized between the associations and the State, except that each and every one of the farmers enjoys relative autonomy, while the State possesses exclusive sovereignty. Nevertheless, the State is faced by an 'insurmountable barrier', (as Gierke phrases it) in relation to the unions; in other words, the State may not infringe upon the special rights of these social unions. Society is not yet, indeed, conceived as such in this view, but it is constituted in its idea; it is not society, but the State under its name, which appears as the 'immortal and eternal society,' as Grotius formulated it, or under its own name as a 'composite society,' in the words of Althusius—the association of associations. But the very fact that all of them are viewed as being linked with one another was in itself something definitely new in sociological thought. This new idea was suppressed for two hundred years by the idea of the unlimited power of the State, which took on a more logically consistent form than ever before.*

In Hobbes' system of thought the intermediate formations are missing as a matter of principle, since he recognizes no stages precedent to the establishment of the State, in which the unorganized individuals unite for fear that otherwise they will destroy one another. Such a unification, which is achieved by means of the subjection of the wills of all the individuals to the will of a single person or a single assembly, is designated by Hobbes in his book *De Cive* as *civitas sive societas civilis*. Here, for the first time as far as I am aware, we have in the writings of a modern thinker the widely disseminated idea of the 'civil society,' which we find again late in the seventeenth century in Locke's essays, in the eighteenth century in Adam Smith's *Lectures on Justice* and in Ferguson's *Essay on the History of Civil Society*, and

---

* This does not mean that in that epoch there was no further development of Althusius' ideas, particularly in the doctrine of Leibniz.

which recurs, in the nineteenth century, in the philosophy of Hegel and the sociology of Lorenz von Stein, as the antithesis to the State. In Hobbes' view, civil society is entirely identical with the State. Hobbes, too, is cognizant of the social principle—in the form of free contracts between individuals for the recognition and preservation of the rights of ownership; he is aware of its existence, and tolerates it in the above sense because he regards the political 'Leviathan' as still incomplete. But the German sociologist Tönnies doubtless apprehends Hobbes' ultimate meaning when he interprets his views in the following terms: 'The State would carry out its idea to perfection if it controlled all the activities of its citizens, if all wills were directed in harmony with a single supreme will. So long as this has not come to pass, society still exists within the State.' In other words, when the State finally becomes complete, it will annihilate the last vestige of society. Such a complete State has been approximated in a considerable degree in our own time by that known as the totalitarian type.

The age of Hobbes saw the rise of the Third Estate, which attempted to supersede the double society of the Middle Ages by a unitary society which did not, however, extend beyond its own bounds and which evoked a liberal attitude on the part of the State towards the individual, but an increasingly illiberal attitude on its part towards associations. The State was prepared to tolerate only a pulverized, structureless society, just as modern industrial capitalism at first tolerated only individuals without the right of association. A little over a century after the appearance of the 'Leviathan,' the physiocrat Turgot declared in the *Encyclopædia* (in an article entitled 'Fondations'): 'The citizens have rights, rights sacred for the actual body of society (by which he meant nothing else but the State); they have an existence independent of it; they are its essential elements . . . but the particular bodies do not exist in their own right and for their own sake. They have been constituted solely for the sake of society, and they must cease to exist as soon as their usefulness is at an end.' Turgot does not, however, include among his 'particular bodies' all the free associations, some of which he lauds in the course of that same article. Yet only five years later Rousseau wrote the contrary in his *Contrat Social* where, in his fundamental concept, the *volonté générale*, the social and political principles are again confused in the most dubious manner, though he was well able to distinguish between the social contract and the establishment of a State in a legal manner: 'So that the common will may be manifested, there must be no partial associations within the State.' In other words, there may not exist within the State any society which is constituted of various large and small associations; that is to say, a society with a truly social structure, in which the diversified spontaneous contacts of individuals for common purposes of co-operation and co-existence, i.e. the vital essence of society are represented. But if 'partial societies' already exist, Rousseau goes on to say, 'their number should be increased and inequalities prevented.' In other words, if it proves impossible to suppress the formation of free associations, their scope should be restricted by creating other associations determined entirely by the purposes and planning of the State; moreover, care must be taken that the free societies should never become stronger than the unfree ones.

In general, the French Revolution could content itself with carrying out the first of these two precepts, especially since it had abolished the right of association (an attempt in that direction had already been made under Louis XVI) because an 'absolutely free State should not tolerate corporations in its midst' (resolution of the Constitutional Assembly, August 1791). On the other hand, both of Rousseau's methods were applied jointly in a large measure during the Russian Revolution.

Only after a fully-fledged bourgeoisie had sprung from the loins of the French Revolution did it become possible to attempt to set the State and Society, as such, over against one another. The first two attempts in this direction were far apart in every respect.

The first of the two attempts was suggested by Saint-Simon. The more or less chimerical plans for reforms of this highly ingenious dilettante were based, in essence, on an accurate and important distinction between two modes of leadership, namely, social leadership, or Administration, and political leadership, or Government. Saint-Simon did not adequately define these types of leadership, but we shall convey his meaning correctly if we say that administrative powers are limited by the technical requirements implicit in the specific conditions and functions of the leadership, while governmental powers are limited, at any given time, solely by the relation between the power of government and that of other factors. Society—by which Saint-Simon means the subject of economic and cultural production—administers, in so far as it is organized; but the State governs. Saint-Simon's proposal to divide the conduct of the State—that is to say, to entrust the conduct of the national affairs to a select group of men, capable and well versed in the sphere of social production, thereby giving it an administrative character, while leaving to the political authorities only the responsibility for the defence and security of the country—this proposal need not concern us here. But it is worth-while quoting what Saint-Simon said in this connection: 'The nation went into the revolution to be governed less; but it achieved nothing except to be governed more than ever.'

The other fundamental division between the social and the political principle, that of Hegel, is antithetical to Saint-Simon's in its evaluation of the two. But its very purpose is different. Unlike Saint-Simon, Hegel compares not two forms of leadership with one another, but civil society in general with the State in general. The two factors are not, however, placed in polar opposition: society stands between the family and the State, between a relative whole and unity and an absolute whole and unity, as an incomplete and disunited multiformity, between form and form as something formless, an offspring of the modern world, an aggregation of individuals in which each is an end in himself and concerned with nothing else whatsoever; and all of them work together only because each uses the others as a means towards his own ends; and the groups and classes composed of individuals obsessed with their own ends get into conflicts which society, by its very nature, is unable to resolve: such power inheres in the State alone, because it prevails over the 'waves of passion' by means of the 'Reason that illumines them.' The State is the 'moderator of social misery' because its substance is not a private matter like that of society, but generality and unity, while its foundation is 'the force of Reason manifesting itself as will.' Such is the result of the most unequivocal distinction ever made between the two principles—a glorification of the State that reminds us of Hobbes. Hegel's critical portrait of society lacks everything that is still to be found in our own age, such as social consciousness, solidarity, mutual aid, loyal comradeship, spirited enthusiasms for a common enterprise; there is no trace whatever of creative social spontaneity which, though it is not concentrated like the power of the State, nevertheless exists in numerous single collective phenomena and, within the social sphere, very quietly counterbalances the conflicting forces. On the other hand, a State is seen here which we know, not from world history, but only from Hegel's system. He tells us, indeed, that in pondering the idea of the State we must not have any particular State in mind, but that 'the idea, this true God, must be considered for itself.' A given historical State exists, so says Hegel, 'in the world, hence in the sphere of arbitrariness, accident and error.' And just as a cripple is a living man for all that, 'the affirmative, life, exists' in spite of the defect; and it is this 'affirmative' which is the essential thing here. But if we apply this to society as well, the whole picture will be completely changed.

With Saint-Simon and Hegel we find ourselves on the threshold of modern sociology. But the society known to this sociology has become something different, namely, the society of the modern class struggle. Two men at that time undertook, each after his own fashion, to create a synthesis between Hegel and Saint-Simon. One was Lorenz von Stein, the founder of scientific sociology, and the other Karl Marx, the father of scientific socialism. The thinking of both men was so deeply rooted in the new situation that, on the crucial issue of the relationship between the social and the political principle, they were unable to take over the heritage either of Saint-Simon or of Hegel. Stein, who was a disciple of Saint-Simon's, could not share his belief that control of the State should be taken over by the leaders of social production because he regarded society only as the main arena of human conflict. He tried to hold fast to Hegel's views concerning the overmastering and unifying function of the perfect State, but did not really succeed. Marx, who adopted Hegel's mode of thought, objected to such a function on the part of the State because, as a 'superstructure,' the latter was necessarily a tool in the hands of the ruling class of society, and he strove to set up in its stead a State that would pave the way for a classless society by means of a dictatorship of the lowest social order, which would then be absorbed into the classless society. Stein, who held that 'the movement of opposition between the State and society was the content of the whole inner history of all the peoples,' attributes supremacy to the State in terms of philosophical abstraction; but in dealing with the concrete reality he affirms society, which is shaken through and through by conflicts; his concern is with that society. Hence the science of social reality begins with Stein (and not with Comte, as some think, because the latter lags behind his master Saint-Simon in distinguishing between the social and the political principle). Marx, who evinced no particular interest in the State in his theoretical thinking, could suggest nothing but a highly centralized all-embracing and all-disposing revolutionary State which leaves no room for the social principle and so thoroughly absorbs the free society that only in a messianic vision can it be merged in it. That is why a socialist movement began with Marx in which the social principle is found only as an ultimate aim, but not in the practical scheme.

Even nowadays, in the midst of wide-ranging and extremely detailed social knowledge and planning, sociology is faced ever and again with the problem of the relationship between the social and the political principle. This relationship must not be confused with that between Society and the State because, as Tarde rightly says, there is no form of social activity which cannot, on some side or at some moment, become political; we must realize that social forms, on the one hand, and State institutions, on the other, are crystallizations of the two principles. But it is most essential that we recognize the structural difference between the two spheres in regard to the relationship between unity and multiformity.

The society of a nation is composed not of individuals but of societies, and not, as Comte thought, of families alone but of societies, groups, circles, unions, co-operative bodies, and communities varying very widely in type, form, scope, and dynamics. Society (with a capital S) is not only their collectivity and setting, but also their substance and essence; they are contained within it, but it is also within them all, and none of them, in their innermost being can withdraw from it. In so far as the mere proximity of the societies tends to change into union, in so far as all kinds of leagues and alliances develop among them—in the social-federative sphere, that is to say—Society achieves its object. Just as Society keeps individuals together in their way of life by force of habit and custom and holds them close to one another and, by public opinion, in the sense of continuity, keeps them together in their way of thinking, so it influences the contacts and the mutual relations between the societies. Society cannot, however, quell the conflicts between the different groups; it is powerless to unite the divergent and clashing groups; it can develop what they have in common, but cannot force it upon them. The State alone can do that. The means which it employs for this purpose are not social but definitely political. But all the facilities at the disposal of the State, whether punitive or propagandistic, would not enable even a State not dominated by a single social group (that is to say, by one relatively independent of social divarications) to control the areas of conflict if it were not for the fundamental political fact of general instability. The fact that every people feels itself threatened by the others gives the State its definitive unifying power; it depends upon the instinct of self-preservation of society itself; the latent external crisis enables it when necessary to get the upper hand in internal crises. A permanent state of true, positive, and creative peace between the peoples would greatly diminish the supremacy of the political principle over the social. This does not, however, in the least signify that in that event the power to control the internal situation of conflict would necessarily be lessened thereby. Rather is it to be assumed that if, instead of the prevailing anarchical relationships among the nations, there were co-operation in the control of raw materials, agreement on methods of manufacture of such materials, and regulation of the world market, Society would be in a position, for the first time, to constitute itself as such.

Administration in the sphere of the social principle is equivalent to Government in that of the political principle. In the sphere of the former, as of the latter, it is essential that experts demonstrate how the wishes and decisions of the union or the association are to be carried into effect; and it is also essential that those appointed to carry out the experts' instructions should follow those instructions, with everyone doing his share. By Administration we mean a capacity for making dispositions which is limited by the available technical facilities and recognized in theory and practice within those limits; when it oversteps its limits, it seals its own doom. By Government we understand a non-technical, but 'constitutionally' limited body; this signifies that, in the event of certain changes in the situation, the limits are extended and even, at times, wiped out altogether. All forms of government have this in common: each possesses more power than is required by the given conditions; in fact, this excess in the capacity for making dispositions is actually what we understand by political power. The measure of this excess, which cannot of course be computed precisely, represents the exact difference between Administration and Government. I call it the 'political surplus.' Its justification derives from the external and internal instability, from the latent state of crisis between the nations and within every nation, which may at any moment become an active crisis requiring more immediate and far-reaching measures and strict compliance with such measures. Special powers must be accorded to the government even in States under a parliamentary régime when a crisis arises; yet in such States also it is in the nature of the case that the 'political surplus' should be indeterminate. The political principle is always stronger in relation to the social principle than the given conditions require. The result is a continuous diminution in social spontaneity.

Yet the social vitality of a nation, and its cultural unity and independence as well, depend very largely upon the degree of social spontaneity to be found there. The question has therefore been repeatedly raised as to how social spontaneity can be strengthened by freeing it as much as possible from the pressure of the political principle. It has been suggested that decentralization of political power, in particular, would be most desirable. As a matter of fact, the larger the measure of autonomy granted to the local and regional and also to the functional societies, the more room is left for the free unfolding of the social energies. Obviously, the question cannot be formulated as a choice between 'Centralization' and 'Decentralization.' We must ask rather: 'What are the spheres in which a larger measure of decentralization of the capacity to make dispositions would be admissible?' The demarcation would naturally have to be revised and improved continually to conform to the changing conditions.

Apart from this change in the *apportionment of power*, it is also in the interest of a self-constituting society to strive towards a continuous change in the *nature* of power, to the end that Government should, as much as possible, turn into Administration. Let us put it in this way: Efforts must be renewed again and again to determine in what spheres it is possible to alter the ratio between governmental and administrative control in favour of the latter. Saint-Simon's requirement, that a society productive in the economic and cultural spheres should have a larger share in shaping public life, cannot be fulfilled, as has been suggested in our own days, by having the administrators seize the government (which would certainly not lead to any improvement), but by transforming Government into Administration as far as the general and particular conditions permit.

Will Society ever revolt against the 'political surplus' and the accumulation of power? If such a thing were ever possible, only a society which had itself overcome its own internal conflicts would ever venture to embark upon such a revolution; and that is hardly to be expected so long as Society is what it is. But there is a way for Society—meaning at the moment the men who appreciate the incomparable value of the social principle—to prepare the ground for improving the relations between itself and the political principle. That way is Education, the education of a generation with a truly social outlook and a truly social will. Education is the great implement which is more or less under the control of Society; Society does not, however, know how to utilize it. Social education is the exact reverse of political propaganda. Such propaganda, whether spread by a government or by a party, seeks to 'suggest' a ready-made will to the members of the society, i.e., to implant in their minds the notion that such a will derives from their own, their innermost being. Social education, on the other hand, seeks to arouse and to develop in the minds of its pupils the spontaneity of fellowship which is innate in all unravaged human souls and which harmonizes very well with the development of personal existence and personal thought. This can be accomplished only by the complete overthrow of the political trend which nowadays dominates education throughout the world. True education for citizenship in a State is education for the effectuation of Society.

The Demand of the Spirit and Historical Reality

(Inaugural Lecture, The Hebrew University, Jerusalem, 1938)

MODERN sociology as an independent science was originally critical and demanding. The man to whose influence its founding can be traced is Henri de Saint-Simon. Although no sociologist and in general no scientist, he may, none the less, be described as the father of modern sociology. Saint-Simon was a social critic and demander who perceived the inner contradiction of the age and designated scientific knowledge of social conditions as the decisive step towards its overcoming. Not incorrectly did one of his contemporaries call his fundamental concept an ideocracy—he discerned in the knowing and planning spirit the dictator of things to come.

Both Auguste Comte and Lorenz von Stein—the men who under his influence undertook in very different ways to found the new science—held fast to the intention of overcoming the crisis of the human race. When Comte turned against his teacher he characterized his programme, nevertheless, as *une régénération sociale fondée sur une rénovation mentale*; his own programme was just this. Already in his youth he saw the 'profound moral and political anarchy' that threatened society with dissolution, and demanded a spiritual establishment of a new social structure. New institutions could not bring salvation if a new spiritual attitude were not prepared beforehand to prevent the degeneration and perversion of the institutions. 'I consider all discussions about institutions pure farce,' wrote Comte in a letter in 1824, 'so long as the spiritual reorganization of society is not realized or at least strongly furthered.'

Comte, to be sure, did not compose a sociology in the scientific sense; what he calls such in his work is only general reflections about the historical workings of different spiritual principles on the social situation and the political condition. Stein was the first to attempt a genuine philosophical comprehension and clarification of basic social concepts. But he, too, wanted to know in order to change. The scientific conception of society as a reality to be distinguished from the state—indeed in many ways to be opposed to it, 'The existence of an independent society'—was evident to him from the serious *disturbances* that carry the social life of our age towards a state of things 'that we could describe as the dissolution of the community and its organism.' This 'the powerful deed of science' shall prevent. The present situation and its origin must be known for the sake of the new order: 'we think of the future when we talk of this present, and it is useless to hide it—*when* it is talked about, it is just for the sake of that future that it is talked about.' Stein sees the necessary knowledge as having already arisen. 'At all points,' he wrote in the book *The Socialism and Communism of Present-Day France* (that appeared in 1842, at the same time therefore as the concluding volume of Comte's major work), 'human knowing begins to receive a new, powerful shape.'

Modern sociology originates, therefore, in the meeting of the spirit with the crisis of human society, which the spirit accepts as its own crisis and which it undertakes to overcome through a spiritual turning and transformation. Sociology is just this insight into the nature of the crisis, its causes, and the problems set by it, the beginning of this turning and transformation.

An American sociologist of our time, Edward Ross, holds that a sociologist is 'a man who wishes to change something.' That says too little and it says too much. One may better describe the sociologist as one who wishes to know what is to be changed. But this is a question of knowing a world *in crisis*, and the knowing spirit knows that it stands with the world in the crisis. Not as if this spirit were merely a piece of social reality. Rather it is its partner, destined to learn from it what is and to show it in return what should be—the crisis embraces them both together. In the

178

new sociological vision the scientist must acquire to know what is to be known, he obtains at the same time a new life relationship in which he is bound with reality without being submerged in it. He obtains a new dialogical relation that purifies him.

In his book *Critique of Sociology* a younger sociologist, Siegfried Landshut, has grasped the character of modern sociology much more profoundly than Ross. 'It only understands itself rightly today,' he says, 'when it comprehends itself as the contradiction of historical-social reality that has come to word.' In it is expressed 'that "Copernican revolution" of public consciousness through which the decisive expectations and claims of the life of personal individuals prepare a way to the *organizations and institutions* of life with one another.' Here an error is joined with an important insight: from being the partner of reality who must, of course, remain wholly turned to it in order to perceive its question aright, the spirit is made into its spokesman in whom it 'comes to word.' But where the spirit becomes the mere voice of reality, it forgets that that altered direction of its expectations, the direction towards organizations and institutions, becomes false in becoming exclusive. Only when it remains the partner of reality does it remain aware of its office of working for the transformation of the spirit, for its own transformation without which the altered institutions must decline to emptiness, to unfruitfulness, to ruin. *Une rénovation mentale*, such as Saint-Simon had in mind, is certainly not sufficient; the spirit of which I speak is not one of the potentialities or functions of man but his concentrated *totality*. Man must change himself in the same measure as the institutions are changed in order that these changes may have their expected effect. If the new house that man hopes to erect is not to become his burial chamber, the essence of living together must undergo a change at the same time as the organization of living. If the representative of the spirit of the new sociological view has merely succeeded in politicizing sociologically, then that is lost which he and he alone can give to reality—he is lost himself. He must also *educate* sociologically, he must educate men in living together; he must educate man so he can live with man.

One will perhaps object that both, the political and the educational influence, overstep the proper limits of sociology. This protest has an historical foundation. From the philosophizing about social subjects that Comte and Stein pursued, as Hobbes and Condorcet pursued it before them, an independent science detached itself in the second half of the nineteenth century and the beginning of the twentieth that retained the name of sociology and set as its goal the description and analysis of social phenomena. From its character as an 'objective' science it frequently deduced the duty to be 'value-free,' as Max Weber and other German sociologists called it; that is, to present and to explain facts and connections without expressing any value-judgment in so doing. But when one of these sociologists, Ferdinand Tönnies, opened the first German congress of sociology in 1910, he began his address with the statement, 'Sociology is first of all a philosophical discipline,' and remarked further that one could call theoretical sociology social philosophy also. He asserted thereby that the observation of the social sphere as a whole, the determination of the categories ruling within it, the knowledge of its relations to the other spheres of life, and the understanding of the *meaning* of social existence and happenings are and remain a philosophical task. But there is no philosophy unless the philosophizing man is ready, whenever the urgent question approaches, not to hold back the decision whether a thought is right or wrong, whether an action is good or bad and so on. The philosopher must be ready on the basis of known truth, to the extent of his knorwledge to make these decisions and implement them without reseve and, to release them thereby as a working force in the world. Philosophical treatment of social conditions, events, and structures, accordingly, includes valuation; it includes criticism and demand —not as something customary, but as something difficult and responsible that one does not shrink from doing it if comes to that.

But can there be an independent valuation of the subjects that concern the relations of classes to one another, the relations of peoples and states? Can the social philosopher keep his knowledge *pure*, and the decisions that he makes on the basis of it? Yet true social thinking comes to a person only when he really lives with men, when he remains no stranger to its structures and does not know even its mass movements from the outside alone. Without genuine social binding there is no genuine social experience, and without genuine social experience there is no genuine sociological thinking.

None the less, all knowledge is an *ascetic* act. At the moment of knowledge the knower must bring something paradoxical to pass; certainly he must enter into the knowledge with his whole being, he must also bring unabridged into his knowing the experiences his social ties have presented him with. But he must free himself from the influence of these ties through the concentration of spiritual power. No one becomes a sociological thinker if his dream and his passion have never mingled with the dream and passion of a human community; but in the moment of thinking itself, as far as it stands in his power, he must exist only as person, the person open to the subject of thought. If this relation is maintained, he need not unduly trouble himself with the question of how far his knowledge was determined against his will by his membership in a group. In the relationship of a man to the truth that he has discovered, freedom and obligation, vision and blindness, are always merged. Our concern is only this—to will with all the power of our spirit to achieve the free vision. On the basis of the knowledge thus won, the sociological thinker may value and decide, censure and demand, when the urgent question approaches, without violating the law of his science. Only so can the spirit preserve itself in the crisis that embraces it and historical reality together. The spirit asserts the demand that reality, the heart of sick reality, demands of it—of it as of its partner, not as its spokesman. The representative of the spirit speaks his word to a generation of the spirit that must be educated, and he speaks it to a world that must be changed.

But what weight has his word, what effectiveness is allotted to him?

The ideocratic certainty of Saint-Simon did not hold its own for long. Since then with ever greater proximity we have become acquainted with that which massively opposes and resists the spirit; this is usually but misleadingly called 'history.' What is meant is that world which in the last hundred years liberated itself anew and ever more completely from all spiritual control, resolved on actual conquest and exercise of power. The demand for the 'value-freedom' of sociology has resulted in a resignation that may be formulated in these words: The spirit is still effective indeed, but only in so far as it places itself under the sway of powerful groups, under the dictates of what rules in history, that is, of power—we wish, therefore, to define its limits as a sphere where spirit is not to act but *only* to know, and within this sphere to guarantee still its independence.

Since then the resignation of Europe to 'history' has progressed much farther. The tempo of its advance in America is a slower one, due probably to the fact that America has not become so intimately acquainted with 'history.' The great historian Jacob Burckhardt, as is well known, once said that power is in itself evil. Power in this sense means power for itself; that is, when it wills itself, when it resists the spirit, when power takes possession of those who use it, penetrates them, permeates them with the drive for power for itself. Since Hegel, power has learned to offer a grandiose justification of its resistance to the spirit: true spirit, so we are told, manifests itself in history, in its struggles for power and its power-decisions. He who serves power, therefore, is proclaimed as the true representative of the spirit, and he who opposes it with criticism and demand has obviously fallen into the impudent madness of believing there is something that is superior to history. Power employs this justification even when the criticism and demand of the spirit have stood at its origin; then that spirit is said to be the right one, whereby the spirit that steps athwart it with criticism and demand is unmasked as a false and unauthorized intruder.

Faced with this situation and its problematic, the social thinker who understands his office must ever again pose the question: How can the spirit influence the transformation of social reality?

Plato was about seventy-five years old when the assassination of the prince Dion, master of Syracuse, his friend and disciple, put an end to the enterprise of founding a republic in accordance with the concepts of the philosopher. At this time Plato wrote his famous letter to his friends in Sicily, in which he rendered an account of his lifelong ambition to change the structure of the state (which for him included the structure of society), of his attempts to translate this purpose into reality, and of his failure in these attempts. He wrote that, having observed that all states were poorly governed, he had adopted the opinion that man would not be free from this evil until one of two things happened: either philosophers be charged with the function of government, or the potentates who ruled states lived and acted in harmony with the precepts of philosophy. Plato had formulated this thesis, though somewhat differently, about twenty years earlier in a central passage of his *Republic*. The central position given the passage indicates that in the final analysis he believed that individuals, above all, leaders, were of more importance than particular institutions—such institutions as the book deals with. According to Plato, there are two ways of obtaining the right persons to be leaders: either the philosopher himself must come to power, or those who rule must be educated to conduct their lives as philosophers.

In his memorable tractate *Towards Perpetual Peace*, Kant opposed Plato's thesis without mentioning him by name. The rebuttal is part of a section which appeared only in the second edition, and which Kant designated as a 'secret article' of his outline of international law. He wrote: 'Because the wielding of power inevitably corrupts the free judgment of reason, it is not to be expected that kings should philosophize or philosophers be kings, nor even to be desired. But one thing is indispensable to both in order to illuminate their affairs, and that is that kings or kingly nations, i.e., nations which govern themselves on the basis of laws of equality, should not dispense with or silence the class of philosophers, but let them express themselves in public.' Previously Kant emphasized that this was not meant to suggest that the state should prefer its power to be represented by the principles of the philosopher rather than the dicta of the jurist, but merely that the philosopher should be heard. This line of thought

183

clearly indicates not only a resignation of but also a disappointment in the spirit itself, for Kant had been forced to relinquish faith in the spirit's ability to achieve power and, at the same time, to remain pure. We may safely assume that Kant's disillusionment is motivated by his knowledge of the course of Church history which in the two thousand years and more between Plato and Kant came actually to be the history of spirit's power.

Plato believed both in the spirit and in power, and he also believed in the spirit's call to the assumption of power. What power he saw was decadent, but he thought it could be regenerated and purified by the spirit. The young Plato's own epochal and grave encounter with 'history' took place when the city-state of Athens condemned and executed his teacher Socrates for disobeying authority and obeying the Voice. Yet, among all those who concerned themselves with the state, Socrates alone knew how to educate the young for a true life dedicated to the community; like the seer Tiresias in Hades, he was the only spiritually alive man amid a swarm of hovering shades. Plato regarded himself as Socrates' heir and deputy. He knew himself called to renew the sacred law and to found the just state. And he knew that for this reason he had a right to power. But while the spirit is ready to accept power from the hands of God or man, it is not willing to seize it. In the *Republic*, Socrates is asked whether the philosophic man, as Socrates describes him, would be apt to concern himself with affairs of state. To this question Socrates replies that the philosophic man in his own state would certainly concern himself with such matters, but this state which he conceives and which is suitable to him would have to be a state other than his native one, 'unless there is some divine intervention.' Even prior to this passage, he speaks of the man who is blessed with spirit confronting a furious mob, confronting it without confederates who could help maintain justice, feeling as if he were surrounded by wild beasts. Such a man, he goes on to say, will henceforth keep silence, attend to his own business, become a spectator, and live out his life without doing any wrong to the end of his days. But when Socrates' listeners interpose that such a man will thus have accomplished a great work by the time he dies, he contradicts them, 'But not the greatest, since he has not found the state which befits him.'

That is the gist of Plato's resignation. He was called to Syracuse and went there repeatedly, even though he suffered one disappointment after another. He went because he was called and because the divine voice might possibly be speaking in the voice of man. According to Dion there was a possibility that then, if ever, the hope to link philosophers and rulers to each other might there be fulfilled. Plato decided to 'try.' He reports he was ashamed not to go to Syracuse, lest he should seem to be nothing but 'words.' 'Manifest,' is the word he once used to Dion; we must manifest ourselves by truly being what we profess in words. He had used the word 'must,' not 'want to.' He went and failed, returned home, went once more and still another time, and failed again. At the third failure, he was almost seventy. Not until then did the man Plato had educated come into power. But before he was able to master the chaos, he was murdered by one who had been his fellow-student at Plato's academy.

Plato held that mankind could recover from its ills only if either the philosophers 'whom now are termed useless' became kings or the kings became philosophers. He himself hoped first for the one and then for the other of these alternatives to occur as the result of 'divine intervention.' But he himself was not elevated to a *basileus* in Greece, and the prince whom he had educated to be a philosopher did not master the chaos in Sicily. It might possibly be said that the peace which Timoleon of Corinth established in Sicily after the death of this prince was achieved under the touch of Plato's spirit, and that Alexander, who later united all of Greece under his rule, certainly had not in vain studied philosophy with Plato's most renowned disciple. But neither in the one case nor in the other was Plato's ideal of the state actually realized. Plato did not regenerate the decadent Athenian democracy, and he did not found the republic he had projected.

But does this glorious failure prove that the spirit is always helpless in the face of history?

Plato is the most sublime instance of that spirit whose intercourse with reality proceeds from its own possession of truth. According to Plato, that soul is perfect which remembers its vision of perfection. Before its life on earth, the soul had beheld the idea of the good. In the world of ideas, it had beheld the shape of pure justice, and now, with the spirit's growth, the soul recollects what it had formerly beheld. The soul is not content to know this idea and to teach it to others. The soul yearns to infuse the idea of justice with the breath of life and establish it in the human world in the living form of a just state. The spirit is in possession of truth; it offers truth to reality; truth becomes reality through the spirit. That is the fundamental basis of Plato's doctrine. But this doctrine was not carried out. The spirit did not succeed in giving reality the truth it strove to impress it with. Was reality alone responsible? Was not the spirit itself responsible as well? Was not its very relationship to the truth responsible? These are questions which necessarily occur in connection with Plato's failure.

But the spirit can fail in another and very different way.

'In the year that King Uzziah died' (Isa. 6.1) Isaiah had a vision of the heavenly sanctuary in which the Lord chose him as his prophet. The entire incident points to the fact that King Uzziah was still alive. The king had long been suffering from leprosy. It is well known that in Biblical times leprosy was regarded not as a mere physical ailment but as the physical symptom of a disturbance in man's relationship to God. Rumour had it that the king had been afflicted because he had presumed to perform in the sanctuary of Jerusalem sacral functions which exceeded his rights as a political lieutenant of God (2 Chr. 26.16–21). Moreover, Isaiah felt in Uzziah's leprosy more than a personal affliction; it symbolized the uncleanliness of the entire people, and Isaiah's own uncleanliness as well. They all had 'unclean lips' (Isa. 6.5). Like lepers, they must all cover 'their upper lip' (Lev. 13.45) lest by breath or word their uncleanliness go forth and pollute the world. All of them have been disobedient and faithless to the true King, the King whose glory Isaiah's eyes now behold in his heavenly sanctuary. Here God is called *ha-Melekh*; this is the first time in the Scriptures that he is designated so plainly as the King of Israel.

He is the King. The leper the people call 'king' is only a faithless lieutenant. Now the true King sends Isaiah with a message to the entire people, at the same time telling him that his message will fail; he will fail, for the message will be misunderstood, misinterpreted and misused, and thus confirm the people—save for a small 'remnant'—in their faithlessness, and harden their hearts. At the very outset of his mission, Isaiah, the carrier of the spirit, is told that he must fail. He will not suffer disappointment like Plato, for in his case failure is an integral part of the way he must take.

Isaiah does not share Plato's belief that the spirit is a possession of man. The man of spirit—such is the tradition from time immemorial—is one whom the spirit invades and seizes, whom the spirit uses as its garment, not one who contains the spirit. Spirit is an event, something which happens to man. The storm of the spirit sweeps man where it will, then storms on into the world.

Neither does Isaiah share Plato's notion that power is man's possession. Power is vouchsafed man to enable him to discharge his duties as God's lieutenant. If he abuses this power, the power destroys him, and in place of the spirit which came to prepare him for the use of power (1 Sam. 16.14), an 'evil spirit' comes upon him. The man in power is responsible to one who interrogates him in silence, and to whom he is answerable, or all is over with him.

Isaiah does not hold that spiritual man has the prerogative of power. He knows himself to be a man of spirit and to be without power. Being a prophet means being powerless, powerlessly confronting the powerful and reminding them of their responsibility, as Isaiah reminded Ahaz 'in the highway of the fuller's field' (Isa. 7.3). To stand powerless before the power he calls to account is part of the prophet's destiny. He does not himself seek for power; the special sociological significance of his office is based on that very fact.

Plato believed that his soul was perfect. Isaiah did not, regarding and acknowledging himself unclean. He felt the uncleanliness which tainted his breath and his words being burned from his lips so that those lips might speak the message of God.

Isaiah beheld the throne and the majesty of Him who entrusted him with the message. He did not see the just state which Plato beheld in his mind's eye as something recollected. Isaiah knew and said that men are commanded to be just to one another. He knew and said that the unjust are destroyed by their own injustice. And he knew and said that there would come a dominion of justice and that a just man would rule as the faithful lieutenant of God. But he knew nothing and said nothing of the inner structure of that dominion. He had no idea; he had only a message. He had no institution to establish; he had only a proclamation, a proclamation in the nature of criticism and demand.

His criticism and demand are directed towards making the people and their prince recognize the reality of an invisible sovereignty. When Isaiah uses the word *ha-Melekh* it is not in the sense of a theological metaphor but in that of a political constitutional concept. But this sovereignty of God which he propounded is the opposite of the sovereignty of priests, which is commonly termed theocracy and which has very properly been described as 'the most unfree form of society,' for it is 'unfree through the abuse of the Highest knowable to man.'* None but the powerless can speak the true King's will with regard to the state, and remind both the people and the government of their *common* responsibility towards this will. The powerless man can do so because he breaks through the illusions of current history and recognizes potential crises.

That is why his criticism and demand are directed towards society, towards the life men live together. A people which seriously calls God Himself its King must become a true people, a community where all members are ruled by honesty without compulsion, kindness without hypocrisy, and the brotherliness of those who are passionately devoted to their divine leader. When social inequality, distinction between the free and the unfree, splits the community and creates chasms between its members, there can be no true people, there can be no 'God's people.' So criticism and demand are directed towards every individual whom other individuals depend upon, towards everyone who has

* Lorenz von Stein, *System der Stastswissenschaft* (1856), II, 384.

a hand in shaping the destinies of others; that means directed towards every one of us. When Isaiah speaks of justice, he is not thinking of institutions but of you and me, because without you and me the most glorious institution becomes a lie.

Finally, the criticism and demand apply to Israel's relationship to other nations. Israel is warned not to engage in the making of treaties, not to rely on this or that so-called world power, but to 'keep calm' (Isa. 7.4; 30.15), to make itself a true people, faithful to its divine King. Then they will have nothing to be afraid of. 'The head of Damascus,' Isaiah told Ahaz in the highway of the fuller's field, 'is Rezin, and the head of Samaria, Pekah,' meaning 'but you know who is the Head of Jerusalem—if you want to know.' But 'If you will not trust, you will not be confirmed' (Isa. 7.9).

There has been much talk in this connection of 'utopian' politics which would relate Isaiah's failure to that of Plato, who wrote the utopian *Republic*. What Isaiah said to Ahaz is accepted as a sublimely 'religious' but a politically valueless utterance, implying one which lends itself to solemn quotation but one inapplicable to reality. Yet the only political chance for a small people hemmed in between world powers is the metapolitical chance Isaiah pointed to. He proclaimed a truth which could not, indeed, be tested by history up to that time, but only because no one ever thought of testing it. Nations can be led to peace only by a people which has made peace a reality within itself. The realization of the spirit has a magnetic effect on mankind which despairs of the spirit. That is the meaning Isaiah's teachings have for us. When the mountain of the Lord's house is 'established' on the reality of true community life, then, and only then, the nations will 'flow' towards it (Isa. 2.2), there to learn peace in place of war.

Isaiah too failed, as was predicted when he was called to give God's message. People and king opposed him, and even the king's successor, who attached himself to Isaiah, was found wanting in the decisive hour, when he flirted with the idea of allying with the Babylonian rebel against Assyria. But this failure is quite different from Plato's. Our very existence testifies to this difference. We live by that encounter in the highway of the fuller's field, we live by virtue of the fact that there were people who were deadly serious about this *ha-Melekh* in relation to all their social and political reality. They are the cause of our survival until this new chance to translate the spirit into the reality we have a presentiment of. We may yet experience an era of history which refutes 'history.' The prophet fails in the hour of history, but not in so far as the future of his people is concerned. The prophetic spirit does not succeed in giving the reality of its hour what it wills to give it. But it instils the vision in the people for all time to come. It lives within the people from then on as a longing to realize the truth.

The prophetic spirit does not believe, like the Platonic, that it possesses a universal and timeless ideal truth. The Hebrew prophet invariably receives only a message for a particular situation. But for this very reason his word still speaks after thousands of years to manifold situations in the history of peoples. He sets no universally valid image of perfection, no pantopia or utopia, before men; he has no choice, therefore, between his fatherland and another land that 'suits him' better; for realization he is directed to the *topos*, to this place, to this people, it being the people that must *begin*. But he lacks, too, unlike the Platonic spirit, the possibility of withdrawing into the attitude of a calm spectator when he feels himself surrounded by wild beasts. He must speak his message. That message will be misunderstood, misjudged, misused; it will strengthen and 'harden' the people still further in their untruth. But its sting will rankle within them for all time.

The social thinker is not a prophet but a philosopher. He does not have a message, he has a teaching. But for the transformation of the social reality he intends what is decisive. This is no Platonic task, no erection of a universally valid image of perfection; it is the prophetic task of criticism and demand within the present situation. Where an urgent question impinges, he cannot, of course, express criticism and demand as a message, but he can certainly express them on the basis of his knowledge.

Must not this social thinker fail, none the less, like his greater predecessors? Even Kant's 'secret article' has not yet come into force: that the kings and the peoples should *listen to* the philosophers.

Up to now the crisis of the human race has made men only still deafer to the spirit. But that condition will surely change in the course of the crisis, only in a late phase, to be sure, when men despair of power and its autonomous decisions, when power for power's sake grows bewildered and longs for direction.

The spirit is hardly called, as Saint-Simon thought, to be the dictator of things to come. But it can be the preparer and counsellor. It can educate men for what is to come. And when a change is accomplished, the spirit must keep watch so that the altered institutions may not fall into corruption and do violence to the life struggling upward.

Amid the confusion and obliteration of basic social concepts, human knowledge of society must today, in many respects, begin anew with a new conceptual clarification, with a cleansing of the type. Perhaps just this silent, difficult work will help society to a new shape, as Lorenz von Stein proclaimed a century ago. Knowledge, he said, will become 'powerful'; we would say rather: knowledge will become effective.

For Jerusalem, however, still more than this is to be said. There are situations in the lives of peoples in which the people becomes, as it were, plastic, and the impossible becomes possible. Perhaps such an hour is near. We think of this 'perhaps' when we perform our service. We would also perform it, of course, if this possibility did not exist. For, resigned or unresigned, the spirit works.

Prophecy, Apocalyptic, and the
Historical Hour

(1954)

I

THE man who, without particularly reflecting on himself, allows himself to be borne along by the bustle of life, still at times unexpectedly finds himself confronted by an hour which has a special and even an especially questionable connection with his personal future. Among his possible reactions, two stand out as essential. The man I speak of can the next instant renounce the beaten track, draw forth forgotten primal forces from their hiding-places, and make the decision that answers the situation; he cherishes the until-now-unsuspected certainty of thus being able to participate on the ground of becoming, in the factual decision that will be made about the make-up of the next hour, and thereby in some measure also about the make-up of future hours. Or, in contrast, he may banish all such impulses and resolve, as one says, not to let himself be fooled—not by the situation, which is just an embroilment, and not by himself, who is just a man come to grief; for everything is linked invincibly with everything else, and there is nowhere a break where he can take hold. He surrenders anew to the turmoil, but now, so he thinks, out of insight.

If, disregarding all differences and complications, we transpose this hour, with its indwelling possibilities of these two basic human attitudes set in polar opposition, from the realm of biography into that of history, we catch sight of a problematic it may be instructive to look into.

But from what standpoint is this problematic adequately to be grasped, as is necessary, so that, gazing with clarified spirit into the depths of reality, we can make the right choice between affirmation of choice and denial of choice? How shall we manage to escape from the dilemma whose discursive expression is the old philosophical quarrel between indeterministic and deterministic views of the world? It is not within the province of philosophical dialectic to offer us help here; the highest that it can attain is, instead of setting the two aspects in opposition to each other, understanding them as two irreconcilable-reconcilable sides of the same event. In this, to be sure, philosophy does justice to the life experience in which the moment of beginning the action is illumined by the awareness of freedom, and the moment of having acted is overshadowed by the knowledge of necessity. But where it is no longer a matter of aspects, either experienced or recalled, and no longer a matter of their connection with each other, but of the soul's innermost question of trust, such philosophizing does not suffice to guide us.

This question is: Do I dare the definitely impossible or do I adapt myself to the unavoidable? Do I dare to become other than I am, trusting that in reality I am indeed other and can so put it to the test, or do I take cognizance of a barrier in my present existence as something that will eternally be a barrier? Transposing the question from biography to history: does an historical hour ever experience its real limits otherwise than through undertaking to overstep those limits it is familiar with? Does the future establish itself ever anew, or is it inescapably destined? For this innermost inwardness of our praxis there is no help besides trust itself or, to call it by its sacral name, faith. But this faith is not our own personal faith alone. The history of human faith also affords us help. Its help is not the kind that simply places the right before our eyes in historical realization as a truth that no contradiction confronts. A glance at man's history of faith may so clarify the antithesis of the two possibilities that the decision between them can take place in full light. In the history of faith, my faith finds irreplacable support even where it receives only a new manner of choosing.

2

In the history of Judaism these two basic attitudes rose into the purity and unconditionality of the religious sphere, being embodied in two great manifestations of the spirit which, by virtue of this purity and unconditionality, assumed a significance for man's way in the world, and particularly for the present stretch of the way, hardly to be comprehended deeply enough.

These embodiments are the prophets in the ages of the kings of Judah and Israel and the apocalyptic writings of Jewish and Jewish-Christian coinage in the age of late Hellenism and its decline. The question here is not one of the changing historical events and the judgments concerning them passed under the divine summons by the prophet or apocalyptic writer living at that time. It is rather a question of two essentially different views from the standpoint of which the prophetic sayings on the one side and the apocalyptic texts on the other are to be understood. Common to both is faith in the one Lord of the past, present, and future history of all existing beings; both views are certain of His will to grant salvation to His creation. But how this will manifest itself in the pregnant moment in which the speaker speaks, what relation this moment bears to coming events, what share in this relation falls to men, to begin with, therefore, to the hearers of the speaker—at these points the prophetic and the apocalyptic messages essentially diverge.

This difference, as has been said, is by no means of merely historical significance: it has something of the utmost importance to teach each generation, and specifically our own. In order to throw this significance into bold relief, I must disregard all that is atypical, elementally significant though it may be. I must disregard the question of what apocalyptic motifs are already, here and there, to be found among the classical prophets and what prophetic motifs are still, here and there, to be found among the late apocalyptics. I must show the essential difference of the basic attitudes through the clearest examples.

3

In a time when the external and internal crisis of the kingdom of Judah began to manifest itself in momentous signs, about twenty years before the destruction of Jerusalem by the Chaldeans, Jeremiah received the divine command to go to the workshop of the potter in the valley below; there God would speak to him (Jer. 18.2). We understand what is meant: the prophet shall contemplate a reality that shall come to him as a revelatory parable in the midst of his contemplation. Jeremiah went down and beheld how the potter fashioned the clay on the double wheels. 'And if the vessel that he made was marred while still in the clay in the potter's hand, then he made out of it again another vessel, even as it seemed right to make to the potter's eye.' Three times, in the great Biblical style of repetition, the word 'to make' is hammered in; the matter in question here is the sovereignty of the making. In contemplating this sovereignty, Jeremiah received the message of God in which, time after time again, that word recurs: 'Cannot I do with you as this potter, O house of Israel? Behold, as the clay in the potter's hand, so are you in My hand, O house of Israel! At one instant I may speak over a nation, over a kingdom, to root out, to tear down, to dismantle—but if that nation turn from its evil for the sake of which I have spoken against it, I am sorry for the evil that I planned to make for it. And again at one instant I speak over a nation, over a kingdom, to build up, to plant, but if it do evil in My eyes so that My voice remains unheard, I am sorry for the good with which I have said I would benefit it.'

We must bear in mind that in just these verbal terms, the young Jeremiah had received two decades before his summons as 'announcer to the nations' (Jer. 1.5, 7, 10). 'To whomever I shall send thee,' it was there said to him, 'thou shalt go; whatever I shall command thee, thou shalt speak.' While he felt on his mouth the touch of a finger, he heard further: 'I have put My words in thy mouth; see, I appoint thee this day over the nations, over the kingdoms, to root out, to tear down, to dismantle, to annihilate, to build, to plant.' The communication to him as the chosen *nabi*, the 'announcer'—that is, the one who utters the speech of heaven—comes to him now in exact relation to the language of the summons, expanded in meaning, while the lower potter's wheel revolves before him and the vessels are formed on the upper wheel, the successes to remain in the world, the failures to be rejected and shaped anew.

Thus the divine potter works on the historical shapes and destinies of human nations. But, in accordance with His will, this work of His can itself will, can itself either do or not do; with this doing and not-doing that it wills, it touches on the work of the Worker. From the beginning He has granted this freedom to them, and in all sovereignty of His fashioning and destroying, He still gives to them, just in so doing, the answer—fashioning and destroying. He 'is sorry for' the planned good when they turn away from Him; He 'is sorry for' the planned evil when they turn back to Him.

But the announcer—this creature God once addressed, 'Thou shalt be as My mouth'—is a part of the happening. For he is obliged at times to say 'what God is working,' as is said in the prophecy of Balaam (Num. 23.23)—to say it to those whom it concerns. He can do that, however, in two different ways. The one way is the open alternative. Thus we hear Jeremiah time after time speak to his people in the most direct manner when he delivers to them the concise saying of God: 'Better your ways and your affairs and I shall allow you to dwell in this place.' But when those so appealed to persistently resist the call, he no longer proclaims the alternative but announces the approaching catastrophe as an unalterable doom. Yet even in this threat the gate of grace still remains open for man when he turns his whole being back to God. Here, too, no end is set to the real working power of the dialogue between divinity and mankind, within which compassion can answer man's turning of his whole being back to God.

This depth of dialogical reciprocity between heaven and earth is brought to its strongest expression by the prophets of Israel—from the early period till the post-exilic epoch—through one of those meaningful word-repetitions and word-correspondences which so richly abound in the Hebrew Bible. The turning of the being of man and the divine response are often designated by the same verb, a verb that can signify to turn back as well as to turn away, but also to return and to turn towards someone, and this fullness of meaning was taken advantage of in the texts. Already, in one of the earliest of the Biblical prophets, in Hosea, we hear God speak first of all, 'Return, Israel, unto the Lord,' and once again, 'Return'; then it says (just as later in Jeremiah), 'I shall heal your turnings away'; but now follows 'I shall love them freely, for my wrath is turned away from them.' This corre- spondence, expressed through the repetition of the verb, between the action of man and the action of God, which is not at all a causal but a purely dialogical connection between the two, con- tinues in a clear tradition of style into the post-exilic age. The late, yet word-powerful prophet, Joel, sees in his vision a terrible enemy approaching, yet the description of the threatening in- vasion is followed by God's statement, 'Return to me with all your heart.' Then the text says once more, 'Return to the Lord your God'; but now it is said, 'Who knows whether He will not return and be sorry.'

The same turn of speech, 'Who knows,' as expression of the timid hope of those turning back, we find again in the late fable of Jonah who, contrary to the prevailing interpretation, seems to me to derive from a time when there was still a living tendency to make clear to the people that the task of the genuine prophet was not to predict but to confront man with the alternatives of decision. It is not mere literature; rather, with all its epigonic character, it is still a real echo of the prophetic language in the shape of a reverent paradigm when the King of the Ninevites first calls to his people, to whom the exact data of their destruction have just been announced, 'Every one shall turn back from his evil way,' and then adds, 'Who knows, God may return, He may be sorry and may turn back from the flaming of His wrath, and we shall not perish.'

What view of the ruling of the Ruler underlies all this? Clearly a view that preserves the mystery of the dialogical intercourse between God and man from all desire for dogmatic encystment

The mystery is that of man's creation as a being with the power of actually choosing between the ways, who ever again and even now has the power to choose between them. Only such a being is suited to be God's partner in the dialogue of history. The future is not fixed, for God wants man to come to Him with full freedom, to return to Him even out of a plight of extreme hopelessness and then to be really with Him. This is the prophetic *theologem*, never expressed as such but firmly embedded in the foundations of Hebrew prophecy.

An apocryphal gospel fragment of Jewish-Christian origin has the Holy Ghost say to Jesus at the baptism in the Jordan that he has awaited him 'in all the prophets.' This historical waiting of the spirit for man's fulfilment of the intention of creation is prophecy's breath of life. The prophetic faith involves the faith in the *factual* character of human existence, as existence that factually meets transcendence. Prophecy has in its way declared that the unique being, man, is created to be a centre of surprise in creation. Because and so long as man exists, factual change of direction can take place towards salvation as well as towards disaster, starting from the world in each hour, no matter how late. This message has been proclaimed by the prophets to all future generations, to each generation in its own language.

4

Many noteworthy mixed forms lead from the historical sphere into that of apocalyptic, but it does not belong to my present task to discuss them. I must, however, call one manifestation to mind because it illustrates not a transitional form but an exception to that type. I refer to that anonymous prophet of the Babylonian exile who has been named after Isaiah, not only because his prophecies have been included in the Book of Isaiah, but also because he clearly understood himself as a posthumous disciple of Isaiah's. Among the prophets he was the man who had to announce world history and to herald it as divinely predestined. In place of the dialogue between God and people he brings the comfort of the One preparing redemption to those He wants to redeem; God speaks here as not only having foreknown but also having foretold what now takes place in history—the revolutionary changes in the life of the nations and the liberation of Israel consummated in it. There is no longer room here for an alternative: the future is spoken of as being established from the beginning.

This transformation of the prophetic perspective was facilitated for 'Deutero-Isaiah' through the fact that he associated himself across the centuries with the great announcer who, as the memoir whose author he was (Chap. VI–VIII) shows, again and again knew himself bound by the cruel duty to withhold from the people the dimension of the alternative and who often can only utter it in symbols. But essentially the transformation had been made possible by the unheard-of new character of the historical situation. Here for the first time a prophet had to proclaim an atonement fulfilled through the suffering of the people. The guilt is atoned for, a new day begins. During this time in which history holds its breath, the alternative is silent. In this moment what is in question is no longer a choosing as a people between two ways but apprehending as an individual the new, higher summons which shall be fulfilled through a series of 'servants of the Lord,' a series at the beginning of which the speaker sees himself. An epoch such as ours, entangled in guilt and far from atonement, can learn something great from this prophet, but it cannot take anything directly from him. Here something not dependent upon our wills shines on us comfortingly.

5

If we aim to set in contrast the historical categories of prophecy and apocalyptic in the greatest possible purity of their distinctive natures, then, just as we proceeded from the prophecy of Jeremiah as one that embodies in the exact sense the prophetic vision of present and future, so for the presentation of the apocalyptic, we shall do well to select one of its two most mature late works— the Revelation of John and the so-called Fourth Book of Ezra. Although the work that closes the Christian canon is the more significant of the two, I still prefer the other for our purpose, since it affords a fuller insight into the relationship of the speaker to contemporary history. The book, whose constituent parts probably originated around the middle of the first Christian century, obviously received its final form only decades after the destruction of Jerusalem by the Romans. Yet the speaker pretends to be living as a member of the king's house in exile just after the destruction of Jerusalem by the Chaldeans.

Such a literary fiction, common to most of the apocalyptic writers, is by no means a secondary phenomenon; the actual historical-biographical situation of the speaker is deliberately replaced by an alien scene taken over as analogous to his own. That fiction plunges us already into the depths of the problematic. The time the prophetic voice calls us to take part in is the time of the actual decision; to this the prophet summons his hearers, not seldom at the risk of martyrdom to himself. In the world of the apocalyptic this present historical-biographical hour hardly ever exists, precisely because a decision by men constituting a factor in the historical-suprahistorical decision is not in question here. The prophet addresses persons who hear him, who should hear him. He knows himself sent to them in order to place before them the stern alternatives of the hour. Even when he writes his message or has it written, whether it is already spoken or is still to be spoken, it is always intended for particular men, to induce them, as directly as if they were hearers, to recognize their situation's demand for decision and to act accordingly. The apocalyptic writer has no audience turned towards him; he speaks into his notebook. He does not really speak, he only writes; he does not write down the speech, he just writes his thoughts—he writes a book.

The prophet speaks the word that it is his task to speak; he is borne by this task, proceeding from a divine purpose and pointing to a divine goal. The spirit moves him; not only his organs of speech but the whole man is taken up into the service of the spirit. The body and life of the man become a part of this service and by this a symbol of the message. The burden of a message is at times laid on individual apocalyptic writers, but this message is not joined to a life task. The author of the Ezra-revelation does not recognize at all a vital task. At the beginning of his book the speaker—we do not know whether it is the actual speaker or only the fictitious one that is meant—lies on his bed and, visited by a great anxiety over the fate of Israel and that of the human race, laments to heaven and complains of the government of the world while relating to God in some detail Biblical history from the creation on, supplemented by critical questions. Conversations with angels follow who disclose to the so-called 'Ezra' the mysteries of heaven and of the coming aeons; visions mingle in the conversations, mostly of a schematic-allegorical nature, and are interpreted piece by piece in an orderly fashion. At the conclusion a task is formulated, but this is merely an ingredient of the literary fiction, and apparently is not even of the original one; for instead of that prince of the sixth century, Ezra the Scribe stands before us. Ezra is commanded to write down the twenty-four books of the Old Testament canon and in addition seventy books of secret teaching; when he has accomplished this he disappears.

Nowhere in the book does there stir the prophetic breath of actually-happening history and its fullness of decision. Everything here is predetermined, all human decisions are only sham struggles. The future does not come to pass; the future is already present in heaven, as it were, present from the beginning. Therefore, it can be 'disclosed' to the speaker and he can disclose it to others. His innermost question, accordingly, is not concerned with what poor man shall undertake but why things happen to him as they do. In this search, to be sure, the question of Jeremiah and Job, why good befalls the wicked and evil the righteous, is again taken up under the aspect of world history. The query is raised why Zion was destroyed and the certainly no better Babylon spared, but to it is joined the new and altogether different question of how there can be wickedness in general: the problem of the origin of the 'evil heart' through whose working Adam and all those begotten by him have fallen into sin and guilt.

Here, however, we must distinguish two stages. In the one a kind of hereditary sin is recognized that was entirely foreign to the Old Testament. There, despite all consciousness of the growing historical burden, each man stood anew in the freedom of Adam; his capacity for decision was not impaired by any inner inheritance. But now the apocalyptic writer writes out, 'Ah, Adam, what have you done! When you sinned, your fall did not come upon you alone but also upon us, we who issue from you. What does it avail us that an immortal aeon is promised us when we have done death's work?' And he has God proclaim with the utmost precision: 'When Adam disobeyed My command, the creature was condemned.'

But the speaker goes further. Adam's sin arose from his own nature, and this he received from God. God had put into him the evil heart, and He had left it in Adam's descendants. Even when He revealed Himself to Israel, He did not take away the evil heart; therefore, the awareness of the truth could not hold its ground against the 'bad seed.' And the answering angel confirms with still stronger statement, 'A grain of evil seed was sown in Adam's heart in the beginning'; now the whole harvest must come up, and only when it is cut can the field of the good appear. This view of the apocalyptic writer contradicts fundamentally the earlier prophetic teaching. It also contradicts the contemporary early-Talmudic teaching, according to which an evil urge was not placed in the heart of man at creation, but only the still neutral passion without which nothing could succeed. It depends on man whether this passion takes the direction towards God or falls into directionless chaos. The intention of creation, accordingly, was that the world should become an independent seat of free decision out of which a genuine answer of the creature to his Creator could issue. The apocalyptic writer, on the contrary, though he knows, of course, of the struggle in the soul of man, accords to this struggle no elemental significance. There exists for him no possibility of a change in the direction of historical destiny that could proceed from man, or be effected or co-effected by man. The prophetic principle of the turning is not simply denied in its individual form, but a turning on the part of the community is no longer even thought of. The turning is nowhere acknowledged to have a power that alters history or even one that manifests itself eschatologically, again in marked contrast to the early-Talmudic tradition which held that the historical continuation of existence depends on the turning.

The mature apocalyptic, moreover, no longer knows an historical future in the real sense. The end of all history is near. 'Creation has grown old, it notes as a point unalterably established; this is stated still more penetratingly in the Baruch apocalypse: 'The procession of the ages is already almost past.' The present aeon, that of the world and of world history, 'hurries powerfully to the end.' The coming age, the transformation of all things through the incursion of the transcendent is at hand. The antithesis of the coming age to all historical ages is expressed most strongly by a sentence of the Johannine Revelation that surpasses all that can be imagined: 'Time will no longer be.' The proper and paradoxical subject of the late apocalyptic is a future that is no longer in time, and he anticipates this consummation so that for him all that may yet come in history no longer has an historical character. Man cannot achieve this future, but he also has nothing more to achieve.

6

Prophecy and apocalyptic, regarded through their writings, are unique manifestations in the history of the human spirit and of its relationship to transcendence. Prophecy originates in the hour of the highest strength and fruitfulness of the Eastern spirit, the apocalyptic out of the decadence of its cultures and religions. But wherever a living historical dialogue of divine and human actions breaks through, there persists, visible or invisible, a bond with the prophecy of Israel. And wherever man shudders before the menace of his own work and longs to flee from the radically demanding historical hour, there he finds himself near to the apocalyptic vision of a process that cannot be arrested.

There is also, of course, an optimistic modern apocalyptic, the chief example of which is Marx's view of the future. This has erroneously been ascribed a prophetic origin. In this announcement of an obligatory leap of the human world out of the aeon of necessity into that of freedom, the apocalyptic principle alone holds sway. Here in place of the power superior to the world that effects the transition, an immanent dialectic has appeared. Yet in a mysterious manner *its* goal, too, is the perfection, even the salvation of the world. In its modern shape, too, apocalyptic knows nothing of an inner transformation of man that precedes the transformation of the world and co-operates in it; it knows nothing of the prophetic 'turning.' Marx could, indeed, occasionally (1856) write, 'The new forces of society'—by which the *pre-revolutionary* society is meant—'need new men in order to accomplish good work,' although, according to the materialistic interpretation of history, new men can only arise from the new post-revolutionary conditions of society. But such flashing sparks of the prophetic fire are certainly to be found in every apocalyptic. No living man who in his personal experience has known free decision and its share in the objective change of situation can persist uninterruptedly in the thought of a smoothly predetermined course of events bereft of all junctures. Nothing in Marx's basic view of history, however, was altered thereby, and three years later Lasalle could write of it with justification that, linking brazen necessity to necessity, it passes 'over and obliterates just for that reason the efficacy of individual resolutions and actions.'

Today, despite all assurances to the contrary, this inverted apocalyptic no longer occupies any considerable room in the real thinking of its adherents. Meanwhile, a directly antithetical apocalyptic attitude has taken shape in Western humanity. This appears to resume some doctrines of the Ezra and Baruch apocalypses after they have been divested of all theology of a coming aeon. The wholly other state of being there promised for existence after the end of our world is now annihilated, but the character of the present as late, all too late, has been preserved. The world, to be sure, is no longer called creation, but its irremediable old age is accepted as self-understood. In contrast to what prevailed a short time ago, no one any longer pushes the analogy with the organism so far that he links to the declaration of old age the expectation of early death; prognoses of this kind have today become rare. The specifically modern apocalyptic is not merely completely secularized, but also, after several more grandiose than reliable starts, it has been thoroughly disenchanted. Prognoses, accordingly have become unpopular, which is to be welcomed at any rate. Instead of assuming this role, the apocalyptic has now, so to speak, expounded itself in permanence. It no longer says, 'One cannot swim against the stream'—the image of the stream, to which an outlet belongs, already appears too full of pathos. It says rather, 'An old period must behave like an old period if it does not wish to be laughed at.' The only poetry that still becomes such an age is one of a self-directed irony; the only art that still fits it is one that atomizes things, to employ a striking characterization of Max Picard's; faith has become altogether unseemly. In an aged world one knows exactly what is legitimate and what is not.

If one comes and rebels against the indirectness that has penetrated all human relationships, against the atmosphere of a false objectivity where each sees the other no longer as a partner of his existence but merely as an object among objects in order to register him in already-existing interconnections of 'objective' utility, he is upbraided by his critics as a romantic beset by illusions. If he resists the flagging of the dialogical relationship between men, he is forthwith reproached with failing to recognize the fated solitude of present-day living, as if the fundamental meaning of each new solitude were not that it must be overcome on a more comprehensive level than any earlier one. If one declares that one of the main reasons why the crisis in the life of the peoples appears hopeless is the fact that the existential mistrust of all against all prevents any meaningful negotiation over the *real* differences of interest, he is set right by a smile of the shrewd: an 'old' world is necessarily shrewd.

The great apocalyptic writings of that earlier turning-point of history were of two kinds. The one held that men could no longer have faith in history's taking a new direction, the other that men could believe in an all-determining God only with a special limitation: God can make everything with the exception of a genuine, free Thou for Himself—that He cannot make. Unbelief and belief were here only the two sides of *one* point of view. Of the two, only the unbelief remains in the broken yet emphatic apocalyptic of our time. It steps forward with an heroic mien, to be sure; it holds itself to be the heroic acknowledgment of the inevitable, the embodiment of *amor fati*. But this convulsive gesture has nothing in common with real love.

As in the life of a single person, so also in the life of the human race: what is possible in a certain hour and what is impossible cannot be adequately ascertained by any foreknowledge. It goes without saying that in the one sphere as in the other, one must start at any given time from the nature of the situation in so far as it is at all recognizable. But one does not learn the measure and limit of what is attainable in a desired direction otherwise than through going in this direction. The forces of the soul allow themselves to be measured only through one's using them. In the most important moments of our existence neither planning nor surprise rules alone: in the midst of the faithful execution of a plan we are surprised by secret openings and insertions. Room must be left for such surprises, however; planning as though they were impossible renders them impossible. One cannot strive for immediacy, but one can hold oneself free and open for it. One cannot produce genuine dialogue, but one can be at its disposal. Existential mistrust cannot be replaced by trust, but it can be replaced by a reborn candour.

This attitude involves risk, the risk of giving oneself, of inner transformation. Inner transformation simply means surpassing one's present factual constitution; it means that the person one is intended to be penetrates what has appeared up till now, that the customary soul enlarges and transfigures itself into the surprise soul. This is what the prophets of Israel understood by the turning in their language of faith: not a return to an earlier, guiltless stage of life, but a swinging round to where the wasted hither-and-thither becomes walking on a way, and guilt is atoned for in the newly-arisen genuineness of existence.

Towards the end of the first third of that same century in which those apocalypses were produced that spoke of the aged world and announced the approaching rupture of history, John the

Baptist had again taken up the cry of the prophets, 'Return!'; and, in complete accord with their belief in real alternatives, he had joined to the imperative the warning that the axe had already been laid to the roots of the tree. He trusted his hearers to trust themselves as capable of the turning that was demanded, and he trusted the human world of his hour to be capable of just this turning, of risk, of giving oneself, of inner transformation. After Jesus and in like manner his emissaries had sounded the call afresh, the apocalyptics and their associates proceeded to disclose that there is no turning and no new direction in the destiny of the world that can issue from the turning. But the depths of history, which are continually at work to rejuvenate creation, are in league with the prophets.

The Validity and Limitation of the Political Principle

(1953)

IT is characteristic of the great imperishable sayings of religious teaching that they are bound to situations. Their place is never beyond human intercourse. They arise as spoken response to some occasions. A group is assembled, whether one that had previously joined the speaker or one that has gathered around him at the moment. To the members of that group the word is directed, perhaps to summon them in a given situation or to answer a question raised just then in connection with a situation. Demanding or demanded, the message of the particular man is addressed to their special circumstances; it concerns itself with the present moment and aims to affect it.

But once this word has spread abroad and has entered thereby into the memory and tradition of other generations, each generation fashions out of that word the counsel and encouragement, the exhortation and comfort, it has need of in the new conditions of its existence. The original saying proves to be able to bestow manifold gifts far beyond its initial intention, gifts for manifold situations in historical and personal life; indeed, we may even say it contains these gifts. Such a message is directed to a particular group, but it is also directed to the human world—not to a vague and universal world, but to the concrete, the actual, historically-burdened and historically-inflamed world. The interpretation will be true to the saying only when it unites to its intention at the hour in which it was spoken, the intention unfolded throughout all the hours of its working and, in a special way, the intention of this hour when the interpretation is made. History not only ex-

208

pands, it also deepens the significance of the saying, for what is successively derived from it penetrates farther into its ground.

Jesus' saying concerning the tribute money, on the basis of which I shall proceed in order to discuss the value and limitation of the political principle as it concerns our historical hour, is a message of this kind. Interpreters of this saying have repeatedly and rightly pointed out that Jesus deduced from the image of Cæsar on the coin the duty not to refuse tax to the earthly ruler. On the other hand, it seems to me an error to understand the duty, as has been done, as lying in the fact that the payment has been described as a restitution. Neither a financial expert nor a normal human being conceives the money that he inherits or earns to be a gift of the state out of its treasury. The relation of the state that coins money to the economic society that employs money, at whose disposal the state places the medium of exchange, is, in fact, a wholly different one. And what is far more important: the giving to God that is enjoined in the latter part of the saying can only by a strained interpretation be explained as a giving back; indeed, this construction would warp the meaning of the saying. The only legitimate interpretation, as has been maintained in this connection,* is one that follows the clue of the sense of the Greek word: 'to render what one has to give in the fulfilment of a duty or expectation.'

But there already begins that necessary striving I have spoken of: to draw close to the original ground of the message that no longer pertains to one time but to all times. What, we ask, does it mean that time after time man can and should give something to God, as time after time he can and should give something to the earthly power ruling over him; and further what does it mean that the subject of that gift is designated as 'what is God's'—or in the translation closer to the original (which is to be assumed when translating the Greek text into Aramaic), 'that which belongs to God' or 'is due' Him, on the same plane with that which belongs to or is due Cæsar. That one should 'give,' that one is obliged to render to Cæsar, the superior power, the state, what the state

* Buchsel in Kittel's *Theologisches Wörterbuch zum Neuen Testament*, II, 170.

legitimately demands of its citizens—namely, what is due to the state on the ground of the reciprocal relationship, a relationship of reciprocal, limited claim—is clear enough. But how can that which he is obliged to give to God be placed on the same level? Is the reciprocal relationship between God and man which each human creature enters into by his existence also one of a reciprocal, limited claim? Does man, then, have any claim at all on God? When he actually turns to God—that is, when he prays in truth and reality—he can hardly persist in a claim for a moment. But if God has a claim on man, how can it be limited? If one begins to measure from the side of Cæsar what a man has to 'give,' shall the remainder, or the actual part of the remainder, fall to the share of God? In this wise it has clearly been understood by those who have explained the saying as meaning that one ought to comply with the worldly power so long as it demands nothing that stands in contradiction to the reverence due God in the form of creed and service, hence nothing such as sacrificing to the Roman emperor as a godlike being. But thereby the sphere of the divine, the sphere in the life of man pledged to God, is inevitably reduced to cult and confession. In other words, instead of being the Lord of existence, God is made into the God of religion.

If, on the other hand, we begin measuring from the side of God and try first, without regard for other claims, to ascertain what is due God without reserve, then we encounter in the depths of man's experience of himself a dark but elemental knowledge that man owes himself, the totality of his existence, to God. From this primal knowledge the central act of the cult, the sacrifice, apparently derives: man understands his offering as a symbolic substitute permitted him in place of himself. Thus the body of the sacrificial animal (as we find again and again, from a Phœnician formula to one of Indian Islam) represents his own body. Later we encounter in the language of that revelation in whose tradition Jesus grew up and to which he fundamentally referred himself, the awesome command he himself cited as the first of all: man shall love God 'with all his might.' If one takes the primacy of this commandment as seriously as Jesus took it, then one must exclude at the outset the acknowledgment of any special sphere to which one has to 'give' anything at all in independence of his relationship with God.

Unless we seek to allay the disquietude aroused in us by the saying about the tribute money through summarily relegating it, as some theologians have done, to the 'enigmatic sayings,' we are obliged to abandon the current interpretation according to which the statement is concerned with a division between different provinces of the same sphere. Building upon the experiences of all the generations that have encountered the sayings of Jesus in their hours of historical decision, and also on the dearly purchased self-understanding of our own generation, we must turn to another explanation. I can indicate it in modern terms alone, since, as far as I know, this explanation has not been previously dealt with. But its basic, non-conceptual content must be numbered among the presuppositions that, though unexpressed, need no expression, since every central figure has them in common with the inner circle of his hearers.

The human person, ontologically regarded, constitutes not a single sphere, but a union of two spheres. By this I in no way imply the duality of body and soul, allotting to one the kingdom of Cæsar and to the other the kingdom of God; such a dualism would be in clear conflict with the teaching of Jesus. Rather, proceeding from that word of Deuteronomy, 'with all thy soul and with all thy might,' I mean the sphere of wholeness and that of separation or division. When, and in so far as, man becomes whole, he becomes God's and gives to God; he gives to God just this wholeness. The realization of wholeness afforded man in any earthly matter is ultimately, and beyond any name that one can give it, connected with this. His human life, imprinted with mortality, cannot run its course in wholeness; it is bound to separation, to division. But he may and should elicit from the former direction for the latter. What is legitimately done in the sphere of separation receives its legitimacy from the sphere of wholeness. In the sermon of Deuteronomy the commandment to love is followed soon after by a noteworthy dual statement. First it is said that God loves the stranger who is a guest among you, and then it bids, 'You shall love the stranger.' Our duty to love the stranger in the sphere of separation follows, if we love God in the sphere of wholeness, from God's love for him, the exposed man.

Thus giving to the state, giving that which is due it in the sphere of separation, is authorized by the sphere of wholeness in which we give to God what is due Him: ourselves. The same insight can be phrased in other categories: those of the direct and the indirect relationship. The being directed to God in his wholeness stands in direct relation to Him; all direct relationship has its ground of being therein, and all indirect relationship can receive measure and direction only from there. Give to God your immediacy, the saying about tribute money says to us, and from so doing you will learn ever anew what of your mediacy you shall give to Cæsar.

Since the time when certain opponents of Jesus—called 'the Pharisees' by the Evangelists, in starkly oversimplified fashion—asked him whether the Judaic man is obliged by God to pay taxes or may exercise passive resistance, generations of world history have met the saying of Jesus with questions born of their particular situations, and these situations have become ever more difficult and contradictory. The question now is not one of foreign rule but of one's own; not one of a government sustained by force but of a government whose legitimacy is willingly acknowledged. The question does not pertain to acts governed by law; it no longer merely concerns carrying out what is ordered. The question in increasing measure is one of man himself. It is not, however, the state in its empirical manifestation that first raised the claim that has put man in question. It is rather the political thinker who elevated the state above the multiplicity of its empirical forms of manifestation into the absolute.

The decisive stretch of this way leads from Hobbes, the hostile son of the English Revolution, to Hegel, the hostile son of the French. Hobbes, to be sure, subjects the interpretation of the word of God to the civil power, but he holds fast to the unconditional superiority of the God who transcends it. Thus there can still persist here, even if only in a secondary and dependent fashion *de facto*, what is God's. For Hegel, who sees in the fact 'that the state is' the 'walking of God in the world' in which the idea, as the 'real God,' 'consciously realizes' itself, for Hegel, who understands the national spirit as 'the divine that knows and wills itself,' there is no longer anything that can be distinguished from what is Cæsar's. If man has 'his being only therein' in what he owes the state, if he has 'his entire value' 'only through the state,' then logically he himself is the tribute he owes to 'Cæsar.' In place of the empirical state, which was not or was not yet able to raise this claim (in its totalitarian form, of course, the state has already since then come quite close to it), it has been raised in the still-unconcluded age of Hegel by the political principle. This principle no longer confronts the individual and places a demand on him, like its predecessor; it permeates his soul and conquers his will.

By 'the political principle' I designate that so-to-speak practical axiom that predominates in the opinion and attitude of a very great part of the modern world. Formulated in a sentence, it means roughly that public régimes are the legitimate determinants of human existence. Chief emphasis lies naturally on the adjective 'legitimate.' The principle does not simply take cognizance of the fact that in the era of the so-called world wars the fate of those involved therein is elementarily and ever-increasingly dependent upon what happens between the states or, more concretely, between their representatives. It aims rather to establish that this is rightfully the case, since the political environment constitutes the essential condition of man, and it does not exist for his sake but he for it. Man, accordingly, is essentially Cæsar's. So far as this practical axiom prevails, the saying concerning the tribute money is virtually nullified. Whether the remainder that is left after the abstraction of the essential can still be booked to the account of 'God'—where this word has largely either been stricken from the current vocabulary or employed only metaphorically or conventionally—is hardly of importance.

In a human world so constituted, to discuss the value and limitation of the political principle in the spirit of the saying about tribute money means to criticize at the decisive point the would-be *absoluta*, the archons of the hour.

It is not the case, indeed, that in our age the absolute character of any kind of being is simply contested. The relativizing of the highest values that marks this age has halted before the political principle. More than that, within the practical pragmatism that is the basic form of this relativizing, the initial individualistic phase, in which the ethical, noetic, and religious values are tested by their utility for the life of the individual and are only sanctioned according to this utility, is succeeded by a second, collectivistic phase. Here truth is no longer understood and dealt with as what is advantageous to me, but to 'us.' This 'we' is ostensibly that of the collectivity, perhaps of the 'people'; in fact, however, it is the advantage of those who are currently ruling. In the interest of the maintenance and expansion of their power, these rulers seek in manifold ways to preserve in the people a belief in the existence of a truth which they themselves no longer share. The individualistic doctrine of relativism which we perceive in its most grandiose form in Stirner and Nietzsche is supplanted—in an order the reverse of the sequence in the history of the sophists—partly by the collectivistic relativism of Marxism, partly by the various species of existentialism, which are in some points singularly close to Marxism. Among these the German variety of existentialism, an ontological affirmation of history, appears to me especially significant. I can touch here only on what directly concerns our problem, in which connection I may note that not only Marx but also Heidegger descends essentially from Hegel.

Marx's so-called 'inversion' of the Hegelian world image is at the same time a reduction, since, following the great Vico, of all that exists, in nature and spirit, he allots to our knowledge only that in whose occurrence we men have historically participated; he combines with this reduction a still more intensive historicization of being than is found in Hegel. Apparently the historical economic process alone is accorded absoluteness—although, of course, only an historically existent one—and the state belongs only to its 'superstructure' and as such is relativized. But since the political order appears here as the bearer of the future change of all things and the highly centralized political concentration of power as the indispensable preparation for it, the unlimited state is postulated as the unconditional determining force until, according to the eschatological myth of the withering away of the state, the miraculous leap from the realm of necessity to that of freedom can be made.

The existentialism of Heidegger is also rooted in Hegel's thought, but in a deeper, indeed the deepest possible, level. For Hegel world history is the absolute process in which the spirit attains to consciousness of itself; so for Heidegger historical existence is the illumination of being itself; in neither is there room for a suprahistorical reality that sees history and judges it. For both philosophers the historical allows itself to be sanctioned in the last resort by its own thought concerning history; here as there, accordingly, reflection on man's boldest concept, that of eternity set in judgment above the whole course of history and thereby above each historical age, is not admitted. Time is not embraced by the timeless, and the ages do not shudder before One who does not dwell in time but only appears in it. The knowledge has vanished that time can in no wise be conceived as a finally existing reality, independent and self-contained, and that absurdity lies in wait for every attempt to reflect on it in this way no matter whether time be contemplated as finite or as infinite. If historical time and history are absolutized, it can easily occur that in the midst of present historical events the time-bound thinker ascribes to the state's current drive to power the character of an absolute and in this sense the determination of the future. After that, the goblin called success, convulsively grinning, may occupy for a while the divine seat of authority.

But how does it happen at all that the state can everywhere be absolutized when it exists in fact only in the plural, as 'the states,' each of them being continually reminded of its relativity through the existence of the others?

Hegel could conceive of the state as absolute precisely because history for him was absolute, and the state that had become representative in any historical epoch signified, in his mind, the current actuality of the being of the state. In Heidegger one may still read something of the same notion between the lines. But in the concreteness of lived life a strange singularizing has been accomplished here; it would call to mind the myths of primitive tribes, in which the creation of the world is related as the creation of the tiny territory of the tribe, were these myths not concerned with something essentially different from the state, with something, in distinction to it, corporeal and pregnant with mystery, the fatherland. Hegel has not noticed this vast difference; thus he can write, 'While the state, the fatherland, makes up the community of existence . . .' Jacob Grimm has come closer to perceiving the true nature of the matter.

On the other hand, all relative valuation of the state rests for the most part just on the fact of plurality, since the defence against the outside world generally asserts itself far more emphatically than a defence against inside perils. Enemy communities are, in general, far more clearly discernible than hostile elements within. The state, of course, only reluctantly leaves the measure of its value to be determined within the limits of actual differences of interest; not infrequently it fosters a perspective which allows differences of interest to appear as radical opposition. The accumulated power of mastery thrives on drawing profit from a —so to speak—latent exceptional condition. Vast sectors of the economy are inclined, understandably, to help perpetuate this tendency. Thus in times like ours the cold war tends to become the normal historical condition. Already at the beginning of our historical period we saw teachers of the law appear who, obedient to this trait of the times, defined the concept of the political so that everything disposed itself within it according to the criterion 'friend-enemy,' in which the concept of enemy includes 'the possibility of physical killing.' The practice of states has conveniently followed their advice. Many states decree the division of mankind into friends who deserve to live and enemies who deserve to die, and the political principle sees to it that what is decreed penetrates the hearts and reins of men.

Note carefully that I do not speak of the conduct of war itself, where personal decisions are, to some extent, taken away beforehand and in the abyss of events killing becomes kindred with being killed. I refer only to that realm of life in which free decision becomes unexpectedly unfree.

The clearest example of this condition is furnished by that certainly most remarkable structure within the public organization that we call the party. Among the members of the political party are people of the most scrupulous integrity in their private lives. Yet when their party has specified who the (in this case internal) 'enemy' is, these same people will day after day, with peaceful and untroubled conscience, lie, slander, betray, steal, torment, torture, murder. In the factories of party doctrine, good conscience is being dependably fashioned and refashioned.

I have no warrant whatever to declare that under all circumstances the interest of the group is to be sacrificed to the moral demand, more particularly as the cruel conflicts of duties and their unreserved decision on the basis of the situation seem to me to belong to the essential existence of a genuine personal ethos. But the evident absence of this inner conflict, the lack of its wounds and scars, is to me uncanny. I am not undertaking to set material limits to the validity of the political principle. That, rather, is just what must take place in reality time after time, soul after soul, situation after situation, I mean only to say that this occurrence has obviously become an exceptional one.

That one cannot serve God and Mammon is an entirely true saying, for Mammon embraces the soul and leaves nothing of it free. On the other hand, I believe that it is possible to serve God and the group to which one belongs if one is courageously intent on serving God in the sphere of the group as much as one can. As much as one can at the time; '*quantum satis*' means in the language of lived truth not 'either-or,' but 'as-much-as-one-can.' If the political organization of existence does not infringe on my wholeness and immediacy, it may demand of me that I do justice to it at any particular time as far as, in a given inner conflict, I believe I am able to answer for. At any particular time; for here there is no once-for-all: in each situation that demands decision the demarcation line between service and service must be drawn anew—not necessarily with fear, but necessarily with that trembling of the soul that precedes every genuine decision.

Another note must still be added. When men of integrity join a party, they do so out of a conviction that the party strives for a goal of the same general character as their own, and that this goal is to be reached solely through an energetic alliance of the like-minded. An actual party, however, consists both of genuinely convinced members and of only ostensibly convinced men who have entered it for all kinds of motives, usually out of an inextricable tangle of motives. It may easily happen, of course, that those of pretended convictions predominate. Be that as it may, it is incumbent on those of genuine conviction to resist the dominance of the fictitious faction within the party without crippling the party's energy. A thorny business this is; but without it one cannot serve God in the party, one cannot render Him in the sphere of political organization what is His, God's. What is at stake here is shown most clearly when means are proposed whose nature contradicts the nature of the goal. Here, too, one is obliged not to proceed on principle, but only to advance ever again in the responsibility of the line of demarcation and to answer for it; not in order to keep one's soul clean of blood—that would be a vain and wretched enterprise—but in order to guard against means being chosen that will lead away from the cherished goal to another goal essentially similar to those means; for the end never sanctifies the means, but the means can certainly thwart the end.

There is, it seems to me, a front—only seldom perceived by those who compose it—that cuts across all the fronts of the hour, both the external and the internal. There they stand, ranged side by side, the men of real conviction who are found in all groups, all parties, all peoples, yet who know little or nothing of one another from group to group, from party to party, from people to people. As different as the goals are in one place and in another, it is still *one* front, for they are all engaged in the one fight for human truth. But human truth is nothing other than the faithfulness of man to the one truth that he cannot possess, that he can only serve, his fidelity to the truth of God. Remaining true to the truth as much as he can, he strives to his goal. The goals are different, very different, but if each way has been trod in

218

truth, the lines leading to these goals intersect, extended beyond them, in the truth of God. Those who stand on the crossfront, those who know nothing of one another, have to do with one another.

We live at a juncture in which the problem of a common human destiny has become so obstinate that the experienced administrators of the political principle are, for the most part, only able to go through the motions of matching its demands. They offer counsel but know none. They struggle against one another, and every soul struggles against itself. They need a language to understand one another, and have no language except the current political jargon fit only for declamations. For sheer power they are impotent, for sheer tricks they are incapable of acting decisively. Perhaps in the hour when the catastrophe sends in advance its final warning, those who stand on the crossfront will have to come to the rescue. They who have in common the language of human truth must then unite to attempt in common at last to give to God what is God's, or, what here means the same thing, since when mankind has lost its way it stands before God, to give to man what is man's in order to rescue him from being devoured by the political principle.

Hope for this Hour*

(1952)

W<small>E</small> ask about hope for this hour. This implies that we
who ask experience this hour not only as one of the
heaviest affliction but also as one that appears to give
no essentially different outlook for the future, no prospect of a
time of radiant and full living. Yet it is such an outlook for a
better hour that we mean when we speak of hope.

Only by the great need of this hour being really felt in common
can our question have a common significance, and only then may
we expect an answer which will show us a way. A hundred or a
thousand men might come together and each bring with him the
daily need of his own life, his wholly personal world- and life-
anxiety. Yet even though each laid his need together with the
needs of the others, this would not produce a common need from
which a genuinely common question could arise. Only if the
personal need of each reveals the great need of man in this hour
can the rivulets of need, united into a single stream, sweep the
storming question upward.

What is of essential importance, however, is that we recognize
not only the external manifestations of that common need perceptible to us, but also its origin and its depth. As important as it
is that we suffer in common the human anguish of today, it is
still more important to trace in common where it comes from.
Only from there, from the source, can the true hope of healing
be given us.

The human world is today, as never before, split into two
camps, each of which understands the other as the embodiment

* Address at a parting celebration held at Carnegie Hall in New York at the
conclusion of the author's lecture tour in the United States.

of falsehood and itself as the embodiment of truth. Often in history, to be sure, national groups and religious associations have stood in so radical an opposition that the one side denied and condemned the other in its innermost existence. Now, however, it is the human population of our planet generally that is so divided, and with rare exceptions this division is everywhere seen as a necessity of existence in this world hour. He who makes himself an exception is suspected or ridiculed by both sides. Each side has assumed monopoly of the sunlight and has plunged its antagonist into night, and each side demands that you decide between day and night.

We can comprehend the origin of this cruel and grotesque condition in its simplest lines if we realize how the three principles of the French Revolution have broken asunder. The abstractions freedom and equality were held together there through the more concrete fraternity, for only if men feel themselves to be brothers can they partake of a genuine freedom from one another and a genuine equality with one another. But fraternity has been deprived of its original meaning, the relationship between children of God, and consequently of any real content. As a result, each of the two remaining watchwords was able to establish itself against the other and, by so doing, to wander farther and farther from its truth. Arrogant and presumptuous, each sucked into itself, ever more thoroughly, elements foreign to it, elements of passion for power and greed for possession.

In such a situation man is more than ever inclined to see his own principle in its original purity and the opposing one in its present deterioration, especially if the forces of propaganda confirm his instincts in order to make better use of them. Man is no longer, as in earlier epochs, content to take his own principle for the single true one and that which opposes it as false through and through. He is convinced that his side is in order, the other side fundamentally out of order, that he is concerned with the recognition and realization of the right, his opponent with the masking of his selfish interest. Expressed in modern terminology, he believes that he has ideas, his opponent only ideologies. This obsession feeds the mistrust that incites the two camps.

During the First World War it became clear to me that a process was going on which before then I had only surmised. This was the growing difficulty of genuine dialogue, and most especially of genuine dialogue between men of different kinds and convictions. Direct, frank dialogue is becoming ever more difficult and more rare; the abysses between man and man threaten ever more pitilessly to become unbridgeable. I began to understand at that time, more than thirty years ago, that this is the central question for the fate of mankind. Since then I have continually pointed out that the future of man as man depends upon a rebirth of dialogue.

I experienced a great satisfaction, therefore, when I read a short while ago the words in which a not just ordinarily competent man, Robert Hutchins, formulated the importance and possibility of a Civilization of the Dialogue. 'The essence of the Civilization of the Dialogue is communication. The Civilization of the Dialogue presupposes mutual respect and understanding, it does not presuppose agreement.' And further: 'It is no good saying that the Civilization of the Dialogue cannot arise when the other party will not talk. We have to find the way to induce him to talk.' As the means to this, Hutchins recommends showing interest and understanding for what the other has to say.

But there is an essential presupposition for all this: it is necessary to overcome the massive mistrust in others and also that in ourselves. I do not mean thereby the primal mistrust, such as that directed against those with strange ways, those who are unsettled, and those without traditions—the mistrust that the farmer in his isolated farmstead feels for the tramp who suddenly appears before him, I mean the universal mistrust of our age. Nothing stands so much in the way of the rise of a Civilization of Dialogue as the demonic power which rules our world, the demonry of basic mistrust. What does it avail to induce the other to speak if basically one puts no faith in what he says? The meeting with him already takes place under the perspective of his untrustworthiness. And this perspective is not incorrect, for his meeting with me takes place under a corresponding perspective. The basic mistrust, coming to light, produces ground for mistrust, and so forth and so forth.

It is important to perceive clearly how the specifically modern mistrust differs from the ancient mistrust, which is apparently inherent in the human being and which has left its mark in all cultures. There have always been countless situations in which a man in intercourse with a fellow-man is seized with the doubt whether he may trust him; that is, whether the other really means what he says and whether he will do what he says. There have always been countless situations in which a man believes his life-interest demands that he suspect the other of making it his object to appear otherwise than he is. The first man must then be on his guard to protect himself against this threatening false appearance.

In our time something basically different has been added that is capable of undermining more powerfully the foundations of existence between men. One no longer merely fears that the other will voluntarily dissemble, but one simply takes it for granted that he cannot do otherwise. The presumed difference between his opinion and his statement, between his statement and his action, is here no longer understood as his intention, but as essential necessity. The other communicates to me the perspective that he has acquired on a certain subject, but I do not really take cognizance of his communication as knowledge. I do not take it seriously as a contribution to the information about this subject, but rather I listen for what drives the other to say what he says, for an unconscious motive, say, or a 'complex.' He expresses a thought about a problem of life that concerns me, but I do not ask myself about the truth of what he says. I only pay attention to the question of which interest of his group has clothed itself in this apparently so objective judgment. Since it is the idea of the other, it is for me only an 'ideology.' My main task in my intercourse with my fellow-man becomes more and more, whether in terms of individual psychology or of sociology, to see through and unmask him. In the classical case this in no wise means a mask he has put on to deceive me, but a mask that has, without his knowing it, been put on him, indeed positively imprinted on him, so that what is really deceived is his own consciousness. There are, of course, innumerable transitional forms.

With this changed basic attitude, which has found scientific rationalization in the teachings of Marx and Freud, the mistrust between man and man has become existential. This is so indeed in a double sense: It is, first of all, no longer only the uprightness, the honesty of the other which is in question, but the inner integrity of his existence itself. Secondly, this mistrust not only destroys trustworthy talk between opponents, but also the immediacy of togetherness of man and man generally. Seeing-through and unmasking is now becoming the great sport between men, and those who practise it do not know whither it entices them. Nietzsche knew what he was doing when he praised the 'art of mistrust,' and yet he did not know. For this game naturally only becomes complete as it becomes reciprocal, in the same measure as the unmasker himself becomes the object of unmasking. Hence one may foresee in the future a degree of reciprocity in existential mistrust where speech will turn into dumbness and sense into madness.

One is still inclined to spare the other in order that one may oneself be spared. If he is ready at times to put himself in question he is generally able to stop in time. But the demonry is not to be trifled with. The existential mistrust is indeed basically no longer, like the old kind, a mistrust of my fellow-man. It is rather the destruction of confidence in existence in general. That we can no longer carry on a genuine dialogue from one camp to the other is the severest symptom of the sickness of present-day man. Existential mistrust is this sickness itself. But the destruction of trust in human existence is the inner poisoning of the total human organism from which this sickness stems.

All great civilization has been in a certain measure a Civilization of the Dialogue. The life substance of them all was not, as one customarily thinks, the presence of significant individuals, but their genuine intercourse with one another. Individuation was only the presupposition for the unfolding of dialogical life. What one calls the creative spirit of men has never been anything other than the address, the cogitative or artistic address, of those called to speak to those really able and prepared to hear.

That which had concentrated here was the universal dynamism of dialogue.

There interposed in all times, of course, severe checks and disturbances; there was closedness and unapproachableness, dissembling and seduction. But where the human wonder bloomed time and again, these checks and disturbances were always overcome through the elemental power of men's mutual confirmation. The one turned to the other as to a unique personal being, undamaged by all error and trouble, and received the other's turning to him. The one traced the other in his being, in that in him which survived all illusions, and even if they fought each other, they confirmed each other as what they were. Man wishes to be confirmed by man as he who he is, and there is genuine confirmation only in mutuality.

Despite the progressive decline of dialogue and the corresponding growth of universal mistrust which characterize our time, the need of men to be confirmed still continues. But for the most part it no longer finds any natural satisfaction. As a result, man sets out on one of two false ways: he seeks to be confirmed either by himself or by a collective to which he belongs. Both undertakings must fail. The self-confirmation of him whom no fellowman confirms cannot stand. With ever more convulsive exertions, he must endeavour to restore it, and finally he knows himself as inevitably abandoned. Confirmation through the collective, on the other hand, is pure fiction. It belongs to the nature of the collective, to be sure, that it accepts and employs each of its members as this particular individual, constituted and endowed in this particular way. But it cannot recognize anyone in his own being, and therefore independently of his usefulness for the collective. Modern man, in so far as he has surrendered direct and personal mutuality with his fellows, can only exchange an illusory confirmation for the one that is lost. There is no salvation save through the renewal of the dialogical relation, and this means, above all, through the overcoming of existential mistrust.

Where must the will to this overcoming begin? More exactly from what spiritual position is the man for whom existential mistrust has already become the self-understood gateway into intercourse with his fellow-man to be brought to self-criticism in this matter of decisive import? This is a position which can be described as the criticism of criticism. It is a matter of showing up a fundamental and enormously influential error of all the theories of seeing-through and unmasking. The gist of the error is this: when an element in the psychical and spiritual existence of man which formerly was not or was too little noticed is now uncovered or clarified, one identifies it with man's total structure instead of inserting it in this structure. A leading methodological postulate of all anthropological knowledge in the broadest sense of the term must be that each newly uncovered and newly clarified element should be investigated in terms of its importance in relation to the other elements, which are already in some measure known and elucidated, and in terms of its reciprocal interaction with them. The decisive questions must be: what proportion exists between this element and the others, in what measure and in what way does it limit them and is it limited by them; in what dynamism of different historical and individual genetic moments of human existence is it to be included?

The first task of science at any given time must be, accordingly, to draw demarcation lines for the validity of theses which may be posited about the newly uncovered or newly clarified element; that is, to determine within which spheres it may claim validity. The theories of seeing-through and unmasking, both the psychological and the sociological, have neglected to draw these lines, and have time and again reduced man to the elements that have been uncovered. Let us consider, as an example, the theory of ideologies, according to which the views and judgments of a man belonging to a particular social class are to be examined essentially as products of his class position; that is, in connection with the action of his class for the promotion of its interests. Were the problem of class position and its influence stated with all clarity, the first scientific question would have to be: Since man is set in his world as in a manifold connection of influencing spheres, from the cosmic to the erotic, one of which spheres is the social level, what is the weight of the ideological class influence in relation to the non-ideological constitution of the person and what is their effect on each other? (In this connection it should be noticed that the influence of social levels, as we know, is in no way a simply positive one, for the rebellion against the class to which one belongs not seldom proves stronger than the tendency to conformity, and thus the idea stronger than the ideology.) For the time being, of course, the answer to such questions can only be set as a goal for scientific thought. But the setting of this goal is an essential precondition for the rightness of this thought.

Instead of this, the theories of ideology have reduced the man who holds opinion and formulates judgments to the ideological. This boundless simplification has contributed decisively to the development of existential mistrust. If we wish to overcome this mistrust, we cannot go back into an uncritical acceptance of men's statements. We must go beyond our present position by setting ever more exact measure and limits to the ideological critique. What I mean is not a vague idealism, but a more comprehending, more penetrating realism, a greater realism, the realism of a greater reality! Man is not to be seen through, but to be perceived ever more completely in his openness and his hiddenness and in the relation of the two to each other. We wish to trust him, not blindly indeed but clear-sightedly. We wish to perceive his manifoldness and his wholeness, his proper character, without any preconceptions about this or that background, and with the intention of accepting, accrediting and confirming him to the extent that this perception will allow.

Only if this happens and in so far as it happens can a genuine dialogue begin between the two camps into which mankind today is split. They who begin it must have overcome in themselves the basic mistrust and be capable of recognizing in their partner in dialogue the reality of his being. It is self-understood that these men will not speak merely in their own names. Behind them will be divined the unorganized mass of those who feel themselves represented through these spokesmen. This is an entirely different kind of representation and representative body from the political. These men will not be bound by the aims of the hour, they are gifted with the free far-sightedness of those called by the unborn; they will be independent persons with no authority save that of the spirit. Today, as we know, the spirit has less authority than ever, but there are world hours in which, despite all obstacles, the authority of the spirit suffices to undertake the rescue of man. Such an hour appears to me to draw near.

The representatives of whom I speak will each be acquainted with the true needs of his own people, and on these needs will be willing to stake themselves. But they will also turn understandingly to the true needs of other peoples, and will know in both cases how to extract the true needs from the exaggerations. Just for that reason they will unrelentingly distinguish between truth and propaganda within what is called the opposition of interests. Only when out of the alleged amount of antagonisms just the real conflicts between genuine needs remain can the consideration of the necessary and possible settlements between them begin. The question one must proceed from will be this, apparently the simplest of all questions, yet inviting many difficulties: What does man need, every man, in order to live as a man? For if the globe is not to burst asunder, every man must be given what he needs for a really human life. Coming together out of hostile camps, those who stand in the authority of the spirit will dare to think with one another in terms of the whole planet.

Which will prove stronger in the final accounting, man's common trust of existence or his mutual mistrust? Even if the representatives I hope for be found, their success will depend on those represented, on their unreserved honesty, their good-will with its scorn of empty phrases, their courageous personal engagement. From this source alone can the power that the representatives need stream towards them. The hope for this hour depends upon the hopers themselves, upon ourselves. I mean by this: upon those among us who feel most deeply the sickness of present-day man and who speak in his name the word without which no healing takes place: I will live.

The hope for this hour depends upon the renewal of dialogical immediacy between men. But let us look beyond the pressing need, the anxiety and care of this hour. Let us see this need in connection with the great human way. Then we shall recognize that immediacy is injured not only between man and man, but also between the being called man and the source of his existence. At its core the conflict between mistrust and trust of man conceals the conflict between the mistrust and trust of eternity. If our mouths succeed in genuinely saying 'thou,' then, after long silence and stammering, we shall have addressed our eternal 'Thou' anew. Reconciliation leads towards reconciliation.

Abstract and Concrete

(1952)

AMONG the statements that have reached my ears concerning my Carnegie Hall address,* were some critical ones that have caused me to reflect. Almost all of them had the same import: I dealt with the 'cold' world war as an 'abstract philosophical' question instead of a 'concrete political' one, which latter treatment obviously amounts to helping swell the literature of invective piling up in both camps. I have finally perceived that I must attempt to clarify this matter.

The inner goal of the approach involved in my summons was just this distinction between the primary 'political' and the secondary 'philosophical' points of view. I have appealed just from politics, from its perspective, its speech, and its usages, but not to any kind of philosophy. Rather I appealed directly to the genuine concrete, to the actual life of actual men which has become smeared over and crusted with the varnish of political fictitiousness. The representatives of one side and of the other insist that the reproaches that they hurl at their opponents make up the only reality of the situation worth considering. Many of these reproaches on both sides are, in fact, realistic enough; but in order for this reality to be regarded *in concreto*, it too must first be freed from its encrustation of catchwords. Enmeshed in the political machinery, we cannot possibly penetrate to the factual. Enclosed in the sphere of the exclusively political, we can find no means to relieve the present situation; its 'natural end' is the technically perfect suicide of the human race.

It is just this impotence of politicism, which the propagandistic rhetoric of the orators of both camps will soon no longer be able

* See 'Hope for This Hour,' p. 220.

to conceal, that must be recognized today before it is too late. It is up to those on both sides who have not yet fallen into the total politization to reflect on themselves, and in so doing reflect in wholly unphilosophical concreteness on existence. Despite the overwhelming phenomenon of groups of states whose teeth are sunk in one another, some such men still exist. If these men, despite the weighty scruples against the opposing system that beset even them, will begin to speak with one another—not as pawns on a chessboard but as themselves, partakers of human reality, a tiny seed of change will have been sown that could lead to transformation of the whole situation. I mean especially those who are basically convinced of the rightness of the idea their régime ultimately stems from, and know, just for that reason, that the catastrophe which would flow from victory would mean the collapse of that idea. They are to be trusted and expected to distinguish between the exaggerated conflicts of interest of peoples and their factual differences of interest, and to understand how to settle these latter.

Today, of course, hardly anything is more difficult, more difficult in every respect, than to move in the struggle for the future destiny of mankind elsewhere than within the figurations on the great chessboard and otherwise than according to the rules set by the constellation of those encamped opposite. But shall so-called history, this time too, alone succeed in determining what will happen?

Genuine Dialogue and the Possibilities of Peace*

(1953)

I CANNOT express my thanks to the German Book Trade for the honour conferred on me without at the same time setting forth the sense in which I have accepted it, just as I earlier accepted the Hanseatic Goethe Prize given me by the University of Hamburg.

About a decade ago a considerable number of Germans—there must have been many thousands of them—under the indirect command of the German government and the direct command of its representatives, killed millions of my people in a systematically prepared and executed procedure whose organized cruelty cannot be compared with any previous historical event. I, who am one of those who remained alive, have only in a formal sense a common humanity with those who took part in this action. They have so radically removed themselves from the human sphere, so transposed themselves into a sphere of monstrous inhumanity inaccessible to my conception, that not even hatred, much less an overcoming of hatred, was able to arise in me. And what am I that I could here presume to 'forgive'!

With the German people it is otherwise. From my youth on I have taken the real existence of peoples most seriously. But I have never, in the face of any historical moment, past or present, allowed the concrete multiplicity existing at that moment within a people—the concrete inner dialectic, rising to contradiction—

* This address was given on the occasion of the award to the author of the Peace Prize of the German Book Trade at Frankfurt-am-Main, in Paulskirche, September 27, 1953.

to be obscured by the levelling concept of a totality constituted and acting in just such a way and no other.

When I think of the German people of the days of Auschwitz and Treblinka, I behold, first of all, the great many who knew that the monstrous event was taking place and did not oppose it. But my heart, which is acquainted with the weakness of men, refuses to condemn my neighbour for not prevailing upon himself to become a martyr. Next there emerges before me the mass of those who remained ignorant of what was withheld from the German public, and who did not try to discover what reality lay behind the rumours which were circulating. When I have these men in mind, I am gripped by the thought of the anxiety, likewise well known to me, of the human creature before a truth which he fears he cannot face. But finally there appears before me, from reliable reports, some who have become as familiar to me by sight, action, and voice as if they were friends, those who refused to carry out the orders and suffered death or put themselves to death, and those who learned what was taking place and opposed it and were put to death, or those who learned what was taking place and because they could do nothing to stop it killed themselves. I see these men very near before me in that especial intimacy which binds us at times to the dead and to them alone. Reverence and love for these Germans now fills my heart.

But I must step out of memory into the present. Here I am surrounded by the youth who have grown up since those events and had no part in the great crime. These youth, who are probably the essential life of the German people today, show themselves to me in a powerful inner dialectic. Their core is included in the core of an inner struggle running for the most part underground and only occasionally coming to the surface. This is only a part, though one of the clearest, of the great inner struggle of all peoples being fought out today, more or less consciously, more or less passionately, in the vital centre of each people.

The preparation for the final battle of *homo humanus* against *homo contrahumanus* has begun in the depths. But the front is split into as many individual fronts as there are peoples, and those who stand on one of the individual fronts know little or nothing of the other fronts. Darkness still covers the struggle, upon whose course and outcome it depends whether, despite all, a true humanity can issue from the race of men. The so-called cold war between two gigantic groups of states with all its accompaniments still obscures the true obligation and solidarity of combat, whose line cuts right through all states and peoples, however they name their régimes. The recognition of the deeper reality, of the true need and the true danger, is growing. In Germany, and especially in German youth, despite their being rent asunder, I have found more awareness of it than elsewhere. The memory of the twelve-year reign of *homo contrahumanus* has made the spirit stronger, and the task set by the spirit clearer, than they formerly were.

Tokens such as the bestowal of the Hanseatic Goethe Prize and the Peace Prize of the German Book Trade on a surviving arch-Jew must be understood in this connection. They, too, are moments in the struggle of the human spirit against the demonry of the subhuman and the antihuman. The survivor who is the object of such honours is taken up into the high duty of solidarity that extends across the fronts: the solidarity of all separate groups in the flaming battle for the rise of a true humanity. This duty is, in the present hour, the highest duty on earth. The Jew chosen as symbol must obey this call of duty even there, indeed, precisely there where the never-to-be-effaced memory of what has happened stands in opposition to it. When he recently expressed his gratitude to the spirit of Goethe, victoriously disseminated throughout the world, and when he now expresses his gratitude to the spirit of peace, which now as so often before speaks to the world in books of the German tongue, his thanks signify his confession of solidarity with the common battle—common also to Germans and Jews—against the contrahuman, and his reply to a vow taken by fighters, a vow he has heard.

Hearkening to the human voice, where it speaks forth unfalsified, and replying to it, this above all is needed today. The busy noise of the hour must no longer drown out the *vox humana*, the essence of the human which has become a voice. This voice must not only be listened to, it must be answered and led out of the lonely monologue into the awakening dialogue of the peoples. Peoples must engage in talk with one another through their truly human men if the great peace is to appear and the devastated life of the earth renew itself.

The great peace is something essentially different from the absence of war.

In an early mural in the town hall of Sienna the civic virtues are assembled. Worthy, and conscious of their worth, the women sit there, except one in their midst who towers above the rest. This woman is marked not by dignity but rather by composed majesty. Three letters announce her name: Pax. She represents the great peace I have in mind. This peace does not signify that what men call war no longer exists now that it holds sway—that means too little to enable one to understand this serenity. Something new exists, now really exists, greater and mightier than war, greater and mightier even than war. Human passions flow into war as the waters into the sea, and war disposes of them as it likes. But these passions must enter into the great peace as ore into the fire that melts and transforms it. Peoples will then build with one another with more powerful zeal than they have ever destroyed one another.

The Siennese painter had glimpsed this majestic peace in his dream alone. He did not acquire the vision from historical reality, for it has never appeared there. What in history has been called peace has never, in fact, been aught other than an anxious or an illusory blissful pause between wars. But the womanly genius of the painter's dream is no mistress of interruptions but the queen of new and greater deeds.

May we, then, cherish the hope that the countenance which has remained unknown to all previous history will shine forth on our late generation, apparently sunk irretrievably in disaster? Are we not accustomed to describe the world situation in which we have lived since the end of the Second World War no longer even as peace but as the 'cold' phase of a world war declared in permanence? In a situation which no longer even seeks to preserve the appearance of peace, is it not illusory enthusiasm to speak of a great peace which has never existed being within reach?

It is the depth of our crisis that allows us to hope in this way. Ours is not an historically familiar malady in the life of peoples which can eventuate in a comfortable recovery. Primal forces are now being summoned to take an active part in an unrepeatable decision between extinction and rebirth. War has not produced this crisis; it is, rather, the crisis of man which has brought forth the total war and the unreal peace which followed.

War has always had an adversary who hardly ever comes forward as such but does his work in the stillness. This adversary is speech, fulfilled speech, the speech of genuine conversation in which men understand one another and come to a mutual understanding. Already in primitive warfare fighting begins where speech has ceased; that is, where men are no longer able to discuss with one another the subjects under dispute or submit them to mediation, but flee from speech with one another and in the speechlessness of slaughter seek what they suppose to be a decision, a judgment of God. War soon conquers speech and enslaves it in the service of its battle-cries. But where speech, be it ever so shy, moves from camp to camp, war is already called in question. Its cannons easily drown out the word; but when the word has become entirely soundless, and on this side and on that soundlessly bears into the hearts of men the intelligence that no human conflict can really be resolved through killing, not even through mass killing, then the human word has already begun to silence the cannonade.

But it is just the relation of man to speech and to conversation that the crisis characteristic of our age has in particular tended to shatter. The man in crisis will no longer entrust his cause to conversation because its presupposition—trust—is lacking. This is the reason why the cold war which today goes by the name of peace has been able to overcome mankind. In every earlier period of peace the living word has passed between man and man, time after time drawing the poison from the antagonism of interests and convictions so that these antagonisms have not degenerated into the absurdity of 'no-farther' into the madness of 'must-wage-war.' This living word of human dialogue that from time to time makes its flights until the madness smothers it, now seems to have become lifeless in the midst of the non-war. The debates between statesmen which the radio conveys to us no longer have anything in common with a human conversation: the diplomats do not address one another but the faceless public. Even the congresses and conferences which convene in the name of mutual understanding lack the substance which alone can elevate the deliberations to genuine talk: candour and directness in address and answer. What is concentrated there is only the universal condition in which men are no longer willing or no longer able to speak directly to their fellows. They are not able to speak directly because they no longer trust one another, and everybody knows that the other no longer trusts him. If anyone in the hubbub of contradictory talk happens to pause and take stock, he discovers that in his relations to others hardly anything persists that deserves to be called trust.

And yet this must be said again and again, it is just the depth of the crisis that empowers us to hope. Let us dare to grasp the situation with that great realism that surveys all the definable realities of public life, of which, indeed, public life appears to be composed, but is also aware of what is most real of all, albeit moving secretly in the depths—the latent healing and salvation in the face of impending ruin. The power of turning that radically changes the situation, never reveals itself outside of crisis. This power begins to function when one, gripped by despair, instead of allowing himself to be submerged, calls forth his primal powers and accomplishes with them the turning of his very existence. It happens in this way both in the life of the person and in that of the race. In its depths the crisis demands naked decision: no mere fluctuation between getting worse and getting better, but a decision between the decomposition and the renewal of the tissue.

The crisis of man which has become apparent in our day announces itself most clearly as a crisis of trust, if we may employ, thus intensified, a concept of economics. You ask, trust in whom? But the question already contains a limitation not admissible here. It is simply trust that is increasingly lost to men of our time.

And the crisis of speech is bound up with this loss of trust in the closest possible fashion, for I can only speak to someone in the true sense of the term if I expect him to accept my word as genuine. Therefore, the fact that it is so difficult for present-day man to pray (note well: not to hold it to be true that there is a God, but to address Him) and the fact that it is so difficult for him to carry on a genuine talk with his fellow-men are elements of a single set of facts. This lack of trust in Being, this incapacity for unreserved intercourse with the other, points to an innermost sickness of the sense of existence. One symptom of this sickness, and the most acute of all, is the one from which I have begun: that a genuine word cannot arise between the camps.

Can such an illness be healed? I believe it can be. And it is out of this, my belief, that I speak to you. I have no proof for this belief. No belief can be proved; otherwise it would not be what it is, a great venture. Instead of offering proof, I appeal to that potential belief of each of my hearers which enables him to believe.

If there be a cure, where can the healing action start? Where must that existential turning begin which the healing powers, the powers of salvation in the ground of the crisis, await?

That peoples can no longer carry on authentic dialogue with one another is not only the most acute symptom of the pathology of our time, it is also that which most urgently makes a demand of us. I believe, despite all, that the peoples in this hour can enter into dialogue, into a genuine dialogue with one another. In a genuine dialogue each of the partners, even when he stands in opposition to the other, heeds, affirms, and confirms his opponent as an existing other. Only so can conflict certainly not be eliminated from the world, but be humanly arbitrated and led towards its overcoming.

To the task of initiating this conversation those are inevitably called who carry on today within each people the battle against the anti-human. Those who build the great unknown front across mankind shall make it known by speaking unreservedly with one another, not overlooking what divides them but determined to bear this division in common.

238

In opposition to them stands the element that profits from the divisions between the peoples, the contra-human in men, the subhuman, the enemy of man's will to become a true humanity.

The name Satan means in Hebrew the hinderer. That is the correct designation for the anti-human in individuals and in the human race. Let us not allow this Satanic element in men to hinder us from realizing man! Let us release speech from its ban! Let us dare, despite all, to trust!